Printed in the United Kingdom

First Printing, 2020

ISBN 9781698945545

http://myelderlyparents.co.uk

CONKERS

12th October 2017

The day after I have moved in, and my mother and step-father are discussing moths. Moths have invaded Anna's cashmere jumpers and wool skirts, the long skirts that she wears to keep warm. I tell them that I will go into the village after breakfast and find some conkers. They look at me for a moment and consider this information and then Dave goes to the long coat cupboard and shows us the plastic covers that Anna should store her skirts in.

"No buggers'll get through these covers," he shouts. He is very deaf so Anna is used to this.

I find my old shoes in the boot of my car under a pile of boxes. I head for the village pond, looking for the orangey-red foliage. Three ducks greet my arrival by skidding across the water towards me, hoping for bread no doubt. No conkers to be seen, so I take the lane up towards the church, past the long yew hedge and the church hall and through the kissing gate into the churchyard. On my left are the graves of villagers whose names I am familiar with. Anna and Dave with their morning muesli talk about the old villagers - their lives and their passing. And then a loud cracking noise behind me, and another. Two glossy cheese-cutters lie exposed in their conker cases.

"You could put these in your jumper drawers," I tell them on my return, tipping my spoils onto the round dining table. Dave looks sceptical but pockets half a dozen.

"I just spray em," he tells us.

Two days later I am driving Anna to the supermarket. She is dozing in the passenger seat where the car has warmed on the driveway. The conker trees look almost metallic in the sun.

I must have voiced my thoughts aloud.

"Conkers..." says Anna lifting her head. Her eyes are still closed.

"Some old biddy came down with a bag of conkers and told us to put them with our jumpers. I've never heard anything like it."

"Who was it?" I ask her, trying to sound detached.

"I don't know... some old biddy..."

Her head falls forward again.

I drive on through the village and up Crook hill, where in the past my old cars sometimes struggled to reach the top. I smile to myself.

And in the trees that line the side of the road the sun is just beginning to show.

It will be a fine day.

EGG SANDWICHES

14th October 2017

. . . .

Moving back to your parents' home in middle age is not an easy decision. I don't know how long it will be for. Weeks? Months?

"I just couldn't do that," my brothers tell me. My friends look sympathetic.

But I am in a housing chain. Until the chain breaks I can't move into my new house. And at least I can find out if they are still coping.

One of the first things I notice at the old cottage is that my mother isn't eating well. My step-father Dave likes to cook her a fish cake in the evenings…but every evening?

I decide to make some changes. Mushrooms on toast, tomatoes on toast, Welsh rarebit, prawns with tomato rice? She opts for egg sandwiches.

I like egg sandwiches too. Dave has bought six brown organic eggs.

"Cos you're fussy about your food." he tells me.

I'm not complaining. Until old Brian stopped bringing eggs up from his chickens, the eggs sat for days mouldering in a wooden holder in the kitchen, eventually decaying into a sticky mess.

I tell Dave to keep them in the fridge.

I choose two and cook them on the Aga hotplate for ten minutes. There is a jar of mayonnaise hidden at the back of the fridge. Anna would probably throw it away if the label wasn't familiar. Black pepper. Salt. Dave is outside looking for Robbie the young robin who has befriended him. Robbie hasn't been seen for two days.

"That bugger of a cat has 'ad 'im," Dave tells us throwing down the lid of the corn bin.

"He'll be back," I say.

Dave stomps inside, cursing the neighbour's black and white cat. I've shelled and chopped up the eggs and I'm spooning the mayonnaise into Anna's white oval dish. Slices of wholemeal bread are waiting for buttering.

"What's up with that smell?" roars Dave behind me.

"Just eggs," I say.

Dave goes to the sink. Then I hear a whoosh of air around me. I turn and Dave is holding a can of air freshener over the sandwiches. The smell fills my eyes and nose.

"That's better," says Dave, "I don't like the smell of eggs."

I go outside and look out across the fields. Better to do that and keep calm. From the heuchera plant on the rockery a pair of bright eyes studies me carefully. Robbie swoops down to the back door mat. He is wondering whether to hop into the kitchen. Don't do that Robbie, I tell him. Old country lore. Dave greets him like a returning hero, offering stale flapjack in the palm of his hand. Calm returns.

I go back into the house and find Anna in her armchair by the Aga. She is always cold despite the autumn sun in the windows. On her lap is a plate of egg sandwiches which Dave has brought her.

I'm not sure what to do with mine.

4

PUDDINGS

16th October 2017

Food is very important to Anna and Dave. Some years ago my son interviewed Dave for a school project about his experiences of the Second World War. Dave was eight when the war started and he lived in the countryside. The account that my son recorded was all about food; from poaching rabbits and befriending the butcher's son, to the delight at the candy from the American soldiers.

Anna's experience of food is quite different. As a young fashion model she was told to lose a stone in weight before starting work. This led to a lifelong fear of fattening food. Yet she has what she describes as a "sweet tooth" so it seems to me that she has sacrificed healthy eating in order to eat the puddings she loves.

Caramel pudding is the favourite. It comes in a packet, and Anna fills the base of small tin bowls with a gooey sticky syrup, and then boils milk and adds a curious yellow powder mixture to the milk. This is stirred for two minutes and then poured into the tin bowls. I know this is the method because she constantly forgets the next step and brings me the packet to read. Once cooled and then chilled in the fridge these little tin bowls haunt my every meal. No sooner have we finished the first course than Anna appears with caramel puddings on a tray. Four, five, six. Dave is always pleased to see them. Sometimes the bowls are only half filled and I am not quite sure where the other half has gone.

I politely refuse, saying that I don't eat puddings. This is not quite true. They are always surprised at this. Dave eats two, his and mine. Anna goes to her faded armchair carrying the tin bowl carefully in one hand. All is silent while they enjoy the caramel taste. Then Dave sits back in his chair.

"I don't know what's up with you lot, you young people, you don't eat nothing normal."

I say again that I usually have fruit for pudding. Dave considers this for a while. Anna has finished her pudding. Her head falls forward slightly and the little bowl tips in her lap.

"You young people you don't like home cooking do you? That's what it is I reckon…you like all this fast food."

I think about the cupboard filled with packets of caramel puddings queuing up patiently for their turn at the table. I can almost them laughing.

But Dave has woken Anna as he pushes his chair back noisily from the table.

"My birds…" he says, "my birds…" as he makes his way to the corn bin. I go to the window to watch a pheasant hurry across the field to the garden rockery. Dave whistles as loudly as I have ever heard anyone whistle. I turn to look at Anna but she is dozing again.

THREE PUDDINGS EVENING

18th October 2017

. . . .

Anna and Dave like to eat early in the evening. He has a big oval dish decorated with pheasants which has been broken and glued back together a few times. He loads it with potato, mashed or boiled, and plenty of meat. Anna has a small plate for a fish cake, two broad beans and half a carrot.

I wait for them to finish this before I cook my evening meal. It's October and the evenings are getting darker. Anna comments on this as she draws the heavy velvet curtains in the dining room. She is so frail that it is a struggle to do this simple task, but if I try to help I sense her resentment.

Finally they are watching the news headlines. The newscaster's voice booms from the sitting room. I am busy peeling and chopping carrots but I am aware of Anna carrying two caramel puddings on her favourite tray to the sitting room. Half an hour or so passes. I'm listening to the radio at the round table and eating my stir-fry.

"Nice lot of veg there," says Dave on his way to the kitchen. I hear the freezer being opened and the clatter of spoons.

"Nothing like stewed apple and ice cream I reckon," he shouts on his way back to the TV.

Hold on. Isn't that two puddings?

I take my dishes to the sink and automatically reach above the cupboard to check that Anna's tablets are safely out of her reach. There's a packet on the shelf beneath which I take down. Cream cakes? A week out of date? Dave inspects the packet I take him.

"I'll eat em now," he says, "cut em in half for me would you..."

I wonder at his appetite, but bring a sharp knife and two plates. Then as I cut the first cake the cream oozes a strange green colour.

"Oh dear." I am not surprised.

"Never mind about that. Chuck that half," Dave tells me, reaching for the rest of the cake.

Anna, who is dozing on the sofa opens her eyes.

"Cake!" shouts Dave.

I take the green halves to the kitchen bin. In the sitting room Dave is telling Anna that what she doesn't eat he will take out to Robbie in the morning. I return to the sitting room and find that all the cake has gone. Dave is watching a programme about the war as usual.

"Have you had pudding dear?" Anna says sleepily. Her head tips forward as she dozes.

There is cake on her cashmere jumper.

HOBBIES

19th October 2017

. . . .

Dave has several hobbies. Gardening for example, cars and motorbikes, sailing, shooting (he was a crack shot he tells us), feeding and watching his birds, fishing, and everything about the countryside. Anna is more difficult.

She loves clothes, art, classical music, opera (but it makes her cry), coffee shops, lunch with her friends, long walks. But it is getting more and more difficult for her to enjoy these things as she becomes more frail and her mind more confused.

At the hospital my screensaver tells me, "Colour me Calm". Lunchtime colouring sessions for staff. I have a great idea! My kind friend at work brings me a grown-up colouring book.

I explain to Anna that it would be lovely if we had some nice pictures for our office walls. She touches the coloured pencils I have brought her.

"You want me to colour these pictures?"

I tell her truthfully that art is not my thing. She went to art school before she became a model so she is the ideal person for the job. She looks sceptical, but starts straight away. Two elephants walking through the jungle.

The detail of one elephant ear takes half an hour, but she is clearly enjoying herself. She is concentrating on her picture.

I make us some tea and read the newspaper. Dave's old grandfather clock counts the minutes. Anna hasn't asked me the time for at least an hour.

I explain what I am doing to Dave. He was always a good artist himself, drawing little cartoons for Anna when they were younger. I send a photo of Anna bent over her colouring book to the family. My brother in Sydney thinks his nine year old daughter would like to share some colouring with her grandmother.

Every day when I return from work I am surprised to see how quickly the pictures are being completed. Elephants, butterflies, windmills, a bridge lit with lanterns. I have to buy more crayons and a sharpener.

This evening I return from work as the evening darkens. The lawn is covered with leaves and the rain is steady. I stop at the front door to find my key and look through the old bullseye pane into the dining room. Dave is at the round table. Colouring pencils in his leathery hand. The book open in front of him. Anna is dozing by the Aga, her mug tilted in her lap.

"It calms me down when she annoys me," he says, as I hang up my raincoat in the long cupboard. "I've nearly finished all the pictures for you."

I make a cup of tea and sit at the round table with him. The rain continues and Anna wakes up to draw the velvet curtains. She comments on the bad weather as she always does.

All is calm.

VESTS

20th October 2017

. . . .

Anna has always been a very private woman, like her mother before her. Sensitive subjects were rarely discussed. When my youngest brother was in his punk phase she asked me to warn him of the dangers of drugs. It wasn't the sort of conversation she would have been comfortable with. I approached him as he combed his long hair into extraordinary patterns.

"Sam," I said, "I have to talk to you about drugs,"

He looked at me for a moment.

"Certainly sister," he said looking innocent, "what did you want to know?"

Nowadays no subject is out of bounds. Dementia has made sure of that. Underwear causes particular difficulties for her. It just doesn't make sense any more. Her tiny vests do not belong to her so they must be Dave's. Someone has put their vests in her chest of drawers. They must be Dave's.

"They've got bloody ribbons on," he roars as she offers him a pair of these intruder vests.

"Anna they're pink," I tell her as she shuffles to the sitting room to offer him yet more vests.

My socks go to Dave's chest of drawers. His enormous stretchy white vests are offered to me. Sometimes there is nothing for it but to put the vests in the clothing bank. Brand new, never worn, but they are certainly not hers! Who on earth left them in her room?

Anna is always cold. The Aga warms the dining room, but she is still cold. The discussion about vests continues. Dave thinks winter vests should have long sleeves for added warmth. Anna thinks this would be too bulky. I have never thought about vests to this extent. I have little to add. The discussion moves naturally on to the forthcoming colder weather. Dave is worried about the Aga because it isn't as warm as it should be. He blames the oil for clogging it up. Additives in the oil are causing the problem. And the additives have come from the EU. (According to Dave)

If I am staying here this winter I hope the Aga doesn't go out. I make Anna a cup of tea and go upstairs to my suitcases.

Did I pack any vests?

WIND

23rd October 2017

. . . .

Anna sees things that we don't see. A very common sight is a fierce and unrelenting wind that, in her own words, bends the trees double and uproots the plants. This wind arrives most days. She was particularly worried about the tulip tree, Liriodendron with its sprawling branches and beautiful blooms. My brother in Devon, who understands these things, had to reassure her that it was a young tree and perfectly safe.

Sometimes Anna talks to something small which is sitting on the carpet by the fire. And when I tell her I am going down the garden to the washing line she often asks me if I am taking my dog. I have no dog though. I try to answer yes or no to this question however, because when she first asked me about my dog I said,

"But I don't have a dog Anna."

And she looked so disappointed with herself.

So when Anna tells me that her adult grandson has been to visit and helped them with colouring their pictures, I agree.

When Anna says that we must be quiet in the evenings because the children are asleep, we say yes, we must be quiet.

When Anna insists that the onion chutney on her morning toast is in fact old Mary's homemade raspberry jam, I say yes.

13

But today I return home from the nearby town where I have bought the ingredients for a lasagne.

"I love lasagne," booms Dave from the sitting room.

I hope this meal will cheer him up. His pheasant plate has broken, and now Robbie hasn't been seen for two days.

Anna is cautiously making her way from the kitchen to greet me. She has to hold on to the wall and then the mantelpiece above the old Aga. Then the back of the chair and the round table. She is looking worried.

Anna was a tall woman in her prime, but she is so tiny now that she looks up at me. Her brown eyes hold a mixture of concern and something like disapproval.

"I just wanted to ask you something ducky," she says, "has your gentleman friend gone from upstairs now?"

I am taken aback by this. My what? My gentleman friend?

Now. If I answer yes to her question as I normally would…

If I answer no to her question…

My mind goes blank.

Distraction is probably the best thing…

"Anna," I say," I think I'll just go and get my dog from the car."

WALKING

27th October 2017

· ·

Anna loved walking when she was younger. She walked in the country lanes around the cottage almost every day. I think she walked primarily for the exercise because I have never seen her as a country lover. I've always felt she was a city girl at heart, and her heart returned to Chester in her old age.

"I want to go back," she told me sometimes, remembering her teenage years.

If her heart was in Chester her mind regularly returned to Birmingham and her beloved parents, and the war. The delayed action bomb that fell in their garden and nearly destroyed their home, the neighbour stuck in the trapdoor that led to their cellar during an air raid, the shopkeeper with shell shock from the First World War.

Of her current home; the home she had lived in for the past forty-eight years, she remembered the walking.

"I wish I could come with you," she would say sadly. And sometimes, on a good day, when the trees weren't bent double under the menacing wind, she would walk around the church with me, clinging to my arm. We would stop to look at the village pond with duck island at its centre, and often we would see someone who knew her.

"But I don't know that person," she would say, once we had passed them.

"Never mind."

Last week one of Dave's relatives from the nearby town brought a walking aid. Four wheels and a pair of handlebars and a comfy seat for when you tire. Anna was horrified.

"Put that thing in the shed," she ordered Dave, with menace in her eyes.

I put it behind her armchair by the Aga, muttering warnings about rust in the shed and rubber-eating insects. Anna was not convinced and glared at it regularly.

But today the sun is shining in the fields and we leave the front door open. I put on my jacket and tell Anna I'm going for a quick walk.

"I wish I could come with you."

"You can," I say, "and we'll take your present with us". I wheel the walking trolley to the doorway. Anna looks cross but to my surprise she shuffles towards it and grasps the handlebars.

Dave's face lights up when I call to him from the lane. Anna watches him stacking logs at the bottom of the garden for a while, and then I suggest we go to see the new houses. A developer is refurbishing the old pub and building two new houses as well.

We walk slowly, but Anna is certainly walking faster than when she clung on to me. The walking trolley is giving her confidence and I am delighted. In fact I am feeling quite smug.

Down the lane the sun shines on the new houses. The refurbished pub makes me a little wistful though as it was once one of the best pubs in the county, famous for its ales and ploughman's and the landlady who had been singing at the piano for most of her life.

Our cottage was where our friends came for pre-drinks, before such a thing was ever invented. The farm next door was where my younger brothers worked when they were small, collecting eggs for the singing landlady in return for bottles of beer.

Now the old pub has turned into a house, smart and modern, almost ready to be sold. We stop and stare at the builders' caravan with logs stacked neatly outside, at the scaffolding and the tarpaulins and the new doors and windows. I wonder how much Anna remembers of the old days at the pub.

I compliment her on steering her new aid this far. She is concentrating on holding onto the brake and hasn't noticed that there is actually quite a strong breeze now. Still I am very pleased that I have achieved this little victory. Now Dave can take Anna shopping and he will be able to carry their grocery bags with ease. I can't help voicing my triumph,

"Now you'll be able to go into town with Dave and you won't have to hold onto his arm," I tell her.

Anna is watching two builders on the roof of one of the new houses; the one nearest the lane.

"Mornin," calls one of the men from the roof.

"Morning," I say, and Anna takes her hand from the brake and gives him a slight wave.

"It's a lovely morning," I say.

"It certainly is, although we have to work of course," he says cheerfully.

I laugh.

Anna raises her voice," Now ducky if you've finished flirting with these men I should like to go home please."

Oh.

Oh dear.

Did they hear her on their roof?

Does she know what she is saying?

I pull my jacket collar up around my ears and start to walk back along the lane. I don't think I will walk this way for a while. Anna is interested in the tulip tree which we can see over the hedge.

"This wind has brought down nearly all the leaves. Dave will have to get the rake out soon."

Down at the sheds Dave is still stacking logs. Robbie is watching him from a nearby bush.

"You had a nice walk?"

"Yes dear," says Anna, "very nice."

We walk on a little further.

Anna looks up at me, "But I don't think I'll do it again ducky."

LEAF BLOWING

28th October 2017

Certain things bother Anna. Things that wouldn't necessarily bother me. Washing on the line after three o'clock, bedtime after nine o'clock, waking up after seven o'clock, old newspapers in the sitting room, too much chocolate in the house, and leaving the washing up for longer than ten minutes after you've eaten. And certain things bother Dave. Leaves on the lawn is a big bother. And difficult to deal with when your knees have stiffened up with age. I like raking leaves into leaf piles, but not every day.

But then my brother from Devon arrives with a leaf blower and Dave is smitten.

"I'm going to order one of them blowers," he tells us, and two days later he proudly unpacks one in the kitchen.

It's a beautiful day and I am not working. The cottage faces south and the sun warms the garden and sparkles in the fields beyond.

I have decided to do some baking. A date cake for David and some flapjack for Anna. And probably some home-made burgers for supper. I've opened the front door onto the garden and one of the dining room windows. This is a small triumph for me as Anna hates having doors and windows open in case the wind comes in. Anna has never spent so much as five minutes in a beauty parlour or nail bar, but she does have certain priorities.

They are long skirts, cashmere polo neck jumpers, matching clip -on earrings and a headscarf in her hair. Her hair is washed and styled every fortnight and Dave drives her to these appointments under protest.

"Why can't you do your bloody hair in the sink under the tap like I do," he protests. She takes no notice of course.

So the danger is that the wind could wreak havoc with her carefully styled hair. She has told me that on some occasions the wind has blown her folded headscarf clean off her head!

I find Dave's mixing bowl in the bottom drawer in the kitchen and measure out the flour and sugar for the date cake on the wall scales. Then I carry the bowl and the packet of dates to the round table in the dining room where Anna is sitting by the Aga. The dates have to be chopped into small pieces on the wooden board.

A sudden noise pop-pops behind me. A chainsaw? Surely Dave isn't chainsawing logs by the house? Then a shout of joy and Dave's at the open window with the leaf blower.

"Look at this!" he shouts pointing the nozzle through the window. Papers on the small table by the window rise into the air. My apron is blown onto the floor. The bowl of flour slides across the round table.

"We can even dry the clothes on the washing line with this," he shouts over the noise, "and dry the cars when we've washed em."

"Yes dear," says Anna automatically.

I wonder why she is not worried by the power and noise of this new gadget, but then I remember that Anna trusts Dave implicitly with these things. There is nothing, in her eyes, that he cannot operate or mend.

The smell of 2-stroke fills the house so that I have to shut the door. Anna doesn't seem to notice, but the smell is filling my eyes and my lungs.

It is too warm to shut the window so the irritating whine of the leaf blower fills the afternoon. Dave doesn't even stop for lunch. Like a shepherd with his sheep he herds the leaves into huge piles on the lawn and then blows the piles through the gaps in the hedge, and into the field. I begin to wonder if he is blowing things around just for sake of it.

The cakes are ready and cooling on an old wire rack I've found next to the fridge. I tell Anna that I am going to the local town to get some shopping.

"Those planes have been flying around the house all day," she says sleepily.

Dave is in a swirl of leaves and doesn't notice as I drive out onto the lane. Half a mile down the road is the recreation ground, deserted today but for a young woman walking two dogs. I wind down the windows, unwrap a piece of flapjack, and enjoy the peace.

CLOCKS

29th October 2017

. . . .

The clocks have gone back today. Simple really, to wind your watch back one hour.

But not here.

There are several clocks in the cottage. I get up at eight am, which is now seven am, and notice that the clocks I pass on the way to the kitchen are telling different tales. The old station clock says nine am and the grandfather clock says seven am. If I sit in Anna's faded patterned armchair by the Aga these two clocks tick alternately, as if talking to each other, which is curiously soothing. I have a quick check in the sitting room. It's quarter to one.

Fortunately I don't have a bus or train to catch. Or an appointment at the dentist.

Time is very confusing to Anna now. She has always worn a wristwatch with two dials; one for UK time, and the other for Australian time. This is so that she knows the best time to ring Sam.

But these days she asks me every few days to tell her the time in Australia.

"I don't want to wake them up do I."

Anna also feels sure that someone has messed about with time. The evenings feel more like mornings. At first I suggest she looks outside and sees the evening darkening. The starlings swarming over the field. The fact that Dave is in his armchair watching TV.

But this does not help. Anna becomes restless and goes to the calendar on the kitchen wall. Days and dates have also lost their meaning. The calendar is long and thin, a month to a page. Decorated with scenes from the New Forest and crossings out and scribbles which are their appointments. I might have wondered if, in this quiet village life, they need to worry about time. Surely they could ignore their clocks and just eat and sleep and talk and watch TV. But they have so many appointments. The GP, the hospital, the podiatrist, the hairdresser, coffee with Meg, coffee with Jean, blood tests, collect tablets, opticians. Sometimes crossed out and then rewritten. Sometimes repeated on two or three occasions. Sometimes missed.

I thought I had the answer. A new calendar with a week to a page. No more calendar muddle. Dave was impressed. He immediately put two appointments on the following week. Anna looked at it suspiciously. We removed the old calendar. The New Forest ponies looked at us mournfully. Anna was enraged and found it hidden under Dave's armchair seat cushion. She clutched the calendar to her cashmere jumper.

The old calendar is back in its place on the hook above the wooden chest of drawers in the kitchen. No fancy granite worktop in this house. Just wood.

Anna is back in her armchair next to the Aga; next to the copper frying pans and the old wooden clothes horse dotted with vests and more vests.

"I still wonder how our parents fed us during the war," says Anna, "they had so little food."

Dave has brought their cereal bowls to the round table.

"I caught plenty of rabbits before school," says Dave, "and I sold 'em for a bob in the village!" He laughs loudly at the memory. This upsets his asthma and causes a coughing fit.

My attention wanders outside to the greedy rooks on the bank above the garden and the nuthatch upside down on the feeder.

Breakfast time.

Anna and Dave have returned to their childhood, happily exchanging wartime memories. I check my iPhone.

Time to get on with the day.

DAVE'S KITCHEN

3rd November 2017

The kitchen in the cottage was originally an attached barn. Dave cleverly converted it when Sam was a baby and put in a floor to create a small sloping-ceilinged bedroom above. The dining room has two entrances to the kitchen, either side of the old Aga. The arched entrance is Anna's. Anna stands in the entrance in the early mornings to put on her make up in the mirror over the sink. Anna stands in the entrance to consult the calendar. Anna stands in the entrance to comment on the weather.

"It's a grey old day," is a favourite expression.

Dave gets grumpy about this entrance being blocked.

"Outta my way woman!" he shouts, pushing past her and kissing her on her papery cheek.

I try to use the other entrance. Dave himself is blocking the arched entrance as he watches his birds feeding under the plum tree.

"That bloody cat! If he gets my birds!".

"I'll shoot that bloody rat! He is talking about a real rat now.

But the other entrance is blocked by Dave's shop.

A vegetable rack filled with bags of potatoes, the food that no meal is complete without. Cooking apples slowly turning brown with age. Bottles of beer.

Washing powder. And tins and tins and tins. Macaroni cheese. Evaporated milk. Mushy peas. Baked beans. Carrots. Spaghetti hoops.

Tin walls. Rarely breached. Rarely opened. Just in case the war comes back again.

I try to clear the entrance. I open the dusty wooden kitchen cupboards to look for space. But the cupboards are filled with tins. Macaroni cheese. Evaporated milk. Mushy peas, baked beans…

I push the tins together. I stack the tins. Vegetables one side. Fruit the other. Evaporated milk in a tin stack of its own. Anna and Dave watch anxiously. Dave's shop is running out of food. Potatoes in a potato bag in the cupboard.

The entrance is clear. I walk backwards and forwards through the entrance just because I can.

"This is much better," I tell them. "Look, we can walk through to the kitchen now."

I am talking to myself. Anna and Dave. Heads bent over a piece of scrappy paper. A biro in Dave's bear-like hands.

"Macaroni cheese, evaporated milk, mushy peas, baked beans…"

I put the heavy kettle on the Aga hot plate and wait for the heat to blow the whistle onto the floor. I take my tea to the porch and sit in the afternoon sun. I hear them in the kitchen as I close my eyes in the sun. Dave's shop is being replenished.

SATURDAYS

. . . .

Saturdays follow a regular pattern. Anna is up early, drinking tea and putting on her make-up. Dave makes the breakfast. The muesli, cornflakes and bran in their favourite bowls. Then they sit together by the Aga and talk about Saturday. Dave's boat. Dave's friends. And Anna's appointments for the following week. All three topics lead to debate.

Will the boat sell before the end of the year? Dave loves the sea, but he is getting too old and tired to cope with the maintenance of a boat. Dave's boat friends are a worry. Gordon is eating too much chocolate. Should Dave have lunch at the boatyard with his friends? If he does he will probably eat too much and feel unwell for the rest of the day.

Anna has a hair appointment on Tuesday and a foot appointment on Wednesday. How will she get there? Will Dave take her? Or should she get a taxi?

"Of course I'll take you! I always bloody well do!" he shouts.

"Ooh that wind's getting up," says Anna. "Poor old garden."

Dave heads off to the village shop. He goes early.

27

The newspapers won't be delivered yet but he can have a chat with the volunteers there and eye up the wonderful cakes that Maggie bakes. Anna is left at the cottage wondering where he is.

"Is he at the boat now deary?" she asks me several times.

Sometimes Alan comes across the fields to the cottage in his corduroy trousers, peaked cap and waxed jacket. I am not sure if he has been a builder or a gamekeeper or both, but he loves to talk about the countryside with Dave over a cup of tea and cake. Not so many rabbits out there now. Big polecats eating rabbits. Was it a stoat? Catch that magpie. Going beating Saturday mate? That ferret Ida. Snatches of country conversation make their way to the kitchen while I wash the dishes and look out across the fields.

Then Dave goes off to the boat, and that really means that he's going for a hefty lunch and brew up at the boatyard. And a good old argument about politics with his mates. Brexit. The NHS. Teresa May. The EU messing with the oil that feeds Agas across the country.

He returns at four pm for a cup of tea in his oversized mug and then off to the sitting room to look at the papers.

Anna is colder still since the clocks changed. She wants him to light the huge woodburning stove. Sometimes one of my brothers rings. One of the boys, Anna calls them. The telephone is very loud and wakes Dave from his nap.

"Get that bloody thing!" he roars, struggling to his feet.

But sometimes it's just someone selling something. Dave doesn't want to know.

The television is disappointing. What's the matter with the BBC? That's what Dave wants to know. I cook mushroom omelettes which they both enjoy. One egg for Anna. Three eggs for Dave. And a pile of potatoes and vegetables.

At last Dave has found a programme to watch. Anna wanders into the other rooms of the house. This is her wandering time. Unable to settle.

I bring her a small glass of red wine and put it on the wobbly stool next to the sofa.

"Thank you deary," she says, closing her eyes, "Is it Sunday?"

"It's Saturday!" booms Dave from his armchair.

"It's getting very dark," says Anna.

The moon is very beautiful above the the fields. The only other light comes from the house across the nearest field. In the cottage Anna and Dave have dozed off in front of the news. And another Saturday comes to a close. All the Saturdays the same. For now.

CATALOGUES

10th November 2017

. . . .

A small triumph! I have managed to get them to allow me to take down the bathroom curtain. A pale chintz blue, fully lined, and thick with dust and mildew. What about a blind? Or even a thinner curtain? Anna looks at me sceptically. Dave doesn't like the idea of a blind.

"I 'ad one once and the bloody thing kept jammin' so I ripped 'im down."

"Yes that's true," says Anna thoughtfully.

So I'm washing the wretched curtain. Anna joins me at the sink.

"Deary I'll get them to come and sort out a new one if you like?"

Who? Not that extremely expensive interior designer I hope.

That's the strange thing about Anna and Dave. The cottage has no central heating, no downstairs loo, no shower, until recently no duvet covers, no electric cooker for when the Aga goes out, no dishwasher or microwave oven. But all the furniture is antique, or from the best shops.

And another very important thing the cottage has is catalogues.

So, no patter of envelopes through the letterbox each morning, but the heavy thud of catalogues hitting the doormat.

Catalogues. They arrive each day. Sometimes two, sometimes three or four. If you want a Marseilles soap dish, an Antigua embroidered pouffe, modern tweed culottes, something in marled linen country flannel, velvet tassel slippers, seeland woodcock breeds or a gents nine-piece manicure set, the catalogue is here. I have hardly touched my books since moving in as there is always a country catalogue to look at which sells things I didn't know existed.

I've only once seen a parcel arrive with catalogue spoils. Three cashmere jumpers for Anna in the loveliest colours. Pale lemon, teal blue and an orangey-pink. Every colour suits her. Black doesn't. But every other colour.

Just one parcel. But still the catalogues arrive. Piled up in the dining room and the sitting room until they are out of date; the season changes; the year passes.

Dave loves catalogues too. For his corduroy trousers and moleskin waistcoats. For his shirts and socks and collection of jackets.

"I used to dress up proper," he tells me, "to take Anna to have a meal at nice pubs. Course I can't take 'er now."

Dave has only ever known a modest income. But he has never begrudged Anna a penny for her lovely clothes. Even now when age has twisted her spine and her memory has deserted her.

And that I think is true love.

HAIR

12th November 2017

. . . .

Pandemonium! The cottage is in turmoil. Dave's birds have retreated back into the safety of the hedge at the top of the bank. The cows have hurried to the other side of the field. Dark clouds creep across the sky from the west.

An argument is taking place. Anna has a hair appointment. It's on the calendar. Twice. Next Tuesday and next Thursday. Dave looks after the appointment cards in a little plastic box behind the cyclamen. This box never lies and it tells Dave that Anna's appointment is on Tuesday the fourteenth. So why the bloody hell does she keep on insisting it's on Thursday the sixteenth? Anna has a way of looking at Dave that makes him furious.

"I'm telling you my appointment is on Thursday," she says coldly.

"Then why does the card say Tuesday?" he roars.

The truth is that Dave is more concerned at this moment about his weekend newspaper. It's missing the Saturday Review section. Without this section Dave can't work out what to watch on television. I show him how to select the menu from the TV remote but he is not convinced. He tells me I should have bought his paper from the old shop in the next village and not from the new supermarket on the estate.

"That's why half the bloody paper's missing."

"So will you take me to the hairdresser on Thursday or shall I get a taxi?" says Anna.

Hmmm. I might just go outside now and let the storm go past. I climb up onto the bank and look across the field which is dotted with rooks. In fact everywhere I walk in the village I'm aware of rooks - arguing, nesting, flying, pulling wireworms and leatherjackets out of the grass, or just watching. At the top of the field the young heifers are pushing and play fighting with each other. Chasing each other across the wet grass.

I go back to the warm kitchen. The argument is continuing.

"So will you take me to my appointment today?" says Anna, peering at her calendar.

"Your appointment isn't 'till Tuesday!" Dave is losing patience.

"It says here it's on the sixteenth!"

"It's Sunday today," I say helpfully.

"My appointment's on Thursday then deary."

"Your appointment's on Tuesday!" Dave is overheating now.

"No my appointment's today!"

Right. Janine the hairdresser runs her own business and I will email her to check the appointment date.

To my surprise the email is answered an hour later. Janine is doing her accounts. Anna has an appointment on Thursday the sixteenth. She understands that Anna has memory problems, so is happy for me to email or ring her to check. By now a tense silence has fallen over the cottage. The cows have tentatively moved closer to the hedge to see if Dave has thrown any apples their way.

I break the news. I explain that the appointment on Tuesday fourteenth was moved to the sixteenth.

"Well who the bloody hell moved it?" says Dave.

"I did," says Anna.

"What for!" roars Dave. "You had nothin' on for the fourteenth, so what did you move it for!"

Anna closes her eyes and sighs. "I wanted to move it, so I did," she says. "Now will you drive me to my hair appointment today or shall I get a taxi?"

SITTERS

18th November 2017

It's a damp grey day. The lanes around the cottage are muddy. I'm watching the sparrows and blue tits on the bird feeder, and a tiny field mouse slipping out of sight between the paving stones below the bank. Dave tells me that we should move my pots of plants closer to the cottage as colder weather is coming. He also tells me that the robin watching us from the bank is Bobby, who has chased his brother Robbie to the bottom of the long garden.

"I'll 'ave to take him some grub down there now. I'll take him a fat ball for himself."

Dave is planning an outing with his friend Ted to a furniture auction. Ted hasn't been well for some months now, and Dave is worried about him.

"We've never fell out, me and Ted. Ever. He's my best mate. He joined the Army and I joined the Air Force."

Dave then tells me the story of how Ted lost control of a tanker he was driving on a narrow bridge near Reading. He ended up in the river, swimming through chemicals and fearing for his life.

"The chemicals melted his clothes clean off him!" says Dave wonderingly, "but 'e survived."

So an outing is planned. But there is a problem. And that concerns Anna. Who will look after her?

Dave could ask Anna's friends, Jane or Anne or Brenda. But he's reluctant to bother them unless it's an emergency. I often sense that attitude here now; the need to feel independent and in control of life.

"What about a sitter?" I ask tentatively.

Dave says nothing. He doesn't like to bring up these subjects with Anna.

Amongst the firelighters and the stove cleaner and books about the war with titles like "Soldier" and "Gulf War", are several pairs of glasses. Anna is trying to find her reading glasses. She no longer holds a book in her lap and reads the same page over and over, but she is at least able to look at the TV pages of the newspaper. I wait until she is sitting down.

"Dave and Ted are going to the auction in Somerset next week," I say, "and I'll be at work, so we were wondering about someone coming to sit with you and have a cup of tea rather than being on you own."

"Like a sitter," I add.

I am a little nervous about this proposal although it should be easy. Before she retired, Anna herself was a sitter. She was self-employed. She didn't wear a uniform. She was like a friend or companion calling in for a cup of tea.

Anna narrows her eyes. I sense that Dave is behind the door listening.

"I don't think that would be a good idea at all."

Her tone is cool.

"But rather than being on your own..."

"I'm perfectly alright on my own. I'm not ill."

"But it would be company for you," I say.

Anna looks down at the newspaper and is silent. The door opens.

"I've been wantin' to take her to the pensioners lunch," says Dave, "There'd be people to talk to and stuff to do..."

"There's a Day centre as well locally," I add.

"The Day Centre!"

Anna is giving Dave one of her looks now.

"Carers and Day Centres and whatever you said are for old people," says Anna firmly. "When I am old and past it we can talk about these things, but until then I am quite happy on my own thank you."

Dave makes a noise like a balloon deflating.

"We can think about it again," I say, as firmly as I can.

I go back into the dining room where the Aga kettle huffs and puffs on the hotplate. A nuthatch looks at me upside-down through the window.

That was not successful. Yet every time I meet a friend or acquaintance and tell them about Anna, they tell me about their own mother, father, sister, brother, grandfather, grandmother, close friend, neighbour...

I must make a plan.

TABLETS

19th November 2017

. . . .

Dave has always worked with his hands, driving machines, chopping logs, splitting logs, lighting the wood burner, tending the garden, working on their cars, to name a few. His hands are old and misshapen now, so small things like tablets are difficult to deal with. Anna has tablets three times a day and Dave is in charge. They're collected each week from the GP surgery and are packed in a tablet house with plastic windows that must be split open at the right day and time.

Dave has his own system. He goes by shape.

"That's the mornin' ones," he tells me. A stone-coloured oval and half a round white one. Afternoon is oval white and a large round white. Night is a round blush nestling with a peach oval, accompanied by two small round sky blue ones. One of these pills lists confusion as a side effect.

That is confusing.

Anna doesn't care about any of these tablets except for the little blue ones. Her sleeping tablets. Anna has been a poor sleeper all her life and has told me she had her first sleeping tablets at the age of eighteen.

At about half past four in the afternoon it is almost dark. I like the way Dave has planted the high bank with hollyhocks, cordyline, and a proud olive tree in its pot. All these shapes outlined in the evening light, and the windows draped with the branches of the grape-vine.

Across the field the sky is pink. Dave tells us there will be a frost tonight. But Anna isn't listening. She wants her sleeping tablets. Now. Dave tells her she can have them at 9 o'clock. But Anna wants her tablets. Now.

I suggest soup and prawn sandwiches. Or cheese on toast. Or even a fish cake. I'm trying to distract her from the sleeping tablets. If she has them too early she will be up and dressed at three in the morning. Wandering downstairs on her own. If I don't distract her she will probably get angry and even swear at us. If I don't distract her Dave will get angry and fed up with asking her to wait until nine o'clock. Sometimes my distraction works and Anna shuffles back to the sitting room to sit by the fire to wait for her supper. Sometimes we have to promise her that she can go to bed now, even if it is only eight o'clock, and we will bring her tablets at nine o'clock.

Tonight Anna has gone to bed early. The grandfather clock ticks monotonously and regularly. The kettle hisses on the Aga. The fridge hums. Bloodcurdling yells and screams from Dave's war films. And Anna sleeps.

I break open the plastic window and put the tablets into the small tumbler and take them up to the bedroom. As I lift the latch Anna stirs and lifts herself slowly on one elbow. She is wearing colourful spotted pyjamas. She looks at me curiously.

"Are my parents here?" she says.

Are her parents here?

I don't know.

"Well I've brought your tablets," I say, handing them to her one at a time. Anna puts down her glass of water and curls under her duvet.

As I go back down the stairs I know that she is already asleep.

OUT FOR LUNCH

23rd November 2017

Anna has always enjoyed going out for coffee or lunch with family or friends. She and Dave have their favourite places, and much depends on the quality of the flat white coffee on offer. They first tasted this in Sydney and have loved it ever since. They call it a "flit wott" for some reason.

This morning Anna looks tired and I am surprised when she says she would like to go out for lunch. Dave is down at the boatyard and it is raining, so I think perhaps she wants a change of scene. There's a textile exhibition at the nearby garden centre so I suggest we go there.

This is not a run-of-the-mill garden centre but a specialist tree nursery in many acres of land. We could walk for hours through the extraordinary autumn colours, and we would have done so once, but not now. Anna clings onto my arm and we walk so slowly that I can comment on each Acer or Sequoia that we pass. I stop and pick up some of their fallen leaves so that Anna can see them more closely.

Lunch is soup, at a round table in the big glass cafeteria. The weather has kept people at home today so only three or four tables are occupied. Anna always has soup. Wherever we go. Then we share some mint chocolate cake.

After lunch we walk slowly around the textile exhibition and buy several Christmas tree decorations. Knitted mauve and pink stars. A tiny tree in green felt with yellow and red beads.

Anna looks pale so I walk her back to the car and we drive home along muddy lanes.

She is quiet on the journey and as I park the car she turns to me,

"I'm awfully sorry but I can't invite you in I'm afraid."

Ah.

I switch off the engine and open the passenger door to help her out.

"I feel very bad about this. Perhaps another time though."

Right.

I unlock the front door.

"Shall I make you a cup of tea before I...er...go?" I ask.

"No I'll be fine thank you."

She is closing the door behind herself.

I crouch down under the dining room window and peep through the branches of the grapevine. Anna puts the heavy kettle on the hotplate and her favourite mug on the table.

It's starting to rain again. I am crouching under the window in the rain.

When I see she is in her armchair I go back to the car and watch the raindrops on the windscreen. Four cyclists pass the cottage at great speed. Then Linda from up the road on her horse. Finally a woman walking briskly down the lane with two small dachshunds.

I lock the car and go back to the front door which I tentatively unlock. Anna lifts her head where she has been dozing.

"Hello," she smiles, "Have you had a nice day deary?"

TED

26th November 2017

. . . .

Once upon a time we always went to the pub at the bottom of the lane. The beer was famous, as were the ploughman's lunches and the ham sandwiches. Dave would meet up with his best friend Ted in the public bar. They would enjoy a pint of HSB and remember the old days.

On Sunday I am driving out of the cottage on my way to the local town. I glance in my mirror and see Ted walking slowly up the lane. I wait for him to draw closer and lower my window. We comment on the weather, the mud, the need to get in as many logs as possible before the cold sets in. I tell him Dave will be pleased to see him. That he and Anna have some banana cake to share. As I drive away I think about how pale Ted looks. As if there is no blood in his veins any more.

On Wednesday Dave hears that Ted has been taken into hospital. He has had a heart attack, and before Dave can get to the hospital Ted has gone. Dave sits very quietly in his armchair in the sitting room, and tells me that Ted was his best mate. He always knew how to find anything Dave wanted. From a spare part for the Aga to an antique chair. He is not sure what to do. All his friends have gone now.

Dave says he will take us to a pub for lunch in the next village, and I offer to drive. We find Anna's warmest coat and thickest gloves. She seems restless and anxious and I think she too is upset about Ted. It's not far; two miles maybe through the lanes. And the pub is glorious.

A huge log fire with tables nearby and a very nice menu. Dave tells us that his father used to drink at this pub during the war, sitting in front of the log fire with the Yanks, as Dave calls them. I can just about remember Dave's father. A man who worked hard and drank a lot. And didn't seem to like Dave very much.

"'E used to walk here across the fields from our bungalow," Dave tells us on the way home. He tries to spot the old bungalow through the trees, but they have grown tall over the years.

"These fields are lovely," I say, thinking how different Dave's wartime childhood was from Anna's.

"The men used to drink so much beer at the pub that they fell over in the fields on the way 'ome and slept all night in the corn!" Dave says, smiling at the memory.

"Is that true?" I say.

"Yep. I saw them in the morning," says Dave, "staggerin' 'ome."

"I used to go out in the fields with my mates to get the veg...the potatoes and carrots from the War Ag Committee fields. My mother weren't half pleased I did."

He explains that during the war the farmers were told which crops they should grow by this organisation, the War Agricultural Executive Committee. Dave was one of five children and there wasn't enough to eat, so it was only natural for him to find what he could in the countryside around them.

"I won't sleep tonight," Dave tells me later that evening, "I'm goin' be thinking about Ted all the time."

We talk about Ted's long, happy life; his family, his work, his love of the countryside. Dave is calmer now. But we know that this is not just about Ted's passing.

Outside it is very dark. Anna always seems surprised by this, as if somehow there should be lights somewhere out there. Perhaps that is her city upbringing. I open one of the curtains in the dining room to see if the moon is lighting the fields. But there are just the dark shapes of the shrubs on the bank, and in the distance the harsh calls of a barn owl.

THE AGA

2nd December 2017

The Aga is the heart of the cottage. It is over eighty years old, according to the Aga company, and it is the only source of cooking here. It has a hot oven, a warm oven, a hotplate and a warm plate. I think Anna struggled with it when they first moved in and it ran on solid fuel. I certainly remember my attempts at baking cakes fell flat. Many people would have an alternative cooker available for the summer months, but not here. So the Aga has always been warm, drying our clothes, drying our dog, drying our shoes and socks, drying my Shropshire brother's horse tackle.

It is nine o'clock in the evening and Dave is watching an aggressive war film while Anna dozes, tilting to the right, as she always does. I am immersed in a catalogue of Christmas cashmere, surprised to learn that cashmere clothes have their own combs and shampoo. I hardly notice Dave staggering to his feet, cursing under his breath, but when he opens the sitting room door I can smell something oily in the air.

"Bloody Aga's going out!" says Dave, making his way across the dining room. He bends down to fiddle with the Aga regulator.

"It's the bloody oil," he roars, "The bloody additives that lot puts in it!"

"What can I do?" I ask helpfully, opening the dining room windows. The oil fumes are awful. I wrap my scarf around my nose and mouth.

But I will have to get out of the dining room. Upstairs is no better. I will have to get some fresh air.

Outside I relax. The fields are dark, but there is a bright moon. The windows are open. The front door is open. Dave is letting the Aga go out. Dave loves oil smells, diesel smells, engine smells. This smell does not bother him. I am standing in the garden in December but Dave is inside, in the long coat cupboard, looking for the electric kettle.

And when I go back inside I find Anna in the armchair by the Aga. The windows have been firmly closed.

"Ooh you must be cold deary!" she says.

I am indeed cold.

"It's the oil fumes," I say, "the smell I mean."

Anna looks at me blankly, "what smell?"

In the morning Dave's friend Tom arrives early with his collie dog. Dave has cleared the blockage and replaced the wick, and the Aga is happily boiling the kettle for their coffee. Anna is pleased to tell me that Dave has also made a chocolate cake.

I am studying the paperwork for my new house and unaware of the time passing. In the other room I hear Dave and Tom talking about dog biscuits and vet bills. Then I smell the chocolate cake. Mmmm.

"Dave," I say, "is the cake cool enough to cut?"

I have to repeat this because of his deafness. He gives me a startled look and lunges at the Aga. I pass him the oven glove. Oh dear.

A burnt chocolate cake. Tom and his collie dog look interested however.

"I was too busy talking," says Dave sadly.

"Perhaps we can rescue some of it," I say, "as it does smell nice."

"What smell?" says Anna from her armchair.

I google this. Lemon, peppermint, fish, roses, leather, orange. Our sense of smell has close links with brain functioning. I remember that Anna couldn't smell the Brasso that Dave uses to clean the old warming pans and horse brasses that adorn the cottage.

I tell Dave about this. He tells me that he has a great sense of smell. Anna has a great sense of hearing.

"So I'll do the smelling and she can do the hearing," he says as he cuts the burnt edges off the chocolate cake.

ADMIRERS

5th December 2017

. . . .

So you may wonder how Dave and Anna, as different as chalk and cheese, could have ended up together. Dave the local lad from a rural family; the oldest of five children, who left school at fourteen. And Anna who grew up in various cities and was educated in convent schools, pronouncing "plastic, elastic and drastic" with a drawn out 'ahhh' sound.

Perhaps I didn't really know the answer to this until I came to stay at the cottage.

The talk turns to tomatoes. The local shop gets tomatoes from a nearby nursery, and Dave heartily approves of local produce.

"Tastes better," he says.

"Do you remember those tomatoes Mr Woolly Hat used to bring you?"

Anna scowls at him from the sofa.

"Tomatoes with love he used to call 'em," says Dave in a mocking tone.

"There were chocolates as well," Anna tells me quietly, so Dave won't hear.

"And all the other bloody vegetables," says Dave.

"His glasses were stuck together in the middle with bloomin' superglue! A great blob of it!"

"So Mr Woolly Hat was an admirer?" I ask.

"Just one of 'em," says Dave.

He goes on to list the admirers.

The teacher at the village school, the scout master, someone on a bicycle who taught art, various chaps at the pub, and the local builder's son who apparently almost pined away with love.

"I had to see him off," says Dave.

There are photos of Anna in her young days in the albums. Wearing beautiful clothes. Evening dresses, wedding dresses, day dresses, party dresses. And many hats. And one I remember with particular interest had a zip in it.

"Why does this hat have a zip?" I asked her as a child.

"For your lipstick," she told me.

Anna never went into detail about anything. I think she has always skated rather successfully along the top of life.

Dave is scathing about these admirers as he calls them, but on the other hand he is secretly delighted to have such a beautiful wife. And also delighted that other men fall for her. And Anna loves a compliment.

The other reason for their success is that Anna loves clothes. Well-made clothes. And Dave loves buying her clothes. And seeing her wear the clothes he buys her.

Anna on the other hand has always been happy to give Dave space. Space to get on with his hobbies whenever he wants.

Sailing on Saturdays, chopping logs and shooting and fishing. Spending hours in his sheds, or riding the lanes on his tractor.

So where did they meet?

Surprisingly it was at the ice rink.

"A whole crowd of us used to go speed skating together," Dave tells me. "I saw 'er sitting there at the side of the rink with lovely blonde hair."

"I was with my sister," says Anna.

"My mate John 'e was smitten," says Dave thoughtfully, "'e just kept doing figures of eight to show off in front of 'er."

They are both quiet for a moment. Anna stares into the fire.

So they met at the ice rink. Was it love at first sight?

No it wasn't.

In fact Anna married John.

But that's another story.

COATS

13th December 2017

. . . .

Foolish me. I sold my house, packed up my belongings and put nearly everything I possess into storage. I brought a few things to the cottage. They fill the "little room" at the top of the house, and cause Anna to shake her head in dismay. Anna doesn't like clutter.

Now the winter is as cold as stone. I haven't seen the cows for days, and Bobby and the other birds hop about on the frozen bank in the morning waiting for Dave to get out of bed.

Anna is always up early putting on her make-up, drinking tea and dozing by the Aga. She waits for Dave to make the breakfast which is four or five different cereals mixed with cold milk. And more tea. Anna likes making tea as it is one of the few tasks she remembers. She cannot read or sew or cook or even make much conversation, but she can make tea and coffee.

I am rushing to get to work and it is a long drive.

"You got no coat then?" says Dave as I search for my car keys. "There's loads in the cupboard." He stomps across the kitchen and opens the door of the long cupboard. I hope he isn't going to offer me one of his.

"Loads of 'em," he says lifting hangers off the rail.

Yes he's right. Short burgundy jackets, a cream fur-lined jacket, a long herringbone coat and a wrap-over dark brown coat, a check jacket, a very expensive herringbone jacket with a suede collar, a brown fur jacket, a navy three-quarter wool jacket. And that's just the front section of the long cupboard. Dave pulls out a long navy coat. It's very stylish.

"Here's a warm one," shouts Dave.

Anna looks at us coldly.

"I need a coat in this weather," she says with ice in her voice.

"Let 'er just borrow this one," says Dave, and hurries me towards the door.

It's a warm coat and it's long. Very long. I feel a bit self-conscious wearing it, as if I am aware of a fashion that no-one else has yet discovered. But I'm glad of it in this weather.

It's dark when I get back to the cottage and the wood-burning stove is roaring. Anna follows me out to the kitchen, her long skirt trailing on the floor.

"Deary I've lost a coat and I wonder if you know where it is?"

Ummmm.

"It's my fur coat, and I need it in this cold weather."

I have never seen Anna in a fur coat, and I tell her so.

She looks furious. These days she gets angry so quickly.

"Of course you have, I wear it every winter!"

"I'll cook you some mushrooms on toast," I tell her, " and we can have a think about your coat."

Dave looks surprised when I ask about the fur coat.

"She looked lovely in that fur coat and she had a Russian hat to go with it," he tells me. "But that was forty years ago and then everyone took against 'em and she gave it to the charity shop!"

He tells me about a furrier who lived in the village at that time.

"He went bust in less than a week."

Within a few days I realise that every time I put on my borrowed coat I am triggering a memory of the missing fur coat for Anna. This is difficult as there is no sign of a thaw in the weather.

Finally I decide to keep the coat in my car. I rush out to put it on in the morning before I scrape the ice from the windscreen. Then I leave it in the car in the evening and shiver in the cold rain on the doorstep until Anna or Dave removes the chain from the door and lets me in.

"Oh dear you must be cold," says Anna when she sees me.

I lift the latch of the door to the long coat cupboard and step inside to look for the old wooden drying rack. I'll dry my gloves and woolly hat in front of the Aga.

There is constant debate about this cupboard. Anna and Dave shake their heads with dismay when it is mentioned.

"Too much stuff in that cupboard," says Dave.

"We have to clear it out," says Anna.

But nothing ever happens. If I offer to help Dave always says,

"When the weather's warmer then."

Or something similar.

I stop and stare in wonder. There on the rail is the long navy wool coat. But it can't be! Surely the long navy coat is in my car?

Then I look closer. It's a different coat. But exactly the same.

"Anna," I say, lifting it out of the cupboard, "This is a nice coat."

Anna is alert to the subject of clothes. "Yes deary, I found that at the back of the cupboard today."

Hooray. There are two coats so now I can wear "mine" without worrying.

Anna is gazing out of the sitting room window across the fields. She turns slowly towards me,

"You can put that wool coat away now deary," she says, "The trouble is you see, someone has been in the cupboard and taken my fur coat."

She sits down and reaches for her mug of tea from the wobbly stool. The fire in the wood-burning stove crackles and hisses.

"I just wish they would give it back. I need it in this cold weather."

MONDAY

15th December 2017

. . . .

The day of Ted's funeral. It is so very cold. The date has been carefully chosen to allow all the gamekeepers and beaters and the guns to attend. I remember Ted from when I was a small child and he always seemed a shy man to me, but with friendly kind eyes. I try to think back to when we first met him.

I remember a dairy farm we used to visit because a chap called Frank lived there with his parents and sister. Frank was a friend of Dave and Ted, and of my father, and he loved collecting guns. Frank's dad was always sitting by the fire when we visited and the family laid a big branch across the floor into the fire and Frank or his dad kicked it into the fire as it burned. Frank's mum wore an old sack around her waist instead of an apron and she had very bright eyes and red cheeks. She would take us to the chicken shed to collect the eggs. I remember that Frank once handed me a shotgun to fire in the farmyard. The kickback knocked me backwards off my feet and everyone laughed.

Maybe we met up with Ted at the Boxing Day meet in the Market Square. Horses and their immaculately turned-out riders holding glasses of sherry. Excited beagles. Shropshire brother and I waiting for the hunt to set off. And me secretly hoping that the foxes would be canny enough to outwit them.

I return to the cottage at the end of the day. The evening is a beautiful mixture of orange sky spotted with dark grey clouds. Anna is making a cup of tea. One of Dave's smart shirts hangs over the back of a chair. Dave is sitting quietly by the fire.

"How did it go?" I ask him.

"So cold," he says, "a lovely crematorium though. It's a new one."

"And the family?"

Dave is quiet for a while.

"I couldn't stay," he says, "I had to sit in the car. I couldn't stay."

"I won't sleep tonight," he adds.

I remember meeting Ted at the old pub down the lane. The pub that will soon be someone's lovely new home. Ted and Dave sitting in the public bar with a pint of HSB and a ploughman's with pickled onions.

Dave shows me the Order of Service. On the cover Ted stands proudly by a stile with his crook stick and his two sheepdogs.

"I made him that stick," Dave says.

The picture inside shows Ted in his flat cap and country jacket, both hands holding a brace of pheasants. And a brace of pheasants over his shoulder.

Dave puts the Order of Service on the mantelpiece above the Aga. Among the Christmas cards. It seems appropriate somehow.

"Look at the sky!" says Anna, calling us to the sitting room. The sky is full of rooks and jackdaws, swooping and circling. We watch as they settle on the telegraph poles and along the wires.

"They have a chat before they roost in the woods over there," Dave tells us pointing beyond the fields.

I glance at Dave to see if he is teasing us, but he looks perfectly serious.

And when I turn back the sky is suddenly empty. The telegraph poles are empty. The wires are empty.

And every rook and jackdaw has flown.

THROWS

16th December 2017

. . . .

Anna feels the cold. Dave says she always has. He would like her to eat more; to wear long-sleeved vests and thicker jumpers. But this isn't going to happen. So Anna often has a hot water bottle and a thin blue blanket on her lap, and still she shivers. Until the wood-burning stove is lit at three o'clock. And then everyone falls asleep in the heat.

I tell them about a big store just outside the city where I work. I show them pictures on my phone of throws; "seriously soft" throws in faux fur. Grey, burgundy, brown and even pink. Anna looks disinterested. Dave is excited. He loved the brushed cotton duvet covers I brought home for them,

"Bloody warm!"

Dave and Anna were ignorant of duvet covers when I arrived and simply sandwiched their duvets between sheets. This caused sheet tangles and sheet disappearances.

At eight-thirty in the morning I am having breakfast at the round table and looking forward to seeing my stepmother for coffee and then making a Christmas visit to my aunt and uncle. Dave and Anna are discussing the trip to the big store. Anna thinks it might be too cold for her to go out. Dave wants to take her to choose the throw, but doesn't want her to turn grumpy on him.

Anna keeps changing her mind about the trip. Finally she goes upstairs to put on her "going out" trousers. Dave goes off to the kitchen to find a fat ball for Robbie.

An hour later and the house is quiet. The postman drops several letters onto the doormat as well as two catalogues. Three of the letters are Christmas cards for me; redirected mail. I put them on the high shelf in the dining room. Then the phone rings and when I answer it is Dave.

"Got a bit of a problem 'ere," he says,"car's gone in a ditch, can you get 'ere and get Anna home and we can tow the car out."

I am shocked to hear this. I always worry about Dave driving, as do my brothers.

He gives me directions but I don't know the names of the lanes as Dave does.

Finally a lane I recognise.

"I'll be with you as quickly as I can," I say.

Should I ring my stepmother and cancel? Has Dave got any motor breakdown cover? Will they be in shock?

All these questions rush through my mind as I drive as quickly as I can past the pub building site, over the crossroads, past the old cottages with the well, avoiding Shady Lane (blind corners and deep ditches) left at the wheelbarrow where I found cooking apples in October, up to the next crossroads. There's the red Volkswagen, leaning into the ditch. Oh dear oh dear.

The first thing to do is to get Anna out of the car and into the winter sunshine. No-one is hurt; just bewildered.

Anna has to be carefully guided out of the car and onto the lane but we are wading through thick wet mud and leaves to get to her. And she is wearing fairy shoes of course.

"No, no, no," she pleads in a trembly voice as we half lift, half carry her through the mud.

"Here's a four-be-four," says Dave as a vehicle comes towards us. The driver spots us straightaway and pulls up just behind my car. I steady Anna against the bonnet of my car in the sunshine. The driver looks anxiously at our situation.

"I can tow you out," he says "but I've got no rope."

"I only pulled over for a p...," Dave tells us helpfully.

The man goes to rummage in the back of his car and his dog jumps out and dashes through the wet leaves. Anna is trembling so I distract her by pointing out that the dog is wearing a high-vis coat. The man returns triumphantly with a plastic strap and is soon inspecting the Volkswagen with Dave. Two more men stop to help and so once the strap is attached to both vehicles the new arrivals can help by pushing the car back onto the road.

"Take a picture to show the council that these verges need attention," says one of the men, so I get out my phone and do as he suggests.

With a final push the car is back on the lane and we thank the men for stopping and helping. We are muddy, leaf-strewn and chilly. The car is covered with wet mud and makes a strange jangling noise when Dave starts the engine.

"I'll go back and make a hot water bottle and some coffee for Anna," I call, as Dave helps her back into his car.

"Just follow me back and take care," I call, as I put my phone back on the passenger seat.

But Dave isn't listening. I realise the jangling Volkswagen is in first gear.

And then. Dave and Anna are driving away. Heading off to the big store to buy a throw.

"Oh," I say to no-one in particular.

I start the engine and drive off towards the pub. Despite the warmth of the winter sun and my car heater I am shivering. It strikes me then that at the end of this little drama I'm the one who is in shock.

SOUP

19th December 2017

. . . .

Anna has problems with packaging. Her frail hands are just not strong enough to open the jar of coffee, the carton of carrot and sweet potato soup, or to pull off the the plastic cover under the milk carton lid. In the past two days I've realised that she cannot light a match for the wood burning stove when the afternoons get cold, nor turn her clothes the right way round when they are inside-out.

I imagine a sort of Senior Supermarket where all these products are made with people like Anna in mind. Somehow the designs will allow frail hands to deal with all those everyday tasks that younger people take for granted. And I'm not just talking about difficult lids, tops or packets.

Labels too are confusing.

Dave has moved his bathing routine from morning to evening. The wood-burning stove heats a radiator in the bathroom, and as the mornings are so cold, it suits Dave better to bathe in the evening. He announces his bathing intention and then disappears for an hour. Anna is sitting in front of the stove wondering where he is.

"Funny soap that blue soap," he grumbles on his return as he sits down heavily in his armchair.

I shut the sitting room door to keep in the warmth and head off to the bathroom. There's the soap that Dave's talking about. It's a clear plastic bottle imprinted with diamond-shapes that catch the light. Very pretty.

Except that this is not soap but multi-surface cleaner, posing as soap. The label is enticingly bath-like, 'Wild mint and green tea. With essential oils'. Writ large. And underneath in small letters we discover that it is for cleaning work surfaces.

"I only used it on my front!" says Dave when I explain.

I'm not sure just using it on your front is any real consolation however.

Anna laughs at Dave's mistake. In fact we all laugh. I realise that this is rare for Anna these days.

But then I wonder if a clearer label would really make any difference.

It's late in the evening when I return to the cottage the next day. Anna is moving damp tea towels around on the Aga rail.

"Have you eaten?" I ask her.

"Oh yes deary, very nice..."

I decide to check with Dave who is watching television at a loud volume.

"Yes I gave 'er that soup," he says.

Soup?

"I've brought some soup back with me though. There was none in the fridge when I looked this morning," I tell him.

"Yes she 'ad soup. She 'ad that date and prune soup."

Date and prune?

Oh heck.

"I think that was yogurt," I say as gently as I can.

"Yogurt!" he booms, "I don't know about yogurt. I just heated it up and she ate it all. And she ate the croutons too."

Date and prune yogurt soup. Warmed and served with croutons?

But then I wonder whether, if Anna cannot smell certain smells, or possibly all smells, has she lost her sense of taste as well? Or do foods taste different? I know there is a link between smell and taste.

"Did you enjoy the date and prune soup for supper?" I ask Anna.

She stops and stares across the room at me and I can almost see her mind trying to figure out what I could be saying.

Then her face relaxes and she gives a slight smile.

"Oh yes deary, it was lovely. I always enjoy Dave's home-made soup."

CHRISTMAS

21st December 2017

. . . .

Four days to Christmas and Dave has taken Anna for a Christmas haircut. It is mild and damp outside. Dave's birds have been hopping about on the bank with apple cores and remnants of Anna's morning toast. Then they are gone in a flurry and, as I move to the dining room window I see hunting cat making her way through the long grass in the field.

"You'll be in trouble if Dave sees you," I tell her.

Hunting cat doesn't care. She is waiting for some poor bird to make a wrong move.

I am writing a Christmas shopping list. Crackers, cocktail sausages, mulled wine. And the vegetables of course. The parsnips, carrots, sweet potato and sprouts that Dave demands and Anna despises. It's been many years since we gathered at the cottage for Christmas Day and I can't help remembering all those other Christmases. My grandmother making a brandy butter hedgehog studded with almonds, the big oval table from the shed joining the round table in the dining room, ginger wine, liqueurs that dribbled over our chins, and various guests. Three jockeys, a long way from Ireland, maybe someone's friend who'd fallen out with parents, a boyfriend, a girlfriend, a hen-pecked chicken from the farmyard down the lane.

As we co-habited, married and had children we spent Christmas Day in our various homes but always gathered at the cottage on Boxing Day for a six o'clock meal. Anna loved this celebration. The preparation, the wine, and especially the puddings. Someone was always late. Usually Shropshire brother hurrying from a race meeting, and on one occasion giving a radio broadcast from the garden with the telephone pulled through the dining room window.

The meal always started well, but often disintegrated as pudding finished. It all began with a sprout. I think that Devon brother threw the first sprout. I am certain Anna retaliated. And then sprouts flew through the air, followed by any other leftovers. Even swede. Dave sat grumpily at the head of the table, refusing to participate in the sprout destruction. Guests were initially stunned, but soon joined in. I remember one year someone's Australian relatives joined us for an international sprout fight.

As the years went by Anna bought dozens of party poppers to the table after the pudding, and followed this with a firework display in the garden. The children loved Boxing Day at the cottage.

This year just a few of us will meet for the Christmas meal. We will drink a toast to absent friends. We will keep our fingers crossed that the Aga behaves itself. The weather will be mild. The sprouts will stay on our plates. Dave will eat too much and Anna will doze in her armchair. Bobby will wait patiently on the bank for a fat ball, and hunting cat will prowl the fields as if it were just an ordinary day.

CHRISTMAS DAY

25th December 2017

. . . .

Shropshire brother is in charge as I have rented an apartment several miles away in the city. I arrive back at the cottage with the young people at eleven o'clock to get ready for lunch. I've already received a text from Shropshire brother warning me that Dave isn't happy about the weather. Too mild. Too wet. Too windy. Too muddy.

For some reason the men are looking at a car engine when we arrive. Anna is snuggled in her new throw by the Aga. Small throw is a fluffy green. Large throw is silvery grey and warms Anna's bed. The turkey is in the Aga. Anna is not quite sure who we are and gives us all the wrong names. We decide that we will stick with the wrong names for today.

Lunch is in two stages as the Aga cannot cope with all the vegetables. So turkey, roast potatoes and sprouts and then turkey, carrot and swede mash and parsnips roasted in honey. We pull crackers. We read the jokes. Anna's paper hat slips over her eyes. We toast Sydney and Devon brothers and their families. We are very noisy, as if to make up for the fact that so many of us are not here today.

Then Shropshire brother leads us on a moonlit walk through the dark muddy lanes. No-one but us.

"Around The Manor," we call this walk. We gaze in admiration at the manor's tall twinkly Christmas tree at the top of the drive.

I try in vain to find the footpath called the Monarch Way, along which Charles II escaped after the Battle of Bosworth all those years ago.

Shropshire brother talks about the pub where Dave's father sat by the open fire with the American GIs.

"Dave told me this morning that he and his friends took guns from their open jeeps as they drank in the pub," he tells us.

We are amazed.

"They oiled them, wrapped them in sacking and buried them in the woods."

"Why?"

Shropshire brother explains that Dave and his friends were going to defend their homes when the Germans invaded.

"But they were only about twelve or thirteen years old!"

We try to imagine the fear and excitement Dave and his friends must have felt as they buried the guns.

Back at the cottage we start a game of Consequences. Dave is hopeless; laughing to himself as he writes. Very slow.

"Hurry up Dave!" we shout, "What was she wearing!"

"Nothing!" Dave giggles.

"What did the papers say?"

"Nothing!"

Anna remembers this game from the past. She writes the names of people she remembers.

We unfold the stories and read them aloud. Everyone laughs; even Anna. There are common themes. Brexit. Mutual friends. Country clothing. Aga parsnips (burnt to a cinder). Donald Trump. Feather boas.

Then we depart with cold turkey and Christmas cake.

"Nothing on the bloody TV!" roars Dave as we say our goodbyes.

"What's wrong with the TV? It's bloody Christmas!"

But we have gone through the muddy lanes, back to the city. Leaving Anna and Dave and Shropshire brother to finish the red wine and ruminate on the day.

ANCESTORS

29th December 2018

. . . .

In those quiet days after Christmas and before New Year's Eve the weather stays cool and damp. The puddles outside the front door never disappear. The patch of churned mud in the field where the cows congregate never dries.

My tall son comes to stay, bringing his laptop. He talks to Anna about word sequences, "apple, table, penny," and spelling words backwards. And when Anna has completed all his tests they play I-Spy, as they did when he and his sister were young. He is patient. He talks to her about her childhood and she mentions an adopted sister who she lost contact with.

"Someone brought her to our door," she says, "Not like it is today. And when she was about eighteen she left to live with some man. I don't know if she married him."

Tall son asks her name. He Googles her. Nothing. How did she spell the surname she kept? After a while he finds an ancestry website. I make coffee and serve chocolate cake, and soon Anna's grandparents are discovered. Then her great-grandparents and great-great grandparents. I ask him to find out more about her maternal grandmother, Florence. I have always heard that she was Irish. That she wrote. That she burned all her writings before she died.

72

"Watford, Hertfordshire," says tall son.

Watford?

Florence, her parents and grandparents. No mention of Ireland to be found. Everyone in Anna's family is from the London area. And further back, Abingdon near Oxford.

Dave is listening.

"I'd like to know about my ancestor. He was a prize-fighter. Went round the villages bare knuckle fighting. Villagers 'ad bets on the fights."

"Was this your grandfather?"

"I dunno who he was," says Dave, "but he weren't my grandfather 'cos grandfather was a water diviner. Found water with a hazel twig and then dug wells."

Dave's ancestry is certainly interesting.

Tall son sets to work on his laptop. Dave sits next to him at the round table. The ticking of the grandfather clock in the background. Anna falls asleep, tired with all the spelling and word sequences.

Dave's family is easy to trace. They have populated this village and the surrounding villages for generations. Many of the men are called Charles. Tall son is amazed at the information that he finds,

"Seventeen children!"

"Four wives!"

"Twelve children here!"

No sign of the prize fighter.

"Podge the cobbler told me about 'im," says Dave, "how he got in a fight in one of the villages one day and two weeks later he were dead! That fight killed 'im."

Dave is losing interest in the search for ancestors. It's all names and dates. Not enough colourful information for him. As well as the prize fighter he wants more detail about his mother's father who fought in the Boxer Rebellion and the Battle of Jutland.

Anna wakes up looking for a cup of tea. Dave is pulling on his Australian boots to go down to the sheds with cake crumbs for Robbie.

"I reckon 'e lives in one of my sheds," he tells us, "and keeps away from his brother."

Tall son closes the laptop and looks around for more chocolate cake.

"Have you saved all this?" I ask.

He gives me an of-course-mother look.

And what about Anna's missing sister? Does she wonder about Anna?

Perhaps for now she will have to remain a mystery.

TIME

7th January 2018

. . . .

One of the first things Anna does in the morning is to put her wristwatch on the round table. When Dave comes down for breakfast he fastens the watch on her tiny wrist. But she always asks us for the time.

"Look at the bloody clock!" roars Dave, "it's right above your chair."

But he tells her anyway. Then he tells her he loves her.

It seems to me now that Anna has no need for time any more. She sleeps when she is tired. She cooks toast or nibbles chocolate when she is hungry. She does her best to light the fire when she is cold.

But Dave manages all the appointments. The doctor. The dentist. The podiatrist. The hairdresser. He brings her cereal. He cooks her lunch. He cooks her supper.

But still Anna is concerned with time, and why 'they' have changed time; turned the evenings into mornings and the mornings into evenings. Time gives structure, and Anna's structure is disappearing. While the weather is so cold and wet Anna doesn't go out very often, preferring to sit by the Aga or the wood-burner. Perhaps she doesn't experience enough changes in her day to be aware of time passing? And then I see that Dave sits by the Aga in the mornings and by the TV in the afternoons.

Usually with a shopping trip somewhere in the middle. Therefore when Dave is with her, Anna has more awareness of time. And when Dave is not in view Anna loses track of time.

This loss makes Anna agitated. By keeping an awareness of time Anna knows what she should be doing even if she cannot do very much. So when Dave is sitting by the Aga she can think about making morning tea. Bringing washing downstairs. Putting on the washing machine. Making a shopping list. Ringing the hairdresser or doctor. When Dave is sitting by the wood-burner Anna can think about ringing family and friends. Bringing in logs from the front porch. Planning supper.

Of course the agitation returns when I come back from work early. Or late. Or they have a visitor. Or someone rings the cottage. If they are family or friend Anna becomes convinced they are coming for supper.

"What will they eat!"

"I've got nothing in the fridge."

Sometimes she confuses a caller with someone who is long dead. Usually someone is coming from Birmingham where she spent her early life during the war.

Dave is baffled.

I suggest he tells her not to worry. That he will go for fish and chips when the visitors arrive.

Anna has stopped colouring. She tells me she is too tired to do this any more. I find my washing has been removed from the Aga rail or the wooden horse and stuffed into a corner of the long coat cupboard. I resort to draping my washing over my car seats.

Anna needs something to focus on.

And then I find the Carer's Group at the hospital.

Thursday afternoons from one-thirty to three-thirty.

I will make a visit.

CARER'S GROUP

11th January 2018

I finish work early on a Thursday and go to the Carer's Group at the hospital. I talk to a kind woman about some of our difficulties. Anna's agitation. Her confusion about time. The long skirts. The refusal to accept mobility aids. Or carers or sitters.

The adviser is thoughtful, and listens, nodding. She gives me leaflets about groups nearer the cottage. As I'm talking to her my eye is drawn to a stand of sparkly woolly squares and rectangles. The adviser explains that these are twiddle mats. They are knitted and decorated by volunteers for the hospital. People with dementia find them comforting to hold and "twiddle". The buttons and felt flowers. The pearl and diamond beads. The small plastic cubes decorated with letters of the alphabet.

I give a donation and take a twiddle mat back to Anna. She is delighted. She loves the stripes of bright wool and the beads and flowers. And she loves the fact that she can warm her cold hands inside the mat, as it is a double layer of wool.

In the evening when darkness surrounds the cottage Anna puts the twiddle mat next to her on the sofa.

"Now be good and stay there, and I will see you in the morning."

Dave lifts his eyebrows but says nothing.

I have an idea.

In the local charity shop I search for a new friend. There is a bin full of soft toys and halfway down I find a rather pale-faced monkey with a very soft black and white coat.

Perfect.

Monkey is sitting on a sofa cushion when Anna brings in her mug of tea.

"What's that?"

She stops. Puzzled.

"Is it real Dave?"

"Course not," shouts Dave over the noise from the TV.

"You're very soft," says Anna stroking Monkey's head.

She sits down and I move Monkey closer to her.

""I'm not daft," she says, "it's not real. I know it's not."

"But friendly," I say.

"You take it home with you deary," she says.

"I think he wants to live with you though," I tell her.

"Don't be silly." She gives me one of her disapproving looks.

The room is very warm from the wood-burner and soon Anna is dozing, woken only by the noise from the television. One of Dave's war programmes.

"Oh it's still there," she says, looking at Monkey next to her.

"He's not a real monkey of course," she tells us.

"Course he's bloody not," says Dave staring at the television. Dave is waiting for his favourite programme about selling antiques.

Anna is thinking about going to bed. She always folds her glasses at this point and puts them on the shelf next to the wood-burner. I hear a woo-hoo call from the fields,

Dave sits upright, "Hark! There's a tawny owl out there!"

We listen for a while and then Anna gets unsteadily to her feet.

Dave," she calls, "when you go to bed tonight you'll have to let this monkey out in the garden for a while you know. We don't want puddles on the carpet."

I can tell just by looking at her that Anna isn't joking.

ELECTRICITY

13th January 2018

. . . .

It's Saturday evening and the day has been very cold. Dave is tired after a day with his boat friends, and is looking forward to a new drama series on television.

Supper has been eaten and the dishes washed and put away. Everyone is settled in their favourite chair by the fire. And then it's suddenly pitch black in the cottage. The lights stutter back on for a second, and then darkness again.

I reach for my mobile and put on the torch. Anna and Dave look startled by the sudden darkness. Then Dave heaves himself out of the armchair and across to the window to see if the house across the field has power.

"Bloody house got all their lights on!" he bellows.

I go upstairs to look at the houses across the lane. Total darkness.

"I think it's a power cut," I call to Dave, who has his head in the fuse box cupboard, "but only certain parts of the village. I'll ring the emergency number. Can you find some candles?"

I think I am expecting tealights.

But when I have established that it is indeed a power cut, and that it will be sorted (hopefully) by ten pm, I find that there are no tealights in the cottage.

Dave lights tall thin household candles and drips the wax onto enamel plates to seal the candles in place.

"We 'ad these plates for our lunches in the RAF," Dave tells us.

The candles wobble precariously on their plates as Dave takes them through to the sitting room.

"We 'ad mugs too," he adds.

"I'm going to bed," announces Anna as we sit down by candlelight.

"Don't be daft," roars Dave, "there's no lights up there!"

"Well I'll put some lights on then," says Anna.

Oh dear.

I try to explain that to Anna that it is safer sitting by the wood-burner until the power is back on.

But Anna wants to go to bed.

"I'll get a torch and go up with you," Dave tells her, "and you 'ave to go straight to bed and no wand'ring about like you do."

"Don't forget my hot water bottle," she reminds him.

There is much cursing and muttering as they struggle up the stairs with wobbly candles and a hot water bottle. But there is only so much I can do to help without causing resentment.

Dave reappears soon after.

"That was quick... is Anna in bed?" I ask him.

He looks fed up.

"She's wandering about with a bloomin' torch everywhere," he says.

Oh dear.

We sit in the flickering candlelight. I'm holding my breath, waiting for a crash upstairs.

Nothing.

My mobile rings again. The electricity supplier rings frequently to update me, as they know there are vulnerable residents in the cottage. Maybe midnight, they tell me.

Alan the builder/gamekeeper also rings my mobile to say that their cottage across the fields has no electricity either.

Dave looks more fed up.

"I can't watch my bloody programme. Might as well go to bed."

I wash and change and sort out my bedding by candlelight. I am surprised by how bright it can be. I imagine the cottage lit by candles or gas lamps many years ago. Dave has told me that a family lived in the cottage with nine children, and that a great-uncle of his also lived here at one time.

Upstairs all is quiet. Anna's room is in darkness so she must be asleep at last. I lie awake for a while, listening to the silence around the cottage.

I must have fallen asleep.

Then suddenly I am awake. The cottage is full of light and sound. Every light and appliance is awake and doing its job. I check my watch and it's one o'clock in the morning.

Oh heck.

Anna has turned on all the sidelights and main lights and radios.

Just as she promised.

I turn off the television and the radio and the dining room and kitchen lights. I lift the latch of her bedroom door as quietly as I can.

She is fast asleep. I turn off all the lights in her room and then the bathroom light. Dave can sort out the lights in his room.

Finally the cottage is all in darkness again. All is silent. I suddenly remember nightingales singing in the lane so many years ago. Walking up from the pub and stopping to listen. Where did they go? Dave said something about their food being scarce. I try to remember what else he said.

But then I am asleep again.

SHEDS

17th January 2018

. . . .

Robbie is enjoying the panettone that Dave has taken down the garden to him. It has to be left on the edge of Dave's trailer, just tucked under the bushes. Dave is worried about the hawk he has seen circling over the fields.

"I saw 'er take a blackbird once," he tells me, "straight off the nest over there," and he points across the lane to the trees in front of the neighbour's thatched cottage. Robbie has become more wary, swooping on the cake and retreating under the bushes. Dave is pleased. But there is also hunting cat to worry about.

"Robbie knows how to look after his-self though," he says.

If Robbie wants to sleep in a shed he has a choice of four. Or is it five? Dave built all the sheds himself when they first moved in, nearly fifty years ago. Corrugated iron and wood, with the smartest shed having a concrete floor. The sheds stand in a muddy puddled area, as the bottom of the lane collects all the water. Dave was always in his sheds a few years ago.

"How's Dave?" I would ask Anna when I rang for a catch-up.

"He's in the shed dear," was her usual reply. Unless it was Saturday when he was "on the boat."

85

When suppertime arrived someone always had to go down the lane to fetch Dave. He didn't want an intercom. A bloke has to have some peace in his sheds.

It's where Dave fixed things. Especially engines. Diesel engines. In fact people brought their engines to him, and it was a bit of a social event. A lot of chatting. Countryside chatting.

Dave always talks about his sheds fondly. One reason why they have never moved to a retirement bungalow or apartment is that Dave would never leave the sheds behind. Where would he put all the tools? The old trailers? The rusty metal things? The old wooden things? The half-finished things?

"I must sort out my sheds," Dave says at least twice a week.

"Yes you must," Anna agrees.

"I'll get a lot of stuff I don't want to the tip," he tells us.

But it never happens.

Nowadays when Dave puts on his old grey jumper and tells us he's "going down the shed," he usually means he is going to chop wood. Dave is proud that he never pays for logs for the wood-burner. He just hears about wood on the grapevine. He brings it back to the sheds and cuts it up.

"I 'ave to 'ave logs to keep 'er warm all the time," he tells me.

Eldest grandson is a special favourite at the moment because he brings logs - a van full of logs. From a fallen tree in his aunt's garden. Or from somewhere up in the woods. Dave marvels at his strength and resourcefulness.

"How does he lift them great logs?" he wonders, shaking his head.

I wonder too. I try to lift the edge of one great oak log, but can't even move it.

"It'll break yer leg if it falls on you," he says cheerfully.

We gaze at the woodpile for a while.

"We'd better check she's alright then," he says, stomping up the lane to the cottage. "I'll get back down tomorrow and get them logs split."

"How does he lift 'em?" he says again, to no-one in particular.

I sense that Dave is happy to replenish his log store. But also a little sad. That he is not able to lift huge logs, spend hours in his sheds or walk for miles with Anna across the fields.

Robbie is hiding amongst the lowest branches of the fir tree. I see him in the corner of my eye as I follow Dave up the lane. The shed doors are locked. The planks of wood are stacked up against them. The woodpile is covered with an old boat tarpaulin. And the rusty tools and engine parts sit silently.

Waiting for Dave's big clear-up.

TEETH

18th January 2018

. . . .

I wake up early on a working day as I have a long drive ahead of me. Anna is usually awake before me, wrapped in her green throw by the Aga drinking tea. Or slowly putting on her make-up in the kitchen mirror. I am not sure why she puts on her make-up at the sink. But then I am not sure why Dave dresses his wild hair with olive oil. Or why they have twelve toothbrushes between them. Or why they had never heard of duvet covers.

This morning Anna looks distracted.

"Are you okay?"

"Yes deary," she says; her voice rather muffled.

"You sound... well...different.."

Anna points to her mouth.

"Tooth problems?"

She nods.

I have to hurry though. I tell her to wake Dave at half past seven and he can call the dentist and make an appointment.

Outside a huge flock of rooks is swooping and circling in the sky. Pigeons and starlings are gathering on the bank for breakfast.

The builders at the old pub down the lane are arriving in a fleet of white vans.

I'm busy at work and forget to ring Dave to see if he has called the dentist. I don't remember until the evening when Anna unlocks the front door and greets me with a worried smile.

"Have you seen the dentist Anna?"

"No deary we're going tomorrow..."

"She's found 'er teeth though," shouts Dave coming down the stairs.

"Oh, she'd lost them then?"

I'm not even sure which teeth we are talking about here.

"Cleaner found 'em. Under 'er pillow. Daft woman." He gives her a loud kiss on her forehead.

"That's good," I say. I'm wondering how you could forget where you'd left your teeth. But then I remember that my ex left his in the loft on one occasion. And on another he dropped them in the yard, thereby running the risk of them being run over by one of our cars.

"So all sorted now?"

"Yes deary, all sorted," says Anna.

I hang up my coat in the long coat cupboard and think about making a cup of tea.

"Why are you seeing the dentist tomorrow then Anna?" I ask her, "now that you've found them."

"No I didn't find them deary, that was Sharon."

"Oh yes, but I mean if you've found your teeth you don't need to see the dentist," I say.

Anna looks confused.

"Dave's taking me to the dentist tomorrow aren't you Dave?"

"Bloody expensive!" roars Dave.

I sense an argument coming.

"Why do you need to see the bloody dentist? You only saw him last month!"

Dave is getting heated.

Anna gives him a harsh look.

"I'm going to see the dentist because I have an appointment to see the dentist tomorrow." she says coldly.

I am confused.

What must it be like for doctors, dentists, hairdressers, podiatrists, to name but a few? People who have many elderly patients or clients? Is this confusion going on day after day in surgeries, clinics and shops all over the country?

Talking to friends, work colleagues, friends of friends, and sometimes even strangers, I do believe it is.

CECIL

21st January 2018

. . . .

So why was Anna and her sister at the ice rink that day? The day she met Dave and John and the other speed skaters. So many miles away from her beloved Chester?

When I was a child Anna always drove old cars. Morris Travellers I remember. Anna didn't care much for cars. She let us climb on the bonnet. But in the boot of her car was a pair of leather gloves. Were they black or brown? Were they edged with fur? They lived in the boot and never left. They had belonged to a man called Cecil.

My brothers and I thought the name Cecil was hilarious. Men in those days were called Brian or Bob or Graham. Not Cecil. When Anna lifted the lid of the boot we would pounce on the gloves and demand to know who they belonged to. To which Anna would reply,

"They were Cecil's."

We would laugh until our sides hurt.

Anna wasn't secretive about Cecil.

"He was my first husband."

But of course there was never very much detail.

Cecil was a Welshman and they had met in Anglesey.

Anna told us that he sang to her. To young children that was as ridiculous as his name. They had married when she was young, seventeen maybe, or eighteen. There was hardly time to get to know each other. But he had an aunt in Chester and so he could stay with her and visit Anna. I think they were married in Wales, and she wore a silver skirt and jacket.

I remember Anna getting a speeding fine and having to fill out a form with her maiden name and her previous married name. I thought she was as exotic as Elizabeth Taylor.

What happened to Cecil though?

"He went to South Africa," was all Anna would say.

Years later I heard a little more. Did Anna tell me? Or my grandmother?

Cecil's company relocated him to South Africa. Was he an economist? He and Anna were newly married. The plan was for her to join him when she had finished her studies at Art college. But one day her parents received a letter.

It was from Cecil and he told them that things had not worked out. His secretary, who was Greek, had handed in her notice because her parents wanted her to return to Greece. When he asked her why, she had apparently told him she was in love with him. The startled man realised that he felt the same way about her. And therefore his marriage to Anna could not continue.

So Anna's father asked for a job transfer and they left Chester. They also left Anna's older sister who was already married.

I cannot imagine the trauma the family must have gone through.

But not long ago Anna told me that it was at her insistence that the family moved. She also told me that she had never forgiven herself.

MEMORIES

27th January 2018

· ·

It's just over two weeks until I move to my new house. It's a much shorter journey to the cottage than from my old house, so I intend to visit at weekends to make sure Anna and Dave are alright.

It is not easy to live here. But I will miss Anna and Dave. Dave is a black and white person who says what he thinks and doesn't hold back. When I asked him about his first marriage; before he met Anna, he told me that Fay was unfaithful to him, particularly with younger men. Dave discovered this because his brother-in-law worked in the local dairy.

"Like a foreman," Dave told me.

"She and this young bloke went to the dairy to get some cream for their tea. And they got spotted. So that's how I knew."

It sounds a little innocent in the telling. Buying some cream for your tea from the local dairy. But that was the end of the marriage. Fay disappeared with her young man, leaving Dave alone in the cottage he had bought and converted for them.

It is not easy to live here. But I will miss finding the Worcester sauce bottle in the laundry basket. Or Anna telling me that they had two sets of callers at the house that morning. Both were asking for spare coat hangers.

I have been amazed at the certainty with which Anna makes such statements. I feel sure that if the whole family had been at the cottage all day, and had told Anna that nobody had called at the cottage asking for coat hangers, she would still insist that she was correct in what she had said.

But perhaps this is what Anna sees. Just like the woman with the child who often comes back to the cottage with me. The visitors from Birmingham who never arrive. And my dog. And the man who sits on the carpet in the sitting room.

I walk around the cottage and realise that it hasn't changed much over fifty years.

Barley twist chair has been sitting outside the long coat cupboard for many years. It is a light-coloured wood and Dave thinks it is pine. The chair used to belong to Anna's mother and so it is a prized possession. One day Anna and I found a bedraggled hen-pecked chicken in the ditch down the lane. Anna has a curious affinity with animals. They like her and she likes them. So Poulet was carried back to the cottage and given a bath in the sink and allowed to perch on the arm of barley twist chair. She spent the night in the porch in a box of straw.

Poulet knew the sound of Anna's car engine and would hurry to meet her at the front door for her evening foot bath, before perching on her chair for the evening, and then retiring to the porch.

Box of sticks has been standing by the cottage door for as long as I can remember. A dozen or so varnished walking sticks. Some have a crook handle; one is topped with a ram's horn. Some are thumb sticks made from deer antlers. Dave has made them all over the years. Anna's walking sticks stand incongruously amongst them.

On the other side of the door are two carved wooden boxes; one was once full of Sydney brother's toy cars.

The other was Anna's sewing box. The contents are still the same. A pincushion with an autumn leaf fabric. A tin, originally a bicycle puncture repair kit, contains needles. A tobacco tin contains pins. Anna was once good at sewing, but now the box lid stays shut.

And everywhere I look I see stone and glass jars and bottles. Fry and Co stone ginger beer. Scrase's brewery limited. Confitures fines Felix Potin Paris. And horse brasses. And copper kettles. Warming pans. Jugs. Bedpans. I wondered whether they had been handed down through Dave's family, as families do. Anna's family doesn't hold on to possessions. But Dave told me that he had found them in house demolitions he had worked on. Or he had dug them out of the ground on building sites

And then there is the brass porthole in the sitting room door. I can understand this if you live in a cottage by the sea. But we are at least an hour from the coast here. The porthole in the door with the rattling latch is there to remind Dave of his boat. The boat he has just sold.

"I'm gonna be sad when she's gone," he tells me, "but trouble is, when she's on dry land I can't get up the ladder no more."

And in truth, I think Dave probably finds it difficult to get up the ladder from the dingy when the boat is in the water.

So the boat has to go, and Dave's world shrinks a little more. But he needs to be home more to care for Anna, who no longer finds walking easy, nor wants to leave the cottage except on rare occasions.

Dave puts a picture of his boat on the mantelpiece above the Aga. Next to a photograph of Anna when she was younger.

Happy memories.

BAD DAYS

28th January 2018

. . . .

Some days are not good. When I went to the dining room to make breakfast I found Anna asleep, wrapped in her throw by the Aga. She slept all morning. Just waking occasionally to ask me strange questions,

"Are Mum and Dad back,"

"What is your dog's name?"

"Where did you put it?"

Put what?

I find I don't have to answer these questions. I can distract her by pointing out the cows staring through the window. One brown cow amongst all the black ones.

"How now..." says Anna sleepily.

And Mr Crow on the fence post, just biding his time.

Anna has soup for lunch and seems to enjoy it. But falls asleep as soon as I take the bowl away.

Dave comes back from his boat friends lunch and tells us that Gordon has had a good idea.

His friend Charlie has a boat but hasn't sailed it for a while. To be honest, says Dave, he's a bit nervous. So we can go with him for a good day out.

Dave is looking a little happier.

"Can I have some breakfast please?" says Anna, opening her eyes.

It is half past two in the afternoon, but I bring her a bowl of muesli, cornflakes and granola. Dave looks bemused but stomps off to light the fire.

Anna shuffles slowly into the sitting room.

"Are you feeling better dear," she asks Dave.

"I'm alright," says Dave surprised.

"It's very cold in here."

"You got your vest on then?" says Dave.

Anna lifts her jumper slightly. No. No vest.

It takes us an hour or so to persuade Anna to find her vest. When she comes downstairs again I am puzzled. She is wearing what looks like her grey vest with a thick red scarf around her neck. The scarf is coming out of the hem of her vest as well.

Dave doesn't understand women's clothing so just looks open-mouthed at her.

"Anna," I say, "shall I get you a jumper to wear over your vest."

"I've got a jumper on." she says icily.

I look again and realise that the red scarf is in fact her jumper. She has put it over her head, but not put her arms through. Then she appears to have put her vest over the top of this.

Anna spends the afternoon dozing by the fire in her unusual outfit. I am painting some chairs in one of Dave's sheds. They are a bit rickety, but with some chalk paint they look much better.

A little damp sunshine filters through the old wooden doors, and outside I can hear the cows sloshing in the mud at the edge of the field.

I lose track of time. It is nearly five o'clock when I head back up the lane to the cottage with my paintbrush and rags. Dave and Anna are in the kitchen pottering about.

I smell something burning in the Aga.

"It's her fish cake!" bellows Dave when I mention this.

I am used to this now.

"What the hell's this?" demands Dave pulling out two dishes from the hot oven.

"My fishcake," says Anna.

"And this thing?"

We all look at the plate Dave holds. It is a cooked pineapple. The pineapple I bought yesterday for pudding. To eat raw. I've read that pineapple is a very healthy food. Now it has been baked.

"Yes that's my fishcake," says Anna.

"It's not a bloody fishcake," says Dave, "it's a bloody pineapple! Why have you put a pineapple in the oven!"

I tell Dave (untruthfully) that cooked pineapple is something I enjoy. Then I settle Anna in the armchair with the fishcake, on the table that slides over her lap.

As I wash the paintbrush I think about Anna's reality. Things are getting worse. In the few months that I have been here I have noticed quite a decline in her mental abilities. And yet she is so convinced by this changing reality. That a vest can be worn over a jumper. That a pineapple is a fishcake.

However Anna still knows that clothes are to be worn and that food can be cooked in the oven. So perhaps her mistakes today are no worse than a drunk person might make? Perhaps her shifts in reality are not so great.

I take Anna a bowl of cooked pineapple and ice-cream.

"This looks nice deary," she says.

And she eats it all.

JOHN

3rd February 2018

. . . .

I don't have many memories of Anna and John together. They were in their early twenties when I was born, and moved between rented properties before finally buying a house when I was about five years old. It was large, semi-detached, 1930s-built and cold, and a mile or so from the town centre.

I do remember being taken to the town park to feed the ducks and play on the swings. And on this occasion Anna was carrying me in her arms on one of the winding paths that ran alongside the river. I think John had disappeared down another path because he suddenly appeared carrying a rose which he shyly presented to her. He must have picked it from one of the neat flowerbeds because, young as I was, I detected Anna's disapproval and delight.

On another day, cold and icy, we drove out to the countryside in John's green Ford Consul. There were not many cars on the roads in those days and we stopped by a pond. Anna and John took their ice-skates from the boot of the car and danced off together across the ice. Leaving me sliding and slipping at the edge of the pond. Like an ugly duckling. I wanted white skates. I wanted to glide across the ice. I was miserably aware of my sensible brown shoes.

The ponds don't seem to freeze over these days. Dave has noticed this too.

He reminds me that my younger brothers used to play on the frozen ice of the village pond. He talks about the hoar frosts that he admired while out shooting. A special frost that covered the trees and shrubs with a feathery dusting. I remember John lifting us onto the green sledge at the top of the hill outside our town, and then we flew to the bottom in a flurry of snow. We had so much energy. Pulling the sledge to the top of the hill again and again.

But today we are all tired.

Anna did not sleep last night. She wandered around the house, sometimes waking Dave. Sometimes waking me. Offering me an extra blanket. Cooking toast. Drinking tea.

I have to go to the bank and do some shopping for my new house. When I get back to the cottage Anna is crying. Quietly. Dave is trying to comfort her. Anna tells us she thinks there is something wrong with her mind. She can't remember who she is sometimes. Or where she is. She thought the cottage was a hotel, and now she realises that it isn't.

Because it's her parents home, she tells us.

All the time she is turning the pages of their telephone book trying to find a number. Whose number?

"My parents," she tells us.

She runs her finger over the pages. Backwards and forwards. But then she finds a number that she likes. It's her friend Brenda. Carefully I take the phone and explain to Brenda that Anna didn't sleep well last night and it would cheer her up to have a chat. Brenda understands immediately.

I make some tea and find a slice of banana cake that Dave hasn't spotted. Anna sits by the window listening to Brenda. Her expression looks happier.

I have a memory of Anna and John that never fades. We are in the sitting room of our 1930s house watching a hospital drama on the black and white TV. Me, John and Shropshire brother. Devon brother must be in bed already. We sit either side of John in our dressing gowns and slippers on the old black sofa by the coal fire. Anna comes to say goodnight to us. Her blonde hair is done up in a French pleat. And she is wearing a coat. Black and white dogtooth check. She kisses Shropshire brother goodnight. And then she bends down and kisses me. I think she is going to my grandmother's house. It's not far. You can walk to her house.

I don't remember what she says to me. If she says anything at all.

But tell me. How do children just know when something isn't right?

CHOCOLATE

10th February 2018

. . . .

A sunny day at the cottage. The bank is dotted with groups of snowdrops and Bobby the robin is investigating an apple core that is bigger than himself. Dave is making stewed apple dotted with dates as Anna loves this pudding with ice cream; in fact she now loves ice cream at every meal, and this means Dave has to drive to the town regularly to stock up.

Dave doesn't mind because he loves driving, although both he and Anna complain about how busy the roads are nowadays; how hurried people seem to be; how often drivers break the speed limit or fail to indicate at roundabouts.

Gordon is different. He doesn't rush about. He's a couple of decades younger than Dave, and they make a good team on the boat. Dave keeping his eye on the engine and the sails, and Gordon organising the food and the paperwork. Gordon is in charge of selling the boat, and he has a box of odds and ends that he's bringing to the cottage. When he comes through the door though, it's clear something is not right. Gordon cannot catch his breath.

He sits in one of the creaky wooden chairs and says he'll have to get back home. That walk up the lane was too far. The box of odds too heavy.

Dave is worried and keeps trying to persuade him to have a tea or coffee. When Dave introduces us I can see that Gordon is not well. Pale. Short of breath.

When Gordon has recovered his breath and gone home I take the box of odds to the kitchen. It doesn't weigh much.

"It's too much chocolate. It's making 'im too heavy. He shouldn't keep eating chocolate I reckon," Dave says, "He likes chocolate with everything. Even soup," he adds.

Anna likes chocolate. And so does Dave himself. And toffees. Cakes. Caramel puddings. Mousses and brûlées. Dave loves to talk about the candy that the GIs gave the children during the war. And the sweet coffee that the Italian prisoners-of-war shared with them.

"I'm damned if I know how they made that coffee..."

When Dave talks about the Italians he always marvels at their hair.

"They was always washing it," he tells us, "and they dressed it with olive oil so it shone in the sun."

How exotic these visitors must have seemed to Dave and his friends, with their shining hair and rich food.

I am interested in the way that Dave eats plenty of sugary food but also drinks the vinegar that his onions are pickled in. The water that he has steamed his vegetables in. A whole raw onion with his bread and cheese. Given the chance, he would cook everything with garlic. Is this what keeps him healthy while others are faltering?

Two days later Gordon is in hospital. Dave is nonplussed at what is happening to his friends.

"I'll stay with Anna if you are going to visit the hospital," I say.

Dave says he will visit that afternoon. "I'd better get 'im some chocolate up the shop."

Chocolate?

I thought Dave blamed chocolate for Gordon's current difficulties.

"Or maybe some grapes?" I say diplomatically.

"He don't like fruit," says Dave.

Right.

Dave returns from the hospital visit looking happier.

"He's cheerful alright. He says they're just getting his heart rate down. It's too fast."

Gordon has suggested Dave asks for a copy of the boat survey to be emailed to him. Dave is wondering how this can be achieved. So I write down Dave's email address for him and tell him he can read the survey on his iPad when it comes through. We practice telling the broker Dave's email address.

"What's this "a" thing!" roars Dave when I show him his address.

He means @.

"Don't forget the dot before com," I say.

"What's the point of a bloody dot!" he bellows.

Needless to say the survey is not emailed.

Dave is getting stressed. If the deal isn't done and the boat doesn't go to the new owner before the end of the month, he and Gordon will have to pay hefty yard fees.

I have no answers. When Dave asks me about heart rates and breathlessness I don't have any answers. For the first time in years Dave doesn't go to the Saturday boat lunch at the club.

"Too cold," he says when I ask.

But Dave is never cold. I've not seen him in a coat this cold winter. Only the old chunky grey jumper topped with his flat tweed cap.

Dave's relief when Gordon rings to say he's back at home is palpable. Even Robbie flies up from the sheds and sits outside the kitchen window.

"He's bloody lucky they got 'im sorted," says Dave putting the phone back on the base. "Got me a bit worried 'e did."

Dave goes to the kitchen to make some tea in his favourite mug. Yorkshire tea. Very strong. Plenty of milk, and a sweetener. He settles down in his favourite chair by the window. It has a good view across the fields.

And what's that he's holding? Two squares for Anna. The rest for Dave.

Ah. Chocolate.

EGYPT

13th February 2018

. . . .

When Anna left that night she never returned. Sometimes when I came home from school she was there looking after Devon brother, but when John came back from work she left again. One afternoon she took Devon brother with her. We must have known he was going because I remember seeing his blond head over the wall of the front garden. John moved into Shropshire brother's room and Shropshire brother moved into Devon brother's room. And then John took to his bed. I think he was ill for about three weeks.

A great-aunt and uncle arrived. They tutted and fussed when they saw John. But I was pleased that they came. They agreed to us eating burgers and ice-cream every day. I liked them although their clothes smelt of mothballs. I liked the jokes great-uncle told us. And great-aunt's brooches and necklaces. And I especially liked the box of dominoes that great-aunt kept in the bureau in their dining room. I liked to line up the dominoes on their sides. A long line of dominoes across the dining table. Then great-aunt would tell us about Egypt.

Great-aunt and uncle had been stationed there in the war and one day visited a pyramid in which you climbed upwards to the main chamber. It was hot, narrow and claustrophobic.

107

"Suddenly someone at the front of the line stumbled and fell backwards into the person behind them," said my aunt, "and then..."

On cue I would push the domino at the front of the line backwards and Shropshire brother and I would shout in delight as the whole line of visitors fell backwards inside the pyramid.

So great-uncle and aunt, who treated John like a son, came to look after him. And after a while he got up and carried on with life. He found a large kindly woman, Mrs H, to look after the house and us children. But that didn't work, because Mrs H wanted to do things her way. And John wanted to do things his way. He had been a Boy Scout. The next housekeeper was a pleasant lady, Mrs U. But when we came home from school we found most of our furniture had been moved around. Mrs U liked to keep furniture moving. Regularly. But John didn't want to discover his bed and chest of drawers in different parts of his room.

Here in the cottage I marvel that so much of the furniture has been sitting in its place for years on end. The dark oak table in the dining room, with its centre post supporting the ceiling above, has been here from the building of the cottage. But even the chairs and beds and side tables and sofas all have their place here. Anna was never interested in spring cleaning or re-arranging the furniture. So it just stayed where it was.

When Mrs U left, I took the washing to the launderette after school. Peeled potatoes for supper. And looked after Shropshire brother.

And then one day John came home and told us that he had found us an au pair. I didn't know what that was. Then he said,

"And not just one au pair, but two!"

I asked no questions. Life was so strange that I decided to wait and see.

CROUTONS

16th February 2018

Oops! Dave has left his home-made croutons in the Aga. Little black coal-like squares emerge from its oven. No croutons for Anna's soup today then.

I moved to my new house a week ago. A bright cold day with not a breath of wind. I loaded my car with bags and boxes and then loaded Dave's old Golf with bags and boxes, and we set off for the city twenty odd miles away. Dave was sad.

"I'll miss our chats," he told me.

Anna was confused by the new house. She sat in one of tall son's camping chairs, but couldn't get out of it. Dave and I explored the empty house. He found the stairs difficult but managed to get to the top of the house and down again. Then they shared a cup of tea (I only had one mug) and drove back to the cottage. I sat in the camping chair and waited for the decorator.

Today the forecast threatens snow. There are puddles of ice by the front door and no sign of robins, crows or cows. There is a tension in the cottage. Not only are the croutons ruined, but Anna is washing her plastic hair comb in Dave's cake tin. It's one of those combs with a steel spike, and I think this was originally for backcombing a bouffant hairstyle.

I remember as a child watching Anna doing her hair in the morning and she lifted the bouffant with the steel spike and then turned up the ends of her hair. It was fascinating to me.

Dave is furious about the cake tin, stomping into the kitchen and throwing the comb into the sink. I can see from the calendar that Anna has a hair appointment tomorrow morning and I am worried about Dave driving her there, but I say nothing.

"Has the new blanket arrived Dave?" I ask innocently. I know full well that the blanket has arrived; the one that Sydney brother has ordered from the internet. But it's best to begin at the beginning.

"It's in the other room," says Dave. He's stirring the caramel mixture into a saucepan of milk on the Aga.

The parcel sits by the sofa, unopened. I take it through to the dining room and show Anna.

"This is your new heated overblanket," I say.

"Very nice dearie," says Anna, as I take out the fluffy blanket from its wrappings.

I plug it into the kitchen socket.

"What about the toaster?" says Dave, "How am I goin' to toast my crumpets?"

The blanket warms up quickly and I gently place it over Anna in her chair by the Aga. She is asleep within ten minutes, tilting to the right. Dave looks concerned.

"It's electric then is it?"

I explain that it won't cost much to run, that once it reaches its heat setting it switches off, and then on again when the temperature drops.

It was minus nine degrees in rural areas last night, and with heavy snow forecast I think the blanket is a good idea. I tell him that all my brothers agree.

"Hmmmm," says Dave.

He is grumpy because now that I have moved he is responsible for their washing, cooking and cleaning, as well as making sure Anna is safe and takes her medicine and gets to all her appointments.

My mobile rings. It is Cherry. I suggest she parks her car near the old pub, where they are building the new houses.

"Cherry's arrived," I tell Dave.

"Cherry who?" grunts Dave.

"Cherry from the charity that helps with central heating," I say. He knows perfectly well that this is why I am at the cottage. Dave has decided that central heating is a good idea. In fact he made the suggestion that we investigate a boiler. But now?

"I've got to go up the shop," he says, "no bloody milk here."

Cherry is knocking at the door. Dave is looking for his old shopping bag and car keys. Anna is gently snoring.

CENTRAL HEATING

16th February 2018

· ·

Cherry is young, friendly and caring. Dave abandons his shopping bag quest and heads for the chair by the window. Anna looks attentive but doesn't smile. Her teeth are a little unsteady these days. I have my pen and paper ready.

Cherry fills out forms about the age of the cottage and its present heating arrangements.

"The Aga's been 'ere since 1935 and it's not going nowhere," Dave says.

Cherry explains that her charity works with the local council to help people keep warm in the winter. That may mean replacing a boiler, fitting a boiler, or simply supplying a free-standing radiator to someone who doesn't have any other heating. So no-one would want to change anything or replace anything without the tenant or home-owner's permission. Then she hands out plastic thermometer cards to read the temperature in the cottage. Mine shows fifteen degrees in the dining room. Next to the Aga. 'Warning,' says my card, ' put on an extra layer or turn up the heating.'

But I am already wearing three layers.

Cherry says that one of the big energy companies may be able to send out someone to assess the cottage's heating needs.

Or perhaps Dave may have some military service in the past? In which case Cherry will contact SSAFA.

Dave is delighted to inform Cherry that he did his National Service in the RAF. He worked for Motor Transport Repair and Inspection on Thorney Island.

"I kept puttin' in for going abroad, but it didn't work out," he tells us, "so I was in the machine shop."

I think it's time to get Anna some lunch. Dave is back in the late nineteen forties. Cheese on toast and chips.

"I've brought you an oil-filled radiator," says Cherry, "I'll fetch it from the car."

"How much?" asks Dave, getting to his feet.

Cherry explains that she will only need a token payment. Dave's face lights up. Anna has dozed off again.

"I'll come down the bottom and 'elp you," he says eagerly, reaching for his Australian boots.

The new radiator warms the sitting room beautifully. Cherry explains about the thermostat; how to keep the radiator clear of the furniture, and shows how it can be wheeled from room to room. Then she departs, promising to contact me when she has investigated funding for an oil-filled boiler.

"I'm off to the shop then," announces Dave, opening the front door. The tension has lifted. The comb-in-the-cake-tin incident forgotten.

"You can sit by that new radiator," he tells Anna, "it'll keep you plenty warm enough 'till I get back."

He blows her a kiss.

Anna scowls and gets to her feet. Unsteadily. Making her way to the sitting room. Touching the new radiator. The intruder in the sitting room.

I think it's all gone rather well. I'm hungry now. But I brought a hummus sandwich with me. The sort of sandwich Dave scoffs at. I sit at the round table with my plate and a coffee. The sky is looking very grey and the sun has all but disappeared.

Anna calls from the sitting room. She wants Dave.

"He's just gone to the shop for milk," I tell her. She looks at me blankly for a while.

"How is your sister dearie?"

"Fine thanks," I tell her. Just lately I've begun to realise that the sister she often asks about is the sister she left behind in Chester.

"Will you move this thing please dearie?" she asks, indicating the new radiator. "I want to light the fire."

I explain that the new radiator is there to warm the room until Dave comes back and lights the fire. But Anna is having none of it.

"We'll just move it out of the way," she says, starting to pull it across the room.

Oh heck.

I unplug the radiator and wheel it over to the other side of the room, under the bay window. My heart sinks. We don't want Anna to light the fire in case she falls and burns herself. But Anna insists. So I fetch kindling and small chunky logs to start the fire. Anna scrunches up newspaper.

The fire catches quickly. Anna closes the door of the wood burner and sits down on the sofa with a contented sigh. Then she picks up a catalogue. Anna likes to look at the pictures. I drink my coffee.

The sky through the window is heavy and grey. The new radiator watches us resentfully, while the wood-burner crackles and glows.

Triumphantly.

SNOW

3rd March 2018

· ·

Anna and Dave are snowed in. At least this is what Dave tells me when I ring the cottage. But in the next breath he tells me that he is going to drive to the village shop to get bananas.

"She's running out of bananas," he says, "and I don't want 'er goin' on at me."

I wonder if the snow is deep. Perhaps it would be safer if Dave walked to the shop? It's about a quarter of a mile. But asking Dave to walk somewhere is like asking a jockey to race without a horse.

"It would be good exercise for your knees," I say. Dave has had two knee replacements; the last one being a year ago.

"And you could take one of your sticks..."

Dave pretends not to hear me. He is one of those men whose car is a part of their personality. Whenever he talks about his younger days he always tells us about the car he was driving at the time. Regardless of the story.

The snow keeps me at home for two days; unpacking boxes and rearranging furniture. Thirteen centimetres of snow lie in the courtyard behind the house, and abandoned cars litter the street. There is a lovely silence over the city.

When the snow clears a little I drive out to the cottage, and notice that the verges and fields are clear as the miles go by. Anna is in the kitchen when I arrive. She is looking for her black waistcoat. I can't see that there's any warmth in it, but it is slim-fitting and elegant, and that's what Anna likes. Here it is. In the long coat cupboard, under one of Dave's jackets.

I think we had more snow when I was a child. I remember the big sash windows at the front of the house where I used to stand and watch the traffic and the passers-by. People holding on to our front garden wall when it was slippery underfoot with ice and snow. There were no net curtains at the windows. Anna made sure of that. There was no central heating when we first moved there, and I remember Anna shivering in front of a fan heater in the big bedroom. And despite the arrival of the boiler and the radiators the house always seemed cold and draughty to me. The au pairs in their mini skirts and jumpers (without vests) danced around the sitting room to keep warm, and encouraged us to dance with them. Sometimes I could hear the music from the top of the street as I walked home from school.

"Are these yours dearie?"

I am shaken out of my daydream by Anna, who is holding up a pair of large white pants.

"No, no those are…"

Whose?

"Dave's?"

"Hmmmmm," Anna is uncertain.

"Actually Anna I think they're yours. Do you remember that I moved to my house? So I don't have any washing here now."

(Thank goodness)

"Oh yes," she says dismissively. I don't think she does remember, but at the same time knows that somehow she should remember. Therefore she always moves on quickly from these conversations.

The front door is flung open. Dave and an empty Panattone box. And snow on his Australian boots.

"That Robbie!" he booms, throwing the box down by the grandfather clock.

"He's seen off his brother. That Bobby came down the sheds after the cake and Robbie flew straight at 'im and sent 'im back up the garden."

He shakes his head in happy disbelief.

Up on the bank outside the window a crow perches on an old post, looking out across the icy fields where patches of snow still cling.

"And 'e can get lost too," says Dave. "I'm not feeding 'im any more today. Them crows just stuff their beaks 'till they're dropping the darned food. Then they go on stuffin' more food in."

The crow shivers slightly on his post and turns his head towards the window, as if sensing Dave's disapproval. And that is the old countryman in Dave. The old beliefs that revere the chat and fear the corvid. Why Dave limps down to the sheds in the snow to feed his robin. But also takes out apple cores and birdseed to the crows and rooks. If you show them respect then their magic won't harm you.

Anna takes no notice. She lives a world away from these old beliefs. And even if she detests the cold it's as nothing compared to the six foot snowdrifts in the Birmingham of her childhood.

It is Dave's job to worry about the wildlife at the cottage.

CUPBOARDS

10th March 2018

. . . .

I ring Dave on Saturday morning to check all is well, and that he intends to have lunch at the boatyard. He sounds tense.

"Bloody cupboard's fell off the wall," he tells me.

Which cupboard?

"In the kitchen. Good job it didn't fall on 'er."

"I'll be over in an hour," I tell him, "I'll give you a hand."

As I drive to the cottage I imagine the bottles of sauces, jars of different mustards, Dave's vinegars, the syrups and spices. Sliding. Crashing.

But at the cottage Anna looks calm. She is folding and refolding the tea towels over the Aga rail. They have all seen better days, but when I bought new tea towels she put them into a drawer and never took them out again

In the kitchen Dave's white hair is standing on end. The cupboard is held up by a car jack. Dave has his toolbox open on the worktop and the kitchen smells of oil and grease. Jars and bottles are stacked on the floor.

"Nothing broke when the cupboard came down then Dave?"

He tells me that the cupboard slipped onto the kitchen scales.

"So they're broke," he says.

While he finishes refitting the cupboard I make some coffee.

"How's your sister dearie?"

I tell her that my sister is fine.

"And how's your father?"

I distract her by pointing out that the narcissi in the pot outside are looking good.

"You're a strange rat," Dave tells her, as he comes out for his coffee. He has heard her questions.

We talk for a little about the family and then Dave puts away the toolbox and heads off for the boatyard.

"Would you like some soup deary?"

I tell Anna that I'm going to load some of my plants into the car to take to my new house, and we'll have some soup when I've done that. However Anna has other ideas, and when I come back inside she is already heating soup on the Aga. The smell is very strange.

"What flavour is it Anna?" I ask.

"I don't know deary. Dave buys the soup."

It looks like chicken and vegetable. But why does it smell so odd?

I go to the fridge and find four large cartons of soup. Yes, the one that is open is chicken and mixed vegetables. Ah. The sell-by date is a month ago. Perhaps I can distract Anna, tip away the soup and replace it with a fresh carton.

But. The next carton I pick up is also last month's. And the next one. And this one behind the egg box.

So do I tell Anna that the soup is off? All the soup in the fridge is off. So there is no soup for lunch?

Behind me Anna has come to find a bowl and spoon.

"I love soup when the weather's cold," she says.

I pour the soup into her bowl, find her apron and take it through to the dining room. I've brought some rosemary focaccia bread as I've read that rosemary improves memory. Anna is intrigued by the herb bread.

As I drink my coffee and Anna enjoys her lunch I realise that she and Dave have probably been eating out of date food for some time. I have never heard either of them mention a stomach upset. I am pretty sure that Anna will suffer no ill effects from the soup, whereas I would possibly be in a bad way.

Anna is tired after lunch. She tries to light the wood-burner without putting any wood in it. She falls asleep as soon as it is lit, and I read the newspaper. Stories of the snow have been replaced by more fears about Brexit, and the poisoning of a Russian spy and his daughter.

Dave unlocks the front door and shuts it behind him with a crash. He is back early.

"I don't like leaving 'er too long?" he says, "she put my pan of apples on the Aga and left it and the darn thing is black now."

Anna stirs but her eyes are closed.

"Don't tell tales," she says.

When she realises I am sitting on the sofa she looks surprised.

121

"How's your sister dearie?"

"It's YOUR sister you're talkin' about," explodes Dave.

"It's ok," I reassure them.

We are quiet for a moment.

"Did your sister ever come to see you when we were young?" I ask her.

"No, I don't think so. We didn't get on..."

"She kept runnin' away when she were young," says Dave.

"I think you once told me that your sister stopped speaking for a long time."

We both look at Anna. Her fingers pull at the green throw on her lap.

"I just can't remember... it was a very long time ago..."

She closes her eyes.

"I never met 'er," says Dave, "only the younger one. And she were alright."

He reaches for the TV remote and then puts on the side light next to him. I will have to go soon. Work tomorrow.

"And now," says Dave, "I'm goin' to watch Flog It."

BIRTHDAY

17th March 2018

. . . .

The forecast is not good. More snow. But it is Anna's birthday on Sunday so I must head to the cottage on Saturday with cards and presents. I've made a chocolate cake but it's a bit flat because I'm still getting used to my new electric oven. So strange after an Aga. The cake is flat but chocolatey. I don't think they will mind somehow.

The lane outside the cottage is muddy and damp as usual, but quiet. The conversion of the old pub is nearly complete. The caravan and the white vans and lorries have gone. If you came looking for the old pub because that's where you had your hen night or your stag do, your twenty-first or eightieth birthday; well, all you would find would be new houses.

Dave has been potting up new plants on the bank. Cyclamen standing to attention. Pink primulas. Miniature daffodils. Dave doesn't really go for tall plants in the garden. Except for hollyhocks and the mauve verbena by the front door which Devon brother gave them.

And Anna has flowers in the cottage for her birthday. She seems pleased to see me, and surprised that I have brought Prosecco and Italian coffee bags and birthday cards.

"I'll have the Prosecco now," she says.

The mantelpiece above the Aga is filled with cards. Old friends from Birmingham, local friends, young friends. One of Anna's gifts before she became ill was the ability to be a great listener. Whenever you arrived at the cottage, at whatever time of day, Anna would make you tea or coffee with home-made cake and sit you in the dining room by the Aga, and just listen. If you were shy Anna would ask the right questions to get you talking.

She still does this. The only difference is that her questions tend to be random.

"How is your dog?"

"How is your sister?"

"How is your father?"

When you have no dog or sister, and your father died a long time ago.

"That sky looks bad," Dave says, as he comes back from feeding Robbie at the sheds.

He has a dusting of snow on his shoulders.

From the dining room window we watch the flakes fall more heavily.

"Don't reckon I'm going down the boatyard."

I feel a bit nervous. If the snow settles the journey back could be difficult.

Dave lights the wood-burning stove. I'm surprised as he usually doesn't allow this until the afternoon. Perhaps this is in honour of Anna's birthday.

The plants on the bank are disappearing under the settling snow, and the lane at the front of the cottage is white.

But then as we drink our coffee and talk about the family, it turns to rain, and the greenness of the fields begins to reappear.

"I'll be going then," says Dave, getting to his feet.

"I'll get some lunch," I tell Anna.

I make a sausage sandwich, but Anna barely touches it. She is more interested in the chocolate cake, so I cut a generous slice and then cut that into small portions for her.

"You have plenty of birthday cards," I say.

"I'm eighty-four," she says thoughtfully.

She's eighty-six today.

I watch her cutting the chocolate cake portions into even smaller slices.

Eighty-six years old. That's a good age. She has had a long life, and has never been ill until now. It would be nice to reflect on previous birthdays. Her seventieth, when family members decorated plates for her. They're on the shelf above the sink. Her eightieth when friends gathered at the Lavender Farm for coffee and cake and speeches. The birthdays before I was born. The birthdays of her childhood.

Instead we sit by the fire, watching the rain blowing across the fields. We talk a little about the friends and family who have sent cards. Anna asks me where Dave has gone. I tell her that he is at the boatyard. That he will be back soon.

And all is quiet.

EASTER

31st March 2018

. . . .

I will need a glass of Shiraz as soon as I get home. A large one. This is not a good day.

The idea was to take an Easter lunch to the cottage. So tall son and I set off with pork casserole, apple crumble and creme brûlée (the latter being one of Anna's favourites).

At the cottage the usual mud and dampness. Dave is chuffed as Mr Pheasant has brought his wife over for breakfast on the bank. I obligingly throw them a handful of corn from the corn bin. They look at me in alarm and back off into the field in a flurry of feathers. An unfamiliar figure.

Anna looks pale and sleepy and the dining room smells of oil.

"Aga playin' up a bit," says Dave.

I put the casserole in the oven and we sit and talk about the family, and how middle grandson has bought himself an electric car.

"Bloody lot of money," says Dave.

The smell of oil is getting worse. Then a loud bang, followed by another bang and a flame from the door of the Aga. Tall son and I look at each other in alarm.

126

I suggest that Anna goes to the sitting room and I will bring her electric over-blanket.

"And my sword please..."

"What the hell do you want a sword for!" booms Dave.

Anna points at the warming oven door.

"My..."

Ah, her neck warmer!

As I help her out of her chair I am a bit shocked to see that she seems unable to look up. Unable to walk forward.

"She fell the other night," says Dave, "twice... and I 'ad to get up and get 'er in the chair and then try to get 'er up the stairs and in 'er bed."

Tall son tells Dave to take her to the GP for a check up. I think we will ring medical daughter too.

There is a loud knock at the door and Alan the builder/gamekeeper is here for a late coffee.

Dave forgets the Aga for a moment and the talk turns to logs.

Alan tells Dave that the man in the house across the field has had a tree taken down and is offering them the wood for logs.

"They're big bounders... big 'uns," says Alan.

"Bloody big logs up there," agrees Dave.

"We don't want no-one gettin' near 'em," says Alan.

"I'll bloody shoot 'em if they go near it."

The talk moves on to tractors. Dave tells Alan he needs two new wings for his tractor. I didn't realise tractors had wings.

"Don wanted a tractor didn't 'e, but the tight bastard didn't want to pay the rate. 'E can get stuffed..."

Dave is obviously a little stressed.

There is another loud bang from the Aga accompanied by a flash of flame. Tall son looks alarmed.

"I'm goin' 'ome," says Alan getting to his feet and buttoning up his long waxed coat.

What about the pork casserole and apple crumble!

We eat them anyway. Dave has second helpings. Even Anna finishes the casserole. The plate of sweet potato has scorch marks across it.

After lunch Dave gets down on the floor to peer into the Aga with a torch. This is no mean feat for an elderly, rather portly man. His white hair brushes the floor. Tall son stands by looking a little anxious. Then he beckons me into the kitchen.

"I'm going to get the walking frame from the shed," he tells me, "and then I'm going to bring up that stairlift Dave keeps on about. The one that Alan gave him. It's obvious Anna can't walk properly. She's going to fall down the stairs one of these nights. I'm going to fit that stairlift today. We can't wait any longer, whatever Dave says."

I look at my watch. It's three o'clock.

I would quite like to go home. The smell of burning oil is overpowering, even with the front door and windows open.

Nothing for it but to go and sit in the garden. Away from the oily smell. The smell that Dave and Anna don't seem to detect.

Ah. Fresh air. I've been here before...

EASTER PART 2

31st March 2018

. . . .

Dave and tall son bring the stairlift up from one of Dave's sheds. It looks far too long so tall son decides they need to cut it with an angle grinder.

"Why are all Dave's tools covered in oil?," mutters tall son as we carry the stairlift to the stone table in the garden. Dave is looking anxious. He wants to retire to the sitting room to watch 'Flog It'. Anna is sitting quietly on the sofa. I am sure there has been a decline in her health, as previously she would have been asking us what we were doing.

Once the stairlift has been trimmed tall son can fix it in place and fit the seat and foot rest. I am holding the lift against the wall at the top of the stairs and tall son is adjusting the four clamps that will hold it in place. Dave is hovering by the sitting room door with one eye on the television.

Suddenly there is a loud bang.

"It's the Aga!" says tall son.

I hurry downstairs. Black smoke is pouring from the bottom door. The smoke alarm springs into action. Dave lurches across the kitchen and throws open the door to the burner, letting out a sheet of flame onto the washing on the Aga rail.

"Dave, move the washing!" I shout.

Tall son pulls the washing off the rail while Dave cuts off the oil supply to the Aga. The black smoke starts to disappear, but the smell of burning oil is terrible. Anna is oblivious. Dave's white hair is in shock.

"Bloody flue's blocked," says Dave, wiping his hands on a tea towel.

"I can't cope with this smell," says tall son under his breath.

We carry the stairlift and its seat and foot rest to the little room above the kitchen.

Tall son promises to return with eldest grandson to get it fitted. Dave looks pleased.

1. Eldest grandson is held in high esteem as a very practical young man.

2. Now Dave can sit down and watch 'Flog It'.

We gather up the casserole dish and pudding bowls from lunch and head back to the city. Our clothes and hair smell of oil. Our noses are filled with the smell of oil. Dave has assured us that that once the Aga has cooled down he will clean the flue and re-light it in the morning.

"That Aga is on the way out," says tall son, "and we need to think about getting them an electric oven. I'm going to call Australia when we get home."

I'm just thankful that we were at the cottage when the Aga decided to explode. I can't imagine what would have happened if Dave and Anna had been dozing in the sitting room.

If the Aga has reached the end of its days I need to hurry on with getting central heating in the cottage so that there is a good source of heating and hot water.

"They should have moved years ago," says tall son. He sounds exasperated. "They need to be somewhere that's easier to cope with."

I couldn't agree more.

MINI OVEN

9th April 2018

On Monday my mobile rings at work. It's Alan the builder/gamekeeper. My stomach lurches.

"It's ok," he says, "I've just 'ad a cuppa with them. But that new alarm keeps goin' off and that's got me a bit worried you know."

"The carbon monoxide alarm!"

Oh heck.

"I'm callin' you cos Dave's took the batteries out to stop the noise."

I thank him and hang up quickly. I need to call Dave.

No answer. I try three times and then call tall son at home. He calls eldest grandson who says he was at the cottage that morning and has booked an engineer. He also told Dave to stop trying to light the Aga.

I call Alan and tell him Dave doesn't answer the phone and I am worried. If Alan was with them this afternoon and the alarm was going off, it can only mean Dave has ignored eldest grandson's warning not to light the Aga. Alan says he will go to the cottage straight away.

He rings me a few minutes later.

"There's nobody 'ere," he says, "I reckon they've gone up the pub now the Aga don't work."

Yes that's probably the case.

I call Dave a couple of hours later. He sounds glum, but assures me the Aga is out.

"Don't know what's up with it," he says, "so we 'ad supper at the pub. She 'ad soup."

Tall son suggests he and Dave go and sort out some alternative form of cooking, and Dave sounds happier.

The following evening when I return from work tall son tells me they have bought a mini oven at Argos. Dave has heated up a pie in it and all is well.

"I think I'll go over tomorrow and just check," I tell him.

When I arrive at the cottage I feel the cold in the dining room. The Aga is cold. Anna is cold. But mini oven sits on top of the Aga, gleaming and triumphant.

Anna greets me with a faint "hello deary." She is wrapped up in her throw on the sofa. I plug in the electric fire. Where did the new radiator go?

Out in the cold kitchen I make tea, and when I return she is asleep. She is not wearing make up or earrings.

I hear the thump of Dave's shoes on the stairs.

"I've made you some tea," I tell him, indicating his Spitfire mug on the wooden side table.

"She's bin asleep all day," he says, staring at Anna, "and she won't eat nothing much."

Hmmm.

"Not even ice cream? Or a glass of red wine?" I ask him, " I've never known Anna refuse a glass of wine."

"Not in front of my father deary."

Anna has heard us. Her eyes are closed, but she is listening.

Dave looks surprised, but says nothing.

Out in the dining room we look over mini oven. Dave is impressed with the speed at which it heats their meals. It has two hot plates and a small oven, which is probably all they need. We talk about the Aga engineer.

"I've bin looking on my iPad at gettin' another Aga if this one's no good any more," he says.

I'm glad he's thinking ahead. I hope the engineer will just clear any blockage and allow the Aga to carry on with the job it's been doing since the nineteen-thirties.

But Anna looks so frail. I was worried when I saw her at the weekend.

As I drive away from the cottage I decide to call Sydney brother. I wonder if he could come to England. Just in case. Just to see Anna for a few days. It's so difficult to know.

At the top of the lane, just after the telephone box which is now a book exchange; just before the sheep field, and just level with the allotments, I see hunting cat, alert and watchful on the grass verge. Hunting cat sees me too and gives me a haughty look. I feel her watching as I drive past the recreation ground with the tall trees, and the pub where Anna enjoys the soup, and up the steep hill.

And then out onto the main road.

CAKE

14th April 2018

....

I call medical daughter and she says she will visit her grandparents with me. She arrives by train with laptop and revision. I warn her that Anna seems very frail and uncommunicative. We set off for the cottage on a dull overcast afternoon and stop at the village shop to buy some home-made cake. Slices of lemon drizzle, Victoria sponge and Bakewell tart.

"Lemon drizzle is my favourite," says medical daughter, "what a lovely shop. Everyone is so friendly."

That's true. The volunteers always ask after Anna and Dave, and hope they will pop in to the shop for a coffee and cake.

At the cottage the door is opened before I have time to knock. To our surprise it's Anna. She recognises medical daughter immediately and hurries us in,

"Out of the cold wind dearies."

Medical daughter throws me a puzzled look. I can't explain this. Only four days ago tall son had rung me to say that Anna was dozing all day on the sofa, barely opening her eyes, barely speaking.

We show her the slices of cake and she goes to the kitchen to fetch plates and napkins.

"Dave made a cake when we heard you were coming," she tells us.

Not only are we having a normal conversation, but Anna is walking far more steadily between the kitchen and the dining room. I feel pleased and rather relieved, but this is tempered by the horrible oily smell of the Aga, that makes me want to leave immediately.

Dave has obviously relit it. Against our advice.

And where is mini oven?

And here is Dave, up from the sheds in his favourite grey wool jumper and flat cap, and pleased to see his grand-daughter who hasn't been to the cottage for some time.

We cut the cake into small portions so that we can have a little of each one. Anna eats one or two tiny pieces and then puts down her plate.

"She's not eating..." Dave tells us, "and she ain't takin' er tablets at night."

"Why? What happened?" I ask.

"She went to bed early three nights ago and she just slept all night," he says, "so she don't need them sleeping tablets I reckon."

He helps himself to another piece of Bakewell tart. Dave always talks with his mouth full. This puzzles me sometimes as Anna was so strict with us when we were young. Elbows off the table. Use your napkin. Cut up your fruit. No milk bottles on the table. Hold your cutlery correctly. It is pudding, not dessert. And certainly do not speak with your mouth full.

Medical daughter wants to see the tablet box. But when Dave brings it to the round table she looks at it in dismay.

"It's a bit of a muddle," she says politely, turning it over.

I'm feeling a bit nauseous and my eyes are stinging, so I go out to the garden and gather up fallen branches and twigs from the huge tulip tree.

When I go back to the dining room Dave gives me a curious look,

"Reckon you got a nose problem," he says.

"The smell of oil is pretty strong," says medical daughter.

"It's alright! Don't know what you lot are worrying about! I got it lit and it's fine!"

Why does it smell so bad then?

We've finished the cake from the village shop and now Dave is cutting the Madeira cake he has made. I'm a bit wary of this cake. Firstly Dave says its home-made. But I've seen the packets of cake mix in the kitchen cupboard. Many of them. Secondly Dave uses margarine to grease the cake tin. That shouldn't be a problem. But he forgets how long the margarine has been in the fridge. He doesn't care really. He will use it even if it is green.

"Never done me no harm," he says.

Medical daughter whispers to me that her eyes are stinging.

"We must head back," I say, getting to my feet.

Medical daughter kisses her grandparents. We drive away. Glad to leave the oily smell behind but a little sad. Anna is so frail.

We discuss speaking to Anna's GP about the sleeping tablets. Medical daughter is worried about Anna stopping them so abruptly. I will call Dave tomorrow. Hopefully the engineer will have been to investigate the Aga. I will go to the cottage at the weekend to see how Anna is. How can she be so alert and mobile? So suddenly.

The journey passes quickly because we are so busy discussing what's going on at the cottage. Once home I put the macaroni cheese in the oven and check my emails. Sydney brother has emailed me. He is coming to England. Soon.

FASHION

21st April 2018

. . . .

I call Dave while I'm having breakfast. He sounds pleased to hear from me.

"I've got the Aga flue cleared right out," he tells me, "it's going a treat now."

It turns out that Dave found a sufficiently long metal pole in one of his sheds to push up through the flue, and clean it out properly. At last.

"So what was blocking the flue?" I ask.

"A ton of soot," he says, "and a bloody great bird's nest. Why the heck would a bird be building a nest there?"

Why indeed?

So I drive over to the cottage on Saturday morning feeling hopeful that the Aga is working properly now.

What did the Aga engineer say?

"I stopped him coming," Dave tells me. "Got it sorted now."

I wonder what eldest grandson thinks of this.

The Aga smell has gone. It is possible to sit at the round table without having to bury your nose in your scarf.

And mini oven is sitting in the long cupboard.

"It's good to have a reserve," Dave says.

And Anna is still on good form. In fact she is quite spiky.

"I see you are wearing my clothes," she says, looking me up and down, as I greet her in the dining room.

I think she's referring to my long tweed skirt and yellow jumper.

"I got them in the cancer research charity shop," I tell her.

"Well I must have put them there!" she snaps.

For some reason I feel cross. But that's ridiculous of me.

"Anna, I say, "I wouldn't take your clothes. In fact I wouldn't fit into them as I'm much bigger than you."

She has that very irritating smile today.

"There's hardly anything of you," she says looking up at me. And smiling.

I remember stories of confusion when my grandparents generation reached this age. Stories about pearl necklaces and valuable rings. Somebody had a necklace. Then it was lost. Did they give it away? Or accidentally throw it in the dustbin? I also remember my grandmother, who had cataracts, tying her house keys to a saucepan lid so she wouldn't lose them. But she still managed to throw the saucepan lid and keys into the dustbin.

So Anna's clothes are as precious to her as jewellery was to my grandmothers and great aunts . She wouldn't want anyone else wearing them. Much of the time I feel that she doesn't really know who I am, and therefore I could be a neighbour or a friend, or perhaps I am the sister she didn't get on with.

Perhaps they borrowed each other's clothes, or even argued about who owned what.

I remember after Anna left John the court said we were to visit her on Tuesdays and Thursdays after school. By this time Anna and Dave had bought an energetic springer spaniel and he and Anna, and my brothers would be waiting outside my school cloakroom in the narrow lane that ran alongside the river. Anna would be immaculately dressed. In summer she wore elegant shift dresses with stiletto heels and slim gold bangles. Her hair in a bouffant style. Always sunglasses in summer. In winter her beautiful coats were long and fitted, and matched with leather gloves and boots. Nobody else's mother looked like this.

I wasn't sure what to think. Part of me liked her elegance. Part of me wanted her to look like the other mothers.

My French teacher, who lived in the same village, once remarked,

"Eet is like she is going to a grand ball."

Well not quite.

But I know what she meant.

Once I had found my summer blazer and straw hat, or my gabardine and felt hat in winter, we would pile into the old Morris Traveller. Then head off to the cottage, with our over-excited spaniel trying to chew my hat on the back seat.

After tea we would often go for a walk. We loved the lanes and footpaths around the cottage. Anna always came with us, in her lovely clothes. No anoraks or wellingtons for her. And certainly not a hat. But always an elegant umbrella in case it rained.

Today she looks beautiful in a long black skirt and yellow jacket.

Since Dave stopped the sleeping tablets her eyes are much brighter. Her earrings match her headscarf. Her posture is more upright.

It is as if she has had a very long sleep. And now to everyone's surprise she has woken up.

MILITARY SERVICE

4th May 2018

....

I'm late getting to the cottage. The traffic is bad.

"It's all them new houses they're building," Dave tells me, "just building going on everywhere. We don't need all them houses."

He shakes his head.

"Mad as a box of frogs," he says to himself as he unfolds his newspaper.

There's a knock at the door and it's Robert from SAAFA. The armed forces charity may be able to help with funding for the central heating. The two men are soon in conversation about Dave's National Service on Thorney Island in the nineteen-fifties. I'm making some cheese on toast in the kitchen for Anna, but I hear snatches of conversation from the dining room concerning aircraft, engines and even talk of an explosion.

It's clear that Dave has always regretted not being given work overseas or permission to fly planes. But then the RAF probably realised his skills lay in the engine shop.

Unfortunately Dave can't remember the date he signed up; the date he left Thorney Island or even his service number. Robert scratches his head thoughtfully.

143

"I'll have to do some searching on the computer," he tells us.

He turns to Anna. She is alert and smiling but I can see that she doesn't know what the men have been talking about.

"Did you have a job when you were younger?" he asks her.

She smiles at Robert.

"She were a model," Dave says proudly.

Robert nods his head and writes this on one of the many forms he has brought with him.

"In Chester and London," says Anna.

The cheese on toast is ready. Robert has all the details he needs for the moment. He politely declines Anna's offer of lunch, puts away the forms in his briefcase and picks up his jacket. Promising to be in touch as soon as possible.

"It would be good to get the heating in over the summer," he says as we shake hands.

Just time to have lunch before the occupational therapists arrive.

Neither Anna nor Dave understands,

1. Why they are having a visit from occupational therapists.

2. What an occupational therapist actually is.

But Lynn and Katie arrive promptly at two o'clock. It is a very warm day. Throughout the year rain from the fields runs down from the bank and onto the paving slabs in the garden. But it is so warm that the usual puddle of water outside the front door has dried up. Dave's pots of pansies below the bank are starting to wilt.

Dave wants to get outside and mow the lawn, but now he has to sit down in his armchair and talk about mobility.

"I've got no problems now I've got my knees sorted," he says, struggling to get out of the sagging armchair. Lynn looks around the room and selects a faded flat velvet cushion that has seen better days. She pushes it under the seat of the armchair, and tells Dave to try getting out of the chair again.

"Simple as that," he says getting onto his feet again.

"That's better," says Lynn.

Katie takes Anna to the foot of the stairs to see how she manages them. Anna is smiling but I sense she is inwardly cross at being asked to do such a ridiculous thing . It's Dave who has the mobility problems isn't it? Lynn and I go to the dining room to fill out forms for a new bath seat. This one will raise and lower the bather in and out of the water. It sounds ideal, as Dave is now struggling to help Anna in and out of the bath.

"I hope you don't mind me saying that I'm a bit puzzled," says Lynn when we are on our own.

"What do you mean?"

"Well the central heating charity sent us out as your mum was so...so frail and immobile."

I explain to Lynn about Dave forgetting the bedtime tablets. How Anna is so much more alert now. And how she walks around the house, and even the garden.

"They've been going out to lunch again at the pub," I add.

Lynn is very surprised. I tell her that I'm planning to talk to friends about this as several of them have elderly relatives in various stages of dementia.

Dave promises to call Lynn when the bath seat arrives so that she can show them how it works. He decides to put the stairlift on hold as he thinks it will be too confusing for Anna.

We go out into the warm afternoon to say goodbye. Anna follows us. Without her stick. She smiles politely and thanks them for coming. She waves as they walk down the lane to their car.

I have a feeling she will be glad to have her peace and quiet back again. To make a cup of tea and watch the cows out in the fields.

Dave has already headed off to the sheds to look for the lawn mower. I was planning to go home now. But I'd better give him a hand with the mower. I follow him down the lane. Dave is happy. It feels like Spring is here.

Now he can get on with the gardening.

COWS

7th May 2018

. . . .

The weather forecast is hot. The sky is a clear blue. I've been visiting tall son at university and missed my usual visit to the cottage. So when I arrive mid morning on Bank Holiday Monday they are pleased to see me. Anna is wearing a floaty summer skirt, far too long of course. Her friend Sara rang me during the week,

"I've just rung Anna and she seems very bright..."

Sara is pleased and puzzled at the same time.

Medical daughter texts me to say that her grandmother has rung her asking for her London address.

"How does Anna suddenly realise that I'm in London?" she asks.

Dave is heading off to the sheds to repair his chainsaw.

"It won't cut straight," he tells me.

He also tells me that Robbie has a mate, and Dave is sure they have young.

"I've seen him goin' in that hedge there with food," he tells me, " in an' out that hedge all day long with food 'e is. His wife keeps 'im busy with the kids."

It's too hot in the cottage with the Aga going, so we sit outside under the huge tulip tree. Anna has brought out a pile of catalogues. She insists that I choose something for my birthday.

"It's not for another eight months," I say.

That doesn't matter. Anna wants to be prepared. The old Anna is back.

"What are you lookin' at all them clothes for, you rat?" Dave asks her fondly as he limps up the garden for a cup of tea.

"There are birthdays to think about," she says, "I'm not looking for myself."

But occasionally she asks me if I like a swing mac in salmon and fawn sateen, or an Italian printed silky jersey blouse.

"I think that might be for a special occasion," I say.

"Not necessarily."

It is so hot that the stems of the bluebells, usually so straight and tall, are bending slightly in the haze. I imagine the villagers along the lane have brought out their deckchairs and their Sunday papers to make the most of the weather.

Dave has taken shelter in the cool of the sitting room with his iPad. Searching for spare parts for his chainsaw. The heat makes him irritable. As do Anna's incessant questions.

"When is the news Dave?"

"What do you want to eat Dave?"

"Is it Monday Dave?"

But yes. It is Monday. Anna is quite correct.

I help him with Google. Dave loves his iPad - "best present ever" - but sometimes its technical demands baffle him.

I find a recent email from Devon. Devon brother looking very handsome in a suit. With a beard. He has a part in a film. Dave and Anna study the photograph.

"He is a very handsome chap," they agree.

I can hear a noise from the bank. A flash of red and green. Mr Pheasant is looking for corn. Better to throw a handful of corn myself. Dave is immersed in chainsaw parts. Mr Pheasant sees me and hurries away across the field.

As the day starts to cool Anna busies herself with cooking a fishcake for her supper, and stacking the little pots of caramel pudding on their shelf in the fridge. I am aware of movement in the field beyond the bank. The cows have left their place under the trees and wandered down to graze near the cottage. I watch them moving slowly across the field or standing staring ahead. Then in the midst of them, staying close to its mother, I spot a small black figure. Wobbling slightly on four skinny legs. Gazing at the cottage with huge eyes.

A new calf. Probably its first venture outside. On such a lovely cloudless day.

A new life.

RINGS

12th May 2018

The washing machine has flooded the kitchen. Dave stands on two old floor cloths - one under each shoe - and does his best to mop up the water. When he sees me he heads off to his chair by the window. With his floral mug of coffee and a piece of Madeira cake. So I clean up the remaining water, and then hang the towels and socks and vests in the watery sun.

"Can we go for a walk deary?" says Anna as I sit down with my coffee.

"Round the church?" I ask her. This is a short walk, with the church about halfway round.

She nods.

Dave is delighted.

"See... I told you them night tablets were no good. She's woke up now."

Dave is cutting his brittle fingernails with the little metal cutter he keeps in the kitchen. It's a horrible sound. And I'm not sure where the cut fingernails are going.

"Shall we walk now?" I ask her.

Dave struggles to his feet and goes to inspect Anna's fingernails.

"What you wearing all them bloody rings for again?" he asks her.

Anna is wearing at least six rings on her left hand.

"One for each of my husbands," she says holding up her hand and smiling.

"She tells everyone that," Dave says dismally as he sits back in his chair.

"Is one of them from my father?" I ask her.

She points vaguely at a plain gold ring. "I can't remember deary."

"What about the ring Dave gave you?"

"This one," she says holding up her little finger. It looks like the sort of ring you might find in your Christmas cracker, but I admire it nonetheless. I don't think Dave remembers either.

We walk 'round the church' admiring the pink azalea outside the neighbour's cottage, and the new oak frame garage up the hill where the old newspaper shop used to be. Shropshire brother used to cycle up to the shop to do the newspaper round after school. The evening paper.

Anna walks steadily and holds my arm lightly, apologising every so often for having to hold on.

"I can never go for a walk on my own again can I," she says sadly.

Almost to herself.

It is all the more sad when I think how important walking has always been in our family.

I tell her that at least she is well enough now to walk with a companion.

"Only a couple of weeks ago you wouldn't have been able to get round the church with me," I say.

She listens and smiles.

"Here's Mrs Jackson's," she says, as we come to a garden gate just before the pond. "Dave and I used to look after her plants when they were away.

Mrs Jackson is in a flowerbed under the front window of the thatched cottage and lets out a shriek of delight to see us. The hand on my arm tenses. Anna has always disapproved of women being loud. Dave and the men of the family could be as loud as they wished. But women.

No.

When I think about it I realise that I cannot remember ever hearing Anna shout, or yell or raise her voice. Or even laugh loudly.

We chat with Mrs Jackson and admire her garden. Anna's hold on my arm grows tighter.

"I think we will go home for a cup of tea now," I say to her.

Two small ducklings skitter away across the pond as we approach. Their mother guides them to the safety of the vegetation at the edge.

We walk slowly up the hill and I draw her attention to the old telephone box near the top.

"This is your village library now," I say.

"Our what?"

We cross the road and I hold the heavy door open so Anna can see all the books inside. I explain how villagers can bring their old unwanted books and swop them.

"I'll tell Dave about this," she says, " I don't think he knows about it."

We turn into the lane, past the row of small cottages.

"But where is the thing that used to be in the box," she says.

"The telephone has gone," I say, "people use mobile phones now."

"So they don't use the telephone box to ring people?" she asks. I can hear the surprise in her voice.

As we make our way towards the cottage I think about how much the world has changed for Anna's generation. How bewildering to find that your adult children don't have landlines any more. That so many people send texts or messages rather than ring. That your village telephone box is filled with books.

At the cottage Dave is fashioning an escape pole from an old garden broom. He tells us that a mouse and its baby have got trapped in the log box.

"This'll get 'em out," he says, "they can climb up the pole."

He ushers us inside so that the mice are not frightened.

From the kitchen window I watch a colourful woodpecker dining out on the fat balls Dave has hung from a branch on the bank.

Anna falls asleep in her armchair after our walk. And Dave sits by the window to observe the log box.

Time passes quietly. Just the ticking of the dining room clocks. The heavy breathing of the cows near the hedge.

And the cheers of two mice running for their lives to the rockery under the bank.

WEDDINGS

19th May 2018

John had a cufflink box that he kept on the mantelpiece in his bedroom. Like Anna he appreciated nice clothes. I particularly remember him wearing pink shirts at a time when men seemed to wear white shirts only. That day he asked me to fetch his mother-of-pearl cufflinks and I ran upstairs to his room and opened the little box. A piece of folded paper fluttered onto the carpet and when I picked it up and read it I knew what had happened to Anna.

The housekeepers arrived and left, and the au pairs brought their boyfriends to lunch and tea. John met a tall dark-haired woman who played football. Who had a child but wasn't married. Then a fair-haired woman he had known when he was younger. And then another model; also called Anna. He nearly married her. Shropshire brother and I were nonplussed.

The house filled with people. Music played. Everyone danced and drank and partied. Sometimes I couldn't sleep for the noise. Richard Harris, Marvin Gaye, Thunderclap Newman, the Beach Boys. Their music filled the rooms.

And then at my grandmother's little house by the abbey we met Dave again. Because Dave and Anna were together.

(It wasn't a surprise to me though. Thanks to the cufflink box).

Buying a little cottage in the country. Buying a dog. Getting married. Having a baby.

Getting married.

I'm not sure when or where.

Or what the bride wore.

Or who the guests were. If any.

We didn't attend the wedding.

Or even know that it was taking place.

As Anna never celebrates anniversaries I don't even know how long she and Dave have been married. But if Sidney brother is about to be fifty, then I guess we must have missed their golden wedding anniversary.

I once asked them about their silver wedding anniversary. What was the date? Dave just looked puzzled. Anna looked vague.

So today we are watching the Royal Wedding on television. Dave should be heading off to the boatyard, but even he is just a little curious. He has delayed his departure.

It is a beautiful day and the cottage door is left open. The fields sparkle and Dave's honeysuckle fills the bank and almost covers the stile. Robbie has left the sheds and hops about on the bank looking for food for his young. Dave proudly announces that Robbie nearly perched on his head when he went out to the corn bin.

"Dunno where his brother's gone though."

I drove past hunting cat at the top of the lane. Skulking in the long grass. Her tail twitching. I don't tell Dave.

Anna isn't really watching the wedding. Too many people. Too many names. Instead she looks through one of her favourite catalogues.

Dave isn't sure what to make of it all. The bride is American or Afro-Caribbean. Her mother is Afro-Caribbean. He isn't sure. The sermon is given by a black American preacher. There is a gospel choir. If the guests look somewhat surprised by the service, then so does Dave.

"Who's that deary?" says Anna occasionally, as someone with a beautiful dress and hat is caught on camera.

"I've 'ad enough of this then," says Dave getting unsteadily to his feet.

"Are you going to see Gordon then?" asks Anna.

"I'm goin' now," says Dave. He throws a backward glance at the television.

"They've been together for two years, so it's not goin' to be much different tonight is it?"

And on that cheerful note Dave heads off down the garden to his old car.

The newly married couple are driven through the streets of Windsor in a beautiful carriage. I turn to say something to Anna but in the heat of the afternoon she has closed her eyes. The catalogue is sliding off her lap and onto the carpet. I pick it up. And the corner of one page is turned over.

An elegant dark haired woman in a floor length evening dress in rose, burgundy and black. A slim silver-haired man in a well-cut suit smiles at her, offering a glass of something.

It must be champagne.

HOME

26th May 2018

. . . .

The cottage was old. Two hundred years maybe. Dave was a busy man, with a family to look after, and a job that sometimes took him to another part of the country. But he was lucky, because my grandmother had a talent for doing up houses.

One of Anna's friends told me about a house that my grandmother had owned. She took out interior walls and doors, and made it open-plan. At a time when that would have been very unusual.

"And the furniture was lovely," said the friend. "Especially a beautiful turquoise sofa."

So Dave and my grandmother knocked down walls, and took out doors to make the cottage open-plan. It took some time because Dave worked long hours on building sites and demolition sites. But his work sometimes paid dividends. I will often admire an old piece of stone in the garden or a plant pot, or a decorated pane of glass in the house. You might expect Dave to say that it had been passed down through his family, generation after generation, or he had bought it on a trip to an antique shop. But instead he will tell you quite matter of factly,

"I dug it up."

Or…

"Found it on a demolition site."

Today the cottage needs some redecoration. The curtains are tired. The plaster on some of the walls is crumbling and peeling. The kitchen units need replacing. The wooden windows need painting. Dave talks about all these jobs. But he's tired. After a morning of Anna's appointments. Then toasting crumpets for lunch, with cheese and raw onion. Making soup for Anna's lunch. Watering the pots of plants outside the front door. Dave just wants to sit down and read the paper and watch television.

And it's no good offering to help with the decorating. There's a big difference between Dave and Anna's generation and mine. My generation has to ask for help with computers and mobile phones. Maybe for help with our televisions. Who do we ask but our children and grandchildren. Dave's generation is different. Only in the past two years has Dave reluctantly had to ask for help. With his iPad, or with the mobile phone he carries in his car but never switches on, or how to make a mushroom omelette for his tea. Now that Anna doesn't cook anymore.

And what's more, Dave and his generation lived through the war. That gives them a special knowledge. How to survive when there's not enough food. How to cope with nights in an underground shelter. How to face an unseen enemy who is trying to take away your freedom. So Dave doesn't like to ask for help even though he will praise the men of the family for their practical skills.

Today Shropshire brother has arrived with his smart baggage. He is always travelling to race meetings or training yards and he has perfected the art of packing. He called about an hour or so before to tell us he was coming to the cottage. Anna's friend Sheila is drinking tea in the sitting room. It is so hot that the cottage feels stifling. Anna is wearing a green cashmere jumper, so clearly she has not noticed the warm May weather.

I am looking out over the fields from the wooden porch where my grandmother used to sit. She liked to be in the garden but not in the full sun. I am thinking about how people just pop in to the cottage. They don't write, or email, or text or even telephone. They just turn up. And it was the same in the house I grew up in with Anna and John. John was very sociable. Dave is the same. Anna is different. She is fearful of social occasions. She will do her best to avoid them. But she is oddly welcoming of visitors to the cottage. To fetch tea and cake and sit in her floral-patterned armchair and listen. One of her seventieth birthday plates is painted with the words, "Cup of tea dear?"

These days some of her friends text or email me. "Will you be there Saturday?" They don't pop in so readily in case she isn't feeling well. So if I am there we can chat instead, and Anna can just listen. This works well.

Sheila is getting ready to go. She has her hand on the door latch of the sitting room. But she is looking at me with a question in her eyes.

"My car's down at the pub," she says.

(We still refer to the pub, even though it is not a pub any more).

Anna and Dave call goodbye to her from the sitting room. I follow her out to the garden and into the lane. We stop outside the old pub. Someone has moved in. I can see three cars outside. Executive cars.

"Anna rang me," says Sheila, "and asked if I wanted to go out for a spot of lunch. I couldn't believe it!"

I explain about Dave forgetting the evening medication. How Anna seems to have recovered her balance, and so much of her cognisance. Sheila was a nurse so she understands what I am saying. But all she says is, "Extraordinary."

Behind us I can see see Stuart cleaning his car in the lovely oak barn.

It used to be the farmyard where my young brothers collected eggs from the chicken houses, but Stuart bought and converted the farm buildings to make a family house.

"I was very worried about your mother," says Sheila, "the last time I saw her she was so upset."

I wait for her to explain.

"She thought someone was trying to harm her."

"The family?"

Sheila nods. "But that's not uncommon with elderly people with memory problems."

I have read about delusions and paranoia linked to dementia. Poor Anna.

"But this is like the old Anna isn't it," says Sheila cheerfully, unlocking her car door. "I will be over during the week and take her to lunch somewhere nice."

She drives away up the lane and I walk back to the cottage. I can hear Mr Pheasant calling from the field. Dave always says the birds have their regular feeding times, and Mr Pheasant visits mid afternoon. Looking for corn. Shropshire brother is watching horse racing on the television. Dave is watering plants. He points out the mauve pansies lifting their faces to the sun. Anna is in the kitchen, slowly drying the plates and cutlery on the draining board. She smiles when she sees me.

"Cup of tea deary?"

AUSTRALIA

2nd June 2018

. . . .

Sydney brother has arrived from Australia and the weather is beautiful. From Heathrow he heads straight to the cottage. Anna sheds a few tears when she sees him. He arrives at my house in the early evening looking jet-lagged but happy. I think he is thinner than when I last saw him. He tells me about a fishing trip to a remote island where it hadn't rained for a year. Where he ended up with a water-borne infection that left him weak and ill for a long time.

Today I am heading to the cottage for a lunch get-together. Sydney brother has gone ahead in his hired car, and he and tall son have found an old trestle table in Dave's sheds, which they've carried into the garden and placed under the tulip tree. One of Dave's pale blue bedsheets is the tablecloth. Devon brother has arrived with Alis his wife and their Lakeland terriers. He has picked flowers from the garden for the table. It is so hot that Dave is fretting about his wilting pansies. We are glad of the shade. Sydney brother has brought bread, cheese and salad and raided the cupboard for Dave's many jars of chutney. Anna is looking lovely in orange and red from head to foot. She recognises everyone but cries a little when she sees Sydney brother, seeming to forget that she saw him yesterday. And the day before.

Shropshire brother arrives from Bath (something to do with horses). His sons, Anna and Dave's eldest grandson and middle grandson will be along shortly, he tells us.

We drink rosé wine and the talk turns to youngest grandson who is fire-fighting in Canada; medical grand-daughter (it must be way too hot to live in London at the moment) and youngest grand-daughter, at home with her mother in Sydney.

Dave is transfixed by Sydney brother's accounts of fishing in Pacific islands. Various pictures of curious iridescent fish are shown to us. Apparently the majority are returned to the water after being caught, and only one fish is saved for the pot. There are strange tales of Sydney brother cutting his arm on a coral reef and then the coral taking root in his body and re-growing in his arm. Anna looks alarmed but is distracted by the rosé wine and a bowl of colourful boiled sweets that she has brought from the kitchen. Today for Anna, boiled sweets and wine are the perfect lunch.

"I want you to choose something from one of the catalogues deary," she tells me, "for your birthday."

"But my birthday is in January," I remind her, "when the weather is cold. Not long after Christmas."

"There's some new catalogues on the sofa deary," she says, ignoring me.

But Shropshire brother has fallen asleep on the sofa on top of the magazines so I go to the dining room to talk to Alis. She tells me that Devon brother is getting many offers of film and television work. He seems happy to follow a script these days. Tall grandson is roaming the garden with his new SLR camera. Photos of cows eating the leaves from a fallen branch of the tulip tree. Cows nudging the stile. Calves looking at our party with wide eyes.

I suddenly remember Beauty, the old black horse who lived in the field with Tom-Tom the donkey, and a sheep whose name I think was Dudley.

Eldest grandson and middle grandson arrive in an electric BMW. Dave is not sure what to make of this. Certainly it is a car. A fast car. A BMW. But it is powered by electricity? Middle grandson explains that this is the sort of car he needs in London. He and eldest grandson sit under the tulip tree with the Lakeland terriers, and Shropshire brother, now awake, makes tea for everyone. I steer Anna back to her deckchair under the tree. Dave has made a Madeira cake which looks nice, but Dave is disappointed. The Aga is not as hot as it should be and he is very sensitive about this. Sydney brother is the Aga's greatest critic.

"That mini oven burns everything," Dave tells us.

"That's because it cooks things properly, and more quickly than the Aga," I say. But I am ignored.

Shropshire brother has taken slices of cake to the garden. Anna cuts hers into tiny pieces and alternates her cake with boiled sweets. I pretend I have eaten too much bread and cheese, and have no room for Dave's cake. There is much talk about fishing because tomorrow there is a special trip in honour of Shropshire and Sydney brothers' birthdays. All the men are going out to fish around the Needles, and it is a very early start to catch the tides. The men discuss the weather forecast and the need for seasickness tablets.

"I only have to look at the sea to feel seasick," says eldest grandson.

Dave is worrying about bait and hooks and rods; unwilling to trust the fisherman who will be hosting the trip. I wander back to the cool of the dining room to make more tea. Outside in the field the young calves wobble on their new legs, enjoying the open air and warm sunshine.

From the window I see Dave dozing in his deckchair while the younger men continue their fishing talk. There is not a breath of wind. The bird feeders hang quietly on the bank. No sign of crows or rooks or even robins. Not even rook leader and his four henchman (which is how Dave described the rooks to Sydney brother).

"Why are we feeding them bread then?" he asked Dave, "Why did you give me bread to throw out into the field?"

Why indeed? Perhaps Sydney brother has been away from the cottage for so long that he has forgotten the old country ways. Or perhaps Dave has only reverted to them in his old age. When the end of life seems closer. And yet conversely when we think more about our youth.

While everyone lends a hand to clear away the remnants of lunch and wash up Dave takes the bread and cake crumbs down to Robbie in the bushes by the sheds. Devon brother walks the terriers round the church. Middle grandson parks his electric car outside the sitting room window.

And Anna looks happy. There is no wind. The day is very warm. She has had a nice lunch. And almost all her family is with her.

FISHING TRIP

10th June 2018

· ·

I am tired. It's an early start to the cottage to look after Anna today. The men of the family set off shortly after dawn to the coast to meet the fishing boat. Anna looks pleased to see me and asks straightaway if we can go out to lunch.

"Where would you like to go?" I ask her.

But she can't remember the names of any cafes or restaurants that she likes, so I tell her we can go to a delicatessen in the local town that I discovered when I was staying with them. For lunch they do poached eggs and spinach with hollandaise sauce. Delicious.

"Let's go now," says Anna heading to the stairs to put on her "going out" trousers.

"Well it's not even nine o'clock," I say, "how about coffee first."

The fridge is awful. It needs cleaning. So does the cutlery drawer. And the mugs. And the pot of teaspoons. Just as I am considering what to do first, there is a knock at the door. It's Sheila.

"Oh Anna left a message on my phone at half past seven. I wasn't even awake. She said she will be on her own today, so I thought I'd better come over."

Anna looks vague. So I make them both some coffee and leave them to chat.

It's a warm overcast day. I wander around the garden admiring Dave's enthusiasm for his plants. Heathers, pansies, verbena, begonias, small palms, and the beautiful honeysuckle bordering the field beyond. Plenty of colour. Randomly put together. Dave doesn't have time for thoughtful colour combinations.

I am thinking about a conversation I had with Devon brother at our recent lunch. He is concerned about the loss of insect life in the UK. It's our farming methods; just growing single crops. It's our gardening methods; mowing our lawns too frequently and cutting the grass too short. It's difficult to get very much detail from Devon brother because he moves so fast, like all my brothers. After the lunch party Shropshire brother took me, tall son, eldest grandson and my brothers on a city walk. Streets, alleyways, meadows, bridges, parks. All disappeared in a flash as we walked. Fast. Just stopping briefly to peer into the rivers to catch sight of a brown trout or a chubb.

"I'm hungry. I think we should go," calls Anna from the dining room. Sheila comes to the door.

"I'll come back in the week," she says. "and I'll take Anna for lunch."

In the car Anna talks about Jean, a woman she used to sit for a few years ago. Jean lives alone; her husband died several years ago. She has been in and out of hospital after having falls.

"Yes, she's had another fall," says Anna.

"Is she in hospital?"

"Oh no deary, it wasn't that bad. She's at home. Dave and I will go and see her this week. Dave will cut the lawn and we'll have a cup of tea."

We get a seat in the window of the delicatessen. Anna likes this, as she can watch people going by.

"Oh do look!" she says, smiling, when a young child goes past the window in a pushchair, or holding its mother's hand.

"Goodness me," when a particularly plump person walks by.

"That wind's getting up," when the branches of the trees quiver slightly in the breeze.

A young man approaches our table. He is very suntanned. He kneels down and addresses Anna.

"Excuse me... are you Sam's mother? I'm James. I met you three or four years ago at your house. I've just been speaking to Sam about meeting up with him. Perhaps going fishing. I've just arrived from Dubai."

I hold my breath.

But Anna smiles and takes his hand.

"Yes of course. James. You were at school with Sam weren't you?"

She gestures towards me, "This is Sam's sister... my daughter."

James reaches across the table to shake my hand. "I didn't realise Sam had a sister."

"No, I didn't live at the cottage for very long. Sam is quite a bit younger than me."

"Well I just wanted to say hello," he says.

Anna loves people who are polite. She takes hold of his bare arm.

"I love your arm," she says. It is covered with tattoos. James laughs. And so do we.

Anna pays the bill. She can't remember her PIN so we are grateful for contactless payment. She also shows the surprised waitress the rings on her left hand, and tells her about her many husbands.

We are not long back at the cottage before the men arrive. Fortunately they caught several fish. Mainly mackerel. They returned them all to the sea. Sydney brother tells me that in his opinion Australians are kinder to their fish, and remove the hook much more carefully from the fish's mouth.

Dave looks happy and a little sunburnt.

"Best trip ever," he tells us.

I am telling Sydney brother about how we met James at lunchtime when I realise that Dave and Anna are talking about Jean's fall.

I stop and listen.

"When did you ring 'er neighbour,"

"Oh after you'd gone fishing,"

"Was the neighbour goin' round there?"

"I don't know dear, do I,"

"I don't think Anna rang anyone other than Sheila," I say helpfully.

"What you ring 'er for then? She don't live near Jean!" Dave is getting agitated.

"I rang her to see if she wanted to come round for coffee," says Anna.

"But what about Jean!" says Dave, getting louder.

"Was Anna supposed to call the neighbour to go and help Jean?" I ask.

Out of the corner of my eye I see Shropshire brother giving me a "don't interfere" look.

"Is she still on the bloody floor?" yells Dave. "Gimme the phone. I'll call the neighbour myself. Where's the bloody phone?"

He stomps off to the sitting room muttering to himself.

My head is crowded with questions. When did Jean have the fall? Why didn't Dave call the neighbour himself? Or call an ambulance? Doesn't Jean have a personal alarm?

The next time I see Dave he is heading down the lane towards the thatched cottage.

"Has Dave contacted Jean's neighbour?" I ask Anna.

"He's taking some machinery to the thatched cottage," she says.

"His leaf blower." says Sydney brother helpfully.

The combination of Dave's deafness and Anna's confusion can be quite daunting at times. I decide to clean the cutlery drawer while I wait for Dave to return. Anna helps by drying all the teaspoons, but I can see that the tea towel has seen better days. My brothers drink tea in the garden and talk about cars and mutual friends. Dave looks puzzled when I ask him how Jean is.

"Neighbour went over. She called them," he says.

"Is she in hospital?"

"She's alright," says Dave, "Neighbour's there. We'll go down after I've been up the shop in the morning."

I can only assume from this that Jean's fall can't have been too serious. Good job she has a neighbour to call on. Dave is draining the tea from his floral mug and putting on his Australian boots.

"Got to cut that grass," he says to no-one in particular.

"Are you going to cut the grass dear?" says Anna.

"Grows fast this time of year," says Dave, unhooking the keys to his sheds.

Yesterday the lawn looked good when we sat outside for lunch. Not too long, I thought. I go into the sitting room and look out at the garden from the bay window. The lawn does look fine. But Dave is already heading to the sheds for the lawn mower.

I don't think Devon brother will be very pleased.

OBSTINACY

23rd June 2018

. . . .

Sydney brother has flown home. He stayed at the cottage for the final night of his visit. Before he left my house I suggested he say goodbye to Anna, and we both knew what I meant. But he said he would come back again if, and when, things got difficult.

The day after he left I received two emails. One from Robert at the armed forces charity and the other from Cherry at the heating charity. They said that all the funding was in place, the central heating installation could go ahead, and the engineers were waiting for a date to start. This was very good news. It would mean that the central heating would be ready for the start of winter.

Last week tall son and I went to the cottage to see Anna and Dave. The day was hot and Dave was in the garden digging at the bank with a spade, wearing his gardening trousers and an old sagging white vest.

"What are you up to Dave?" said tall son.

Dave put down his spade and wiped his forehead with a faded blue and white spotted handkerchief.

"Them blokes that deliver the oil said the tank up on the bank 'ere was tipping over so they won't deliver. I'm goin' to make it more level."

171

"But aren't you getting a new tank for the central heating system?" I asked.

"Well reckon I might do. We'll see," said Dave.

We went into the cottage to see Anna, and Dave soon followed for a cup of tea and cake. He was reading the newspaper when we left.

The following day I called the engineers to see when they could start the fitting. The woman who answered the phone gave me a date to start in ten days time. This is the best date for them, but I am not sure that Dave will have a new oil tank in place. The engineers told me that they cannot complete the work if a new tank is not ready. I decided to call Dave.

"I'm waitin' for them farmers across the field to come and take the old tank out. They'd 'ave to take it across the field. Get it over the hedge."

"Have they told you when they can do this?" I asked him.

"They're bringin' in the hay right now," he said.

Oh heck.

"Do the farmers know this needs to be done in the next ten days," I said.

"I told 'em that, but they're bringin' in the hay right now."

"So should we perhaps get someone else to supply a new tank, and take away the old tank at the same time?" I said.

There was a sort of explosion at the end of the phone.

"I'm not paying some bloke to come in with a crane and take the tank over the top of my carport! That'll cost an arm an' a leg! Them farmers can lift it over the hedge and take it up the field!"

Right.

So the tank has to be lifted over the hedge and into the field. Rather than being taken through the carport and onto the lane.

Why can't it be taken through the carport? Or be drained of its oil and cut up into pieces?

No. It has to be lifted over the hedge by the farmers across the field. And that is that.

I call Shropshire brother. But he is driving between racecourses and the phone signal keeps fading. The gist of the conversation is; Dave is pretty stubborn.

I explain all this to tall son and he calls eldest grandson. Between them they decide to call the central heating company for advice. The central heating company wants to know that the new oil tank is in place before they start the work. They give tall son the name of an oil tank fitter, and remind him that the fitting needs to be done by a certified installer. I am not sure that the farmers across the field are certified installers. But I don't really want to tell Dave that.

Tall son calls the farmers. Yes they install oil tanks, but they don't provide all the certification for signing off the fitting. Tall son calls the oil tank fitter recommended by the central heating company and arranges to meet him at the cottage the next day. Now all that needs to be done is to explain all this to Dave.

It is a very hot and humid day. Tall son is making a planter box for my courtyard and we have bought cordylines and a miscanthus to plant in it. My mobile rings and it's the central heating company wanting to know if the new oil tank will be installed by Monday. No chance. But they agree that if we have an oil tank fitter and a date for the installation, and we put this in writing, they will start work as arranged.

Tall son will have to call Dave, who will be finding the day too hot. The news about the tank too complicated. The thought of a new installer taking the oil tank through the carport too much to bear. Although tall son and I are not sure why this would be.

Dave answers the phone at the cottage. I hear tall son patiently explaining the situation. Dave's hearing aids are working quite well today which is good. My phone call to him last week was a disaster. He couldn't hear a word I said and so he just talked throughout the call until I had to shout that I wanted to talk to him about central heating. Today Dave is disappointed. He cannot understand why the farmers can't do the job. What is all this paperwork for? Is it something to do with the EU? I think he is finding all this too much to cope with. If only he had thought about all this ten years ago. Tall son explains that he will be at the cottage in the early morning to meet the tank installer to discuss what needs to be done.

We have an early supper and admire the planter box, complete with its minimal planting. I try not to think about central heating, or oil tanks, or farmers.

 But I can't help thinking about a remark that Dave made recently to eldest grandson about the proposed central heating.

"They can put it in, but it don't mean I'm putting the bloody thing on."

WEED KILLER

30th June 2018

. . . .

Anna is just coming out to the garden when I arrive this morning. She stops suddenly when she sees me. She looks concerned.

"Deary I'm deformed!"

"What do you mean?"

She takes my hand. "I've seen myself in the mirror, and this hip is lop-sided." She indicates her left hip.

Certainly Anna's spine has been curved for the past three or four years, but it seems that she has only just realised this.

"I think it's osteoporosis," I tell her, "I saw it mentioned in one of the letters from the hospital. "But your walking is much better than it was, now that you are not so sleepy. And I wouldn't really notice your hip because of your long skirts."

That isn't strictly true, but I have found that when Anna gets upset about what she can't remember, or what she looks like, I can cheer her up by emphasising the things that are positive.

Anna goes to the porch where my grandmother used to sit. I make some coffee and bring it out to her and show her the photos of my new planter box.

And then she wants to read the television guide (for some reason) so I take my coffee to the stone seat outside the front door. When they first bought the cottage Dave built the rockeries and seat from stone slabs that he found on building sites. Then he added a stone table with an uneven top. The overall effect is a hotch potch of different stones. Rather too much stone in my opinion. Usually we have to bring out cushions for the seat, but not today. It is so hot.

I hear Dave and tall son coming up the lane. They've been splitting logs down at the sheds. Dave is wearing his baggy white vest and working trousers. He looks tired. While he goes into the kitchen to make a mug of tea, tall son tells me that Dave is very worried about the oil tank. He just cannot understand why jobs have to be signed off.

"Next door 'ad a new tank and the farmers fitted it alright," he complains.

Tall son once again explains that the central heating engineers cannot sign off the heating until the oil tank has been replaced and a new one connected. If they cannot sign off the heating job they won't get funding from the charities.

"I reckon it's the EU doin' this," says Dave.

Tall son is endlessly patient. Dave has gone to fill the watering can and throw some corn to Robbie and the blackbirds who are hopping about on the bank.

"His brother's got a nest over the neighbours," Dave tells us.

I explain to tall son that Dave is talking about robins.

"They're fightin' all the time, Robbie and his brother," Dave says.

"That tree will probably have to come down," says tall son quietly, "the new tank will be bigger."

Oh dear. The tree with the bird feeders. The tree where all the robins and blackbirds and woodpeckers and rooks gather. The tree that shelters Mr Pheasant and all the Mrs Pheasants when it rains. The tree that has been growing on the bank all these years.

"Don't tell Dave until we know for sure," I warn him.

"Some of the branches are dead anyway," he says.

Anna is still reading the television guide. Tall son is washing his car on the driveway. Dave appears in the porch with a bottle of weedkiller and starts filling his pressure sprayer from the outside tap. I am enjoying my cup of coffee on the stone seat.

Dave is limping towards us with the pressure sprayer, stopping to spray tiny weeds pushing their way between the paving stones. Surely he is not going to spray the stone seat?

Surely not!

Good grief he is!

I stand up. Just in time. I dash into the kitchen with my hand over my mouth and nose.

Anna sits happily in the porch, oblivious.

I google the brand of weedkiller to see how dangerous it is. (The packet is sitting on the log store).

'SIGNIFICANTLY TOXIC TO HUMANS…'

"Anna, do you want to come in for another cup of coffee while Dave sprays the weeds?" I ask her, "there's some chocolate cake here."

Anna shuffles into the kitchen at the mention of chocolate cake. I shut the front door. And the dining room window. Dave sprays the stone seat and the patio, whilst on the bank Robbie and the sparrows pick at the corn that Dave has thrown them.

Tall son has finished cleaning his new car.

"I'll be over in the morning when the central heating guys arrive," he tells Anna and Dave.

"I hope they'll know what they're doin'", Dave says grumpily.

"It'll be fine," says tall son, heading for the door.

"I just hope Dave doesn't try to tell the central heating people what to do," I say, as we drive up the lane. "Dave doesn't trust anyone younger than himself to do any job."

"Mmmmmmmm," says tall son, looking at his mobile. He isn't really listening. "Don't worry, I'll be there to keep an eye on things."

The village rooks are gathering on the overhead power lines opposite the recreation ground. They shuffle and flap their wings, trying to get the best position.

This week is not going to be easy. Why would I think it would be? This week could be very difficult indeed.

HEATING WEEK

2nd July 2018

My mobile rings as soon as I reach the office. It's the central heating company.

"Your stepfather is refusing to accept the new combi boiler."

Oh no.

I call tall son, who is on his way to the cottage.

"I'll call you back as soon as I can," he tells me.

I try to focus on my job, but it is difficult.

An hour later I get a text from tall son.

'All sorted. Lots of drama but I've told them to ignore everything Dave says.'

Oh ok.

Fortunately Dave has respect for tall son and eldest grandson who are practical people. Perhaps things will be alright now.

But tall son comes home in the evening looking exhausted.

"Dave just keeps telling them how to do their job. And he argues about everything. He thinks they're all apprentices!"

Poor central heating engineers.

At the end of Day Two tall son looks just as tired.

"I don't think they've ever seen anything like the cottage," he tells me.

"What do you mean?"

"Well the state of the walls where they're trying to fit the radiators. The state of the wiring. They've had to re-wire Dave's bedroom. And as for the Aga installation!"

"What about it?"

"Dave's been telling them he's been maintaining it all these years... they really don't want to know this."

"Oh I see... because he should have had proper servicing?"

But tall son has fallen onto the sofa and closed his eyes.

Day Three is the hottest day so far. Tall son tells me that the apprentice engineer has got sunburnt working on the boiler. The poor young man is also being bothered by Anna who is fascinated by his tattooed arm. Apparently Anna also asks him to walk her around the garden, and brings him small squares of cake as a reward.

"But I've told them not to eat anything Anna brings them."

Quite difficult then!

Day Four sees the arrival of the groundworker to give a quote. He will be preparing the ground for the new oil tank. This involves digging out the bank and then laying a concrete base for the tank to sit on. Tall son and I are not looking forward to this, because this is the type of work Dave used to do before he retired.

So if he thinks he knows best how to fit central heating, heaven help the poor groundworker.

In the evening tall son reports that Dave thinks he should be the one doing the groundwork. He intends to drive a small digger across the field to start the job. At eighty-seven years old I do not think this is a good idea. Perhaps the best idea is to tell him that the charity expects the work to be done by an approved contractor?

Day Five and Dave is distressed by the mess and rubble. He complains that the house is full of dust. Tall son texts that Dave has taken a giant sandwich and some avocado to the bottom of the garden to get away from it all.

'I've never seen him eat avocado?' I text back.

Apparently Shropshire brother brought the avocado for Anna, but Dave has forgotten this.

The central heating engineers have got as far as they can. Now we must wait for the groundwork to be completed and the new oil tank to go in.

Tomorrow I'll go to the cottage to vacuum the carpets and sweep the floors.

"I don't think the heating engineers have ever had a job like this one," says tall son, 'it's certainly one they'll remember."

We are having supper in town, and it is so hot that we are outside at a pavement table. Tall son looks very tired indeed.

"It's having to stop Dave pestering them so they can get on with their work. And Anna wandering around with cake and cheese straws. And rubble and dust everywhere. And the hot weather. And they haven't got any hot water until the tank's connected."

"So they can only wash in cold water for now?"

"Well they didn't seem particularly worried."

"Never mind," I say in a motherly fashion. "It's a week until the groundwork starts, so you can relax for a bit."

We walk back through the town. Everywhere people out enjoying the warm evening.

There's a message on my answerphone when we reach home.

"Bloody water pressure's blown the bloody taps off. I can't sleep with all the taps dripping!"

Oh heck.

"I'll have to fit new taps," says tall son miserably.

Half an hour later he looks more cheerful.

"I think this might be an opportunity to fit a shower in their bathroom..."

A shower indeed!

I wonder what Anna and Dave will make of that.

THE FETE

7th July 2018

. . . .

Saturday morning promises another hot day. As we drive towards the cottage tall son notices a banner for the village fete.

"Anna might like that," he says.

Anna always took us to the fete. Tall son and his sister would search the stalls for bargains, and Anna, in a long summer skirt, sunglasses and colourful headscarf, would buy tea and cakes and exchange greetings with other villagers. Dave was always at the boatyard on fete day.

The cottage has had a difficult week. I start by vacuuming upstairs, then sweeping the dining room and kitchen floors. Dave wants to show me how to use the vacuum cleaner, which is faintly irritating. Why is there so much dust around the front door? Then I hear Dave telling tall son how the leaf blower has been so useful in removing the dust from the rugs and mats.

The leaf blower? Indoors? No wonder there's a strong smell of petrol.

Tall son looks puzzled. He tells me later that Dave says he uses it to blow down the cobwebs in the cottage. And dry his car after washing it.

183

The cottage looks faintly surprised at the changes that have been made. New taps and a shower head in the bathroom, copper pipes and brand new radiators, strange bare patches on the bedroom walls.

"The plaster's come off... must be wattle and daub underneath," says tall son

As we leave the cottage to walk up to the recreation ground, tall son and Anna are talking about the rings on her left hand.

"My four husbands," she tells him.

"Who was the fourth one then?" says tall son.

"I can't remember his name, but I can see his face deary,"

"Well there was Cecil, and then John, and now Dave," I say, "when did you marry someone else?"

"Hmmmmmmm,"

Anna takes tall son's arm to steady herself.

"Well he was in the Army, I remember. Yes, I can see his face...

"It must have been a short marriage."

"Oh yes deary, they were in those days."

I make a mental note to ask Dave about this. Anna and tall son are talking to the ducks and chickens that live in the garden at the top of the lane, and admiring the carp pond in the garden opposite.

It's a slow walk to the recreation ground, and when we finally arrive the events in the show ring have finished.

"I need a cream tea," says tall son, "Come on Anna."

He steers her towards the tea tent. Anna stops every so often to catch her breath and smile at the children running around excitedly. Her attention is caught by a baby just learning to crawl on wobbly arms and legs. His parents have put him down on the dry grass and every so often he lies down and rests. Various people greet Anna.

I am not sure if she knows who they are but she smiles graciously and asks after their families.

And then an older woman walks towards us. She has curly white hair, and an orange dress and bright earrings. She hugs Anna and talks quietly to her, and Anna cries a little.

"Ted's wife," says Anna, wiping her eyes, when the woman has gone.

We sit for a moment and listen to the country music in the next tent. Played rather too loudly.

Anna has eaten her chocolate cake and drunk her tea, and is ready to walk home. We look at the stalls as we pass. Gift cards, second hand books and toys, home-made bead jewellery.

"A bit sedate," says tall son, "where's the plate-smashing? You'd enjoy that Anna wouldn't you?"

Anna loves being teased. Especially by the men of the family.

Back at the cottage Dave is reading a war book that I found in the telephone box library the previous week. We admire the red and pink hollyhocks on the bank outside the sitting room window.

"Good year for 'em" says Dave, "and for the roses."

"I've got some catalogues for you deary," says Anna touching my arm.

"Oh don't forget you've bought me a birthday present," I say, "do you remember you ordered that skirt. It must have arrived by now."

Anna looks at me blankly.

"Skirt?"

"You probably put it upstairs," I say.

"Not that bloody skirt you were wearin' yesterday?" says Dave, putting down his book.

"That was a strange skirt," says tall son.

"Why strange?" I ask them.

"Had a bloody slit all the way up the side," says Dave interrupting, "good job she had a thing on, or them builders wouldn't know where to look,"

"Petticoat?" I say helpfully.

Anna and I go upstairs and look through her wardrobe. The skirt is on a hanger with all the other skirts. And yes, it looks like the skirt that we ordered for my birthday (in six months time). But the catalogue didn't mention the side split. I don't think I would have wanted a skirt like that.

"Funny that your skirt hasn't come yet," says Anna, sitting down on the bed.

Yes, funny.

I tell her that I will contact the catalogue company and ask what has happened to the order. But I think in reality there is nothing I can do. I won't mention it again, and Anna will forget about it by tomorrow. Perhaps Dave can smuggle it out of her wardrobe and take it to a charity shop.

Downstairs the men are discussing the groundworks, due to start the following Saturday.

"I don't like that tank outside the window," says Anna as she negotiates the stairs.

"It's just a holding tank for your oil. It will go when the new tank is in place," I tell her.

"Oh no I don't think so deary."

One thing I have noticed since Anna recovered her mobility and became more alert, is that she has become more argumentative. Although we've told her several times that the holding tank is temporary, she forgets this, and seems quite cross when I remind her. She also nags Dave endlessly to paint the banisters, and to paint the outside front wall of the cottage. In this heatwave I doubt Dave is going to take on jobs like that however.

"And I'm not 'avin that tree coming down," says Dave, yet again, "so if them groundwork blokes think that, they can think again! I've got nowhere else to put my bird feeders and fat balls."

Tall son looks exasperated. It's too hot for arguments. Dave is adamant. Dave is always right.

And, after all, he knows that Robbie and Bobby and all the other birds would agree with him.

GROUND WORKS

13th July 2018

Tall son has escaped to London for a few days, leaving me to sort out any problems at the cottage for the start of the ground works. I am not looking forward to this. It seems to be even hotter and dustier today, and the grass verges are turning a pale brown.

I leave my car by the telephone box library and the hedges threaded with bindweed, and walk down the lane to the cottage. I'm always more alert at the house with the carp pond, subconsciously remembering the two alsatians who snarled and barked at me as I walked back from the bus stop after school. But they have long gone. And their owners too. I walk past the row of cottages where Shropshire brother's girlfriend lived. Their front gardens full of roses and honeysuckle. Past the strange modern house that many in the village objected to, with its huge windows and boxy shape.

And up the lane comes a man steering a small dumper truck, and he turns into Dave's carport. As I draw nearer I hear loud voices and laughter, and the sound of spades hitting stones.

Dave and the two groundworkers. The man with the dumper truck is small and slight. He is digging at the bank and pulling away the old concrete bunker that has been there for years.

Every so often he hands the spade to his companion; a tall well-built man with a faded woolly hat on his head. A woolly hat in the heat.

The tall man and Dave are chatting like old friends. Dave introduces me. This is his sister's husband's cousin's son, he says. Or something like that. The tall man smiles.

They are talking about things they have dug up over the years.

"Found an inkwell today," says the tall relative.

"Here in the bank?" I ask.

"Yep," says Dave.

"Dug up plenty of stuff on jobs," says Dave's relative.

"What sort of things?" I ask.

Bottles with stoppers.

"Filled 'em upside down they did," says the smaller man, handing the spade to his companion.

"Marble in the neck," adds Dave.

"Oh and shells of course," says the relative.

"Yeah, plenty of them," says Dave.

Shells. How nice.

"Near the coast?" I wonder.

"Nah, live shells," says the smaller man.

Military shells?! Crikey!

"Did you have to get the Army out? Or the police?" I ask them.

"Nah, defused 'em ourselves," says Dave, "easy if you know what yer doin."

Really?

The three then share a story about ground workers finding a shell in the garden of a house owned by an elderly woman. They took it into her shed to defuse it. Wondering where they'd gone, the elderly woman came down the garden and saw them through the shed window. She banged hard on the window with her cane, and laughed uproariously as they fled in panic from the shed.

I leave the three men chuckling to themselves over this old story, and go to find Anna in the cottage. The talk of digging up objects has reminded me of the Roman coin that John showed me when I was a child. One of the digger drivers at work had found it. I thought it was wonderful that something so old could have remained hidden under the earth for so long.

But if the Roman coin was exciting, what about the meteorite that Dave dug up years ago. Was it an actual meteorite? I remember its beautiful sparkly surface, and I liked to imagine that it really had come from outer space.

"Cup of tea deary?" says Anna when she sees me.

We sit in the dining room and drink our tea. It seems strange that the Aga is cold. Mini oven is back in the dining room, looking pleased with itself.

"Dave does keep burning his supper though," says Anna.

"I guess he's getting used to electric cooking being so much quicker," I say.

"We'll be glad when the Aga's going again though deary."

"But it must be better in this hot weather to have the Aga off?"

"Well deary, we need it to dry our washing as well."

Oh yes, I had forgotten that Anna doesn't like washing on the washing line. She doesn't like the neighbours seeing it.

Dave comes stomping into the dining room, looking for a cup of tea.

"They've finished now. Gone home. Bloody good chaps. Done a bloody good job."

Hurray! Something has gone well. Dave seems happy.

"Bloody hot out there though. Diggin' in that weather is hard work," he says, "an we've got no bloody hot water still. Havin' to boil up kettles all the time to wash with."

"What about wet wipes?" I suggest, "you could get a big box when you next go shopping."

To my surprise Dave and Anna seem happy with this idea. Dave reckons the local supermarket will have them.

Later in the afternoon I leave the cottage to head home, having established with Dave that the ground workers will be back on Monday to lay the concrete base. I can see an end in sight, and that's good news. Dave is already settled in his armchair in the sitting room with his wartime novel. Sydney brother and tall son always say that everything stops at the cottage at three-thirty in the afternoon, and that's the time they always plan to leave.

My car is uncomfortably hot. The steering wheel almost burns my hands. A rustle in the undergrowth near the telephone box library.

Hunting cat.

She sits quietly, almost placidly on the dry grass under the shade of the bushes. For a moment I wonder if it is really her.

I am so used to seeing her in hunting mode, crouched, tail twitching, back legs ready to pounce.

But it is her. It is too hot to hunt. Too hot to run. Too hot to dig. All over the village, people sit and read in the shade. Or doze in their deckchairs. Or stay indoors. Wondering at the heatwave. How long will it go on? When will it rain? The lawns are so dry. The pots have to be watered all the time. The roads are melting.

Only Anna seems oblivious to the weather. Happy in her polo necks and long skirts. Drinking tea to keep herself warm. And looking forward to the return of the Aga.

FRUSTRATION

18th July 2018

My mobile rings at work. My colleagues look at me expectantly. They know that today, being Wednesday, the ground works are to be completed. It's Dave. I can tell from his tone of voice that something is not right.

"They can't get the bloody truck in. Those builders down the pub have taken all the spaces. Can't get the truck in so they've gone 'ome."

Oh no.

"Yep the ready-mix lorry had nowhere to go. 'Ad to go 'ome."

"So they were going to park at the old pub and bring the cement up the lane were they?" I say, trying to grasp what's going on.

"Yep, but they've gone 'ome now."

"Surely one of the builders would have moved their van for you? It's public land isn't it?"

Dave is so cross that he can't take in what I'm saying. He just talks over the top of me.

"Are they coming back tomorrow?" I manage to ask.

"Yep an' I'm goin' to be down that pub at the crack of dawn, an' I'm goin' to make sure our lorry can get in there."

Right ok.

So things aren't going well. My work colleagues sympathise. They know I am very keen to get this work finished. I ring Dave the next day. It's lunchtime, and I'm wondering if they've gone out because he takes a long time to answer. When he does, he has to adjust his hearing aids. This takes a few minutes while he grumbles and mutters to himself. Finally he can hear me.

"Yep got a space today. Slab's laid. Very nice. Bloody good job."

Good news.

So what's next?

Now the oil tank can be delivered. I text Cherry at the charity to let her know. The message comes back that the tank will be delivered Tuesday morning. I will wait until Tuesday lunchtime before contacting the heating engineers. Just in case. But a call comes from Dave at eleven-thirty on Tuesday morning. Very cheerful. Very pleased. The tank is in place. Now let's turn on the oil supply. Let's get the Aga running again.

"Hold on Dave," I say, "I'll call the engineers and see when they can come out."

Half an hour later I am messaging tall son. 'Please call Dave and let him know the engineers can't come out for at least another week. Pressure of work. I really can't bear to tell him myself!'

Silence.

By six o'clock in the evening I have to know what's happening. I call Dave. Tall son has already told him. He is not happy.

"A week! No hot water! Another week! Anyone can connect it up!"

Well. Not really anyone.

"Don't you worry," says Dave, with menace in his voice, "I'll get that Aga goin' again. I'm not waitin' another week."

"But you've got mini oven to cook on," I protest, "and I thought you were buying some boxes of wet wipes for washing with."

"Wet wipes!" explodes Dave, "and that oven burns everything,"

"Only because you're not used to an oven cooking so quickly," I say.

Time to end the call. Dave is going to do what Dave is going to do.

"Don't worry," says tall son, "he can't do much harm."

The evening is oppressively warm. I sit outside in my courtyard garden. Doing nothing. Just watching the evening approaching. Watching the bees hovering on the verbena. Watching the blackbird on my neighbour's fence. The sun's rays sliding off the garden wall.

And above my head the elusive swifts. Screaming and diving, twisting and turning in the heat.

High above the houses.

IVY

28th July 2018

. . . .

I've decided I need a variegated ivy in my new garden. Just a small plant to trail from the top of the wall. The specialist nursery near the cottage is the ideal place to visit today.

Dave is in France. He and Gordon took the car ferry early this morning. This is an annual wine and cheese expedition with a hearty lunch at midday. When I arrive at the cottage Anna is looking bright and cheerful.

"I'd like to go out for some lunch deary..."

As it's only nine-thirty I suggest coffee and then I will make some flapjack. The Aga is still out. When I rang Dave to make arrangements for today he told me that the oil tank fitter had advised him to wait for the central heating engineers. Anna misses the Aga.

"I can't use this electric oven," she complains, "and Dave burns everything."

"He's just not used to it," I tell her.

The new oil tank stands proudly on its cement base on the bank. Dave's tree stands beside it, although most of the branches look as if they are dying.

"Can't we cover up the tank thing deary?" Anna wants to know.

Hmmmmm.

"We could look at a bamboo screen maybe," I tell her, "after lunch."

We walk around the garden admiring the hollyhocks and pansies. It is another hot and still day. Then a faint smell of burning drifts from the front door.

Not the flapjacks!

Yes. Mini oven has burnt the flapjacks. Fortunately still edible, but burnt nonetheless.

"I did tell you deary."

The lunch menu at the garden centre cafe is on a blackboard on the wall. Anna finds this difficult to navigate so I read out some of the options.

"I'll have baked beans on toast I think..."

I didn't mention baked beans.

"What about mushrooms on toast?" I suggest.

"Oh yes that would be nice."

Anna smiles at a family with very young children at the table next to us. I order the lunch, and two flat whites of course. Anna insists on paying. While we eat we talk about the family and I have to remind her where everyone is. Quite by chance both tall son and medical daughter are moving house the following weekend. Eldest grandson and middle grandson have joined Sydney brother for a holiday in Indonesia. Shropshire brother is holidaying in Majorca. Youngest grandson is sending pictures of forest fires in Canada.

Anna listens carefully although I know that in an hour or so she will have forgotten where everyone is again. Even Dave.

"Is he at the boat deary?"

Then her smile fades. "I want to tell you something."

"Go on,"

"The other day... when I was at the top of the stairs... I nearly...I nearly fell backwards."

She stops and looks at her coffee sadly.

"You lost your grip on the handrails?"

"Something like that deary,"

Anna is never precise about events. She was never precise. She was always vague. No fuss.

So I must be careful what I say.

"Were you going up to the bathroom. Was Dave out somewhere?"

"Yes... yes the bathroom. He must have been out shopping."

We sit quietly for a while. A cheerful woman clears our lunch plates and cutlery. The family with the young children say goodbye to us.

"We could clear the long cupboard of coats and maybe put a downstairs loo in there?" I say tentatively.

Anna doesn't say anything.

"I could help you clear out the cupboard. I know there's a lot of coats in there."

"We've nowhere else to put them," says Anna.

"Maybe they could go upstairs in your wardrobes?" I say.

Anna and Dave have three wardrobes between them. There must be some space somewhere.

Anna takes my arm and we walk around the nursery. We look at a variety of wooden garden screens and I take photos to show Dave. I find a variegated ivy. The day is too hot to be out for long.

Back at the cottage we drink tea and Anna fetches the calendar. The week-to-a-page calendar. The calendar that was supposed to be much easier to her to use than a month-to-a-page.

"Excuse me, what day is it deary," says Anna turning the pages.

I tell her it is Saturday. I am looking at all the coats in the long cupboard. And the boxes of tea bags. And shoes. And parts of vacuum cleaners. And carrier bags. And pegs.

While Anna is engrossed in the calendar I go upstairs and take a quick look in Dave's wardrobe. Three shirts and several pairs of trousers. That's about it. There's plenty of room for some of the long cupboard coats.

"Ah there you are," says Anna as I return to the dining room. "What day is it deary?"

I find a scrap of paper and pencil and write down the day and date for her. I drink my tea and look out at the hollyhocks on the bank, tall and proud in the hot sun. A luscious pink.

"That's Dave back," says Anna looking up from her calendar to the window that looks out onto the lane. Her hearing is very good.

"I'll just give them a hand," I tell her.

As I walk down the lane towards the sheds I can hear the sound of Gordon and Dave unloading their shopping.

There will be plenty of olive oil. Plenty of French cheese. And plenty of red wine.

Anna will be very pleased.

SHOWERS

4th August 2018

. . . .

When I arrive today Dave hands me bottles of olive oil and red wine from his French trip. Anna has already poured herself a glass from the wine box in the kitchen. Although it is overcast and windy today the dining room is very warm. Because the Aga is running. It takes a long time to boil the kettle, but Anna and Dave are delighted nonetheless.

"Much better now," says Dave looking fondly at the Aga.

"And I've been havin' showers. Very nice. Very hot. Got to get 'er showered soon, haven't we rat."

Anna looks bored, "Yes dear."

When I speak to tall son later that evening he tells me that Dave found the shower rather confusing at first.

"He didn't understand about the mixer tap," he tells me.

"How do you mean?"

"He told me that he ran the shower but had to keep stepping out of it because it got too hot. So I told him to run the cold tap, but he said he didn't want cold showers. Then I realised he didn't understand how to use the mixer tap."

Crikey.

However, things are back to normal in the cottage. There are radiators in every room. If Dave uses the central heating in the winter the dining room will be warm enough to sit in during the day, and the bedrooms upstairs will be cosy and less damp. I take a photograph of Anna and Dave outside, by their new boiler, to send to Cherry and Robert at the charities. Dave has a huge smile. Anna has an amused smile.

It's time for Dave to head to the boatyard. He has a final look round the garden for Robbie, who hasn't been seen for two days.

"That wind's getting up," says Anna peering out of the window. I have to agree with her. The trees on the bank are being blown about. Will there be rain today? Anna hopes so. The lawn is dry and yellow and littered with leaves and small branches from the tulip tree. I realise, that with very little to do during the day, Anna notices every variation in the weather.

During the week, when I was looking for an envelope in my desk I came across my diary. 1969 to 1973. Anna had been gone for about four years. We spent our school holidays with the great-uncle and aunt who had lived in Egypt. In 1969 my writing is very child-like. Rounded upright letters. I write about the weather almost every day. A hard frost. A bit warmer. Wet day. Cold dry day. Mild frosty day. Stopped raining. Perhaps there just wasn't very much to write about? Perhaps there was too much to write about. Either way I mention the weather in every diary entry. Just as Anna and Dave discuss the weather every day. Now that they are old. And there is so much time to fill.

I drive Anna to the garden centre for lunch; as we did last weekend. Today Anna has a tuna panini. She doesn't seem familiar with the idea of a panini, but enjoys it all the same. There is just the faintest of showers outside, not enough to make a difference.

We talk about family and friends as usual and Anna's sadness about not being allowed to drive any more.

To take her mind off this I lead her around the nursery, admiring the colours and shapes of the plants, stopping to read their Latin names. Sometimes we spot a lovely flower and try to guess what it is before we look at the label.

Back at the cottage the sky is darkening. The latch on the bathroom door is rattling in the wind from the open window. Anna is nervous.

"There's someone upstairs deary!"

I tell her it is just the stormy weather, but she is not convinced. I have to go upstairs and call down to assure her that everything is alright.

But now she is worried that the neighbour's tree might fall on the cottage. I tell her that if it did fall, it would hit Dave's carport, rather than the cottage.

And now she is worried about the tulip tree. Supposing it fell. It is a huge tree. It would flatten the cottage. I tell her it is a young tree, and Devon brother says it is very unlikely to fall.

Fortunately at that moment Dave comes through the front door. Anna is immediately calmer.

And the telephone rings. Devon brother must have known I was talking about him. He is making bookcases in the big barn.

Dave shouts at him down the phone. I catch chunks of conversation.

"Bloody great fire. Lightening started it off. Gorse and bracken fired it up. Bloody great dark clouds and no rain."

I think they are talking about the wildfires on Saddleworth Moor.

Dave passes me the phone. Devon brother has been filming in London.

The temperature was thirty five degrees and they were all in medieval costume. Some of the cast were overcome with heat, especially if they were in full armour.

Poor Anna. In the past she would have been so interested to hear about these things. We can take a short walk, or go out to lunch, or talk about the war and her childhood. But nothing outside of her immediate experience, nothing in the news, nothing beyond the boundaries of the village makes much sense any more.

Dave has headed off to the garden with his mug of tea, inspecting the pansies and begonias and grumbling that he will have to get out the watering can. Anna is dozing on the sofa. Upstairs the latch on the bathroom door continues its rattle in the wind.

We are waiting for rain.

LAVENDER

11th August 2018

. . . .

Shropshire brother calls me on my mobile. He is visiting the cottage and taking Anna and Dave out for coffee. Do I want to join them? There's a cafe out in the countryside which sells lavender plants. We decide to meet there.

It's sunny, but not as hot as it has been. I get to the cafe before them, which is not really a surprise as Shropshire brother is always running late. It gives me time to wander around and admire the cafe gardens. I talk to one of the gardeners about the lavender season. It really finishes in early August he tells me. The lavender fields beyond the cafe are slowly losing their colour. But in the gardens the different shades of mauve are still vibrant.

I order a coffee and find two tables close together under a gazebo. Anna loved to sit in the sun when she was young, but since middle age she has avoided it. So we always head to a table in the shade. Shropshire brother appears from the cafe and behind him I see tall son with Anna holding on to his arm. Dave is in the distance looking at the pots of lavender and roses.

"I've ordered some coffee and cake," says Shropshire brother, pulling the tables closer together.

"He had a winner at Goodwood," says tall son, helping Anna into one of the garden chairs.

205

"A big win?" I ask.

Shropshire brother smiles but doesn't answer, "I'm whacked. Been working flat out. Got to go to a party tonight as well."

I greet Anna and Dave. Anna looks lovely in a long floaty skirt, cream shirt and matching earrings. Dave always looks slightly confused on these occasions. I suspect his lack of hearing is to blame.

"All them cyclists all over the lanes," he says loudly. Very loudly.

"We 'ad trouble just gettin' past 'em!"

The couple at the next table have heard him.

"Dave!" I scold him, "not so loud. Most people have probably cycled here today."

Dave snorts with displeasure.

Then he starts a conversation with the people next to him about the problems of cyclists. Fortunately they share his opinion.

Dave looks pleased when the coffee arrives. With three enormous helpings of chocolate brownie, decorated with a sprinkling of icing sugar and sprigs of lavender. He helps himself to one of the plates of brownie; gives another to Anna, and pushes the third towards us.

"Looks good," he says happily.

Tall son (who loves chocolate brownie) looks slightly startled. Shropshire brother looks surprised.

We talk about horse racing, tall son's new job, the extraordinary weather. I share the third piece of brownie with Shropshire brother and tall son. It is delicious. Light but gooey. Very chocolatey. We are all secretly watching Anna.

Finally she puts down her fork and daintily wipes her mouth with her napkin.

"Very nice cake deary."

She has eaten the whole piece. Now she and Dave are admiring the roses trailing over the gate behind us.

"I thought she'd just have a tiny piece of cake!" whispers Shropshire brother.

"I think we're all surprised," I whisper back.

I drive tall son back to the cottage so that we can stop on the way at the vintage furniture shop in the local town. Tall son has nothing but a mattress to sleep on in his new flat.

At the cottage we discover that Shropshire brother has headed home.

"He said goodbye deary," says Anna.

Dave is down at the sheds thinking about the wood he will need for replacing the fence behind the new oil tank.

"He's worried the cows will push the tank over," Anna tells me when I ask.

"I'm going to get a drill and finish off the shower fitting," says tall son.

Anna has wandered into the kitchen.

"Would you two like some cake?" she calls.

Cake?

"It's chocolate cake. Dave made it yesterday," she adds.

"Um no thanks, I'm going to make some lunch," I tell her.

I'm looking for some pittas and hummus that I've packed in a cold bag.

Anna reappears from the kitchen, walking very slowly and carrying a plate of chocolate cake. She sits in the armchair by the Aga and cuts the cake into small squares.

Tall son returns from the sheds.

"Extraordinary," he says when he sees Anna.

"What deary?" says Anna.

"Uh, extraordinary weather," says tall son, on his way upstairs.

With the shower fitting completed we sit down for warm pitta breads with hummus and tomatoes.

"Would you like some cake deary?" says Anna as Dave puts his head through the dining room window.

More cake?

"Reckon I need to get that leaf blower out again. Bloody leaves everywhere on my lawn."

He stops when he sees Anna. "Is that my chocolate cake?"

"Yes, do you want a piece?"

"Cut me a bit then. I'll 'ave it in a minute. Just measuring up for that fence."

"Would you like some pittas and hummus Dave?" I ask him, "I can heat up some more."

He thinks for a minute. "Nah, I dunno. I've just got no appetite today. I just get days like that." He wanders off to look at pieces of wood.

Tall son looks at me. I look at tall son. We look at Anna eating chocolate cake. The look on tall son's face says that sometimes elderly people are very puzzling.

"I think I'll take Anna and Dave to see my new flat this evening," he says, "and we can have a pub supper afterwards."

That's ambitious. But possible. Unfortunately Anna and Dave don't particularly like the nearby city. It's where Dave's first wife, Fay lives with her much younger husband. But tall son doesn't know anything about this. Or the betrayal in the dairy. All those years ago.

I think I had better join them on this trip.

THE CITY

18th August 2018

. . . .

Supper in the city went well. Anna and Dave admired tall son's new rented apartment, although Dave looked ill-at-ease in the modern surroundings.

"Wouldn't want to be without a fireplace," he told us.

Tall son patiently explained that modern buildings are usually well insulated, so a fireplace isn't always necessary.

"It's something to sit round though," argued Dave.

"And it's not as good as your city," he had told me, as we walked back from supper at the local pub.

I personally prefer tall son's city to mine, but I think Dave's opinion is probably swayed by the memory of Fay.

Anna, on the other hand, looked quite at home. She was brought up in cities, and I think would happily live in one now. Although these days, when she talks about Birmingham, there is often fear in her voice.

"We were so scared... in the war I mean... all the bombing. We didn't know if we would wake up in the morning."

When I discovered my teenage diary recently, I also discovered the transcription of a conversation I had had with her. The date was 1988.

I can't remember why I recorded it. Anna is talking about being in Birmingham during the war. She says,

"I don't remember that it was anything really terrible. It was all rather fun - I suppose it would be when you're only seven. I can't really remember any of the nasty things that must have gone on. I remember going down into the shelter which was the cellars under our house. There were beds in there. We used to go down there when the sirens started and it was great fun - well, especially at first. Our neighbour on one side had a son called Norman who was about nine years old, and I adored Norman!

My father was a member of the ARP - I don't quite remember what that stands for now. He worked in a central office in Birmingham - he mapped the progress of the bombs as they dropped. There was an enormous map on the wall, and the calls would come through that a bomb had dropped, and he'd stick a little flag on the map. And I know this particular night there was no room left on the map. Birmingham was so badly bombed that the flags were packed solid on it. And the call came through about another bomb, and my father said, 'My God, that's my house!' and a chap said, 'well you'll know where to stick that one won't you.' And I often think now that my father had to stay there all night having no idea whether we'd been killed, whether the bomb was on the house, or where it was."

Thirty years ago Anna told me how exciting it was that the Army had arrived at the house the next morning to defuse the bomb, which had made a huge crater in the garden, but had not detonated.

Today she tells me how terrifying it was to see their garden destroyed - just a gaping hole.

Perhaps when Anna was younger she played down the fear that she had felt, in case she frightened us. Or perhaps that was just part of her character; the rather vague and elusive person.

Perhaps now, being more frail and confused about life in general, the old memories of the war have become more frightening. More real. And yet, many years ago I remember her hiding in the long cupboard in thunderstorms, and when the Red Arrows once flew over the cottage.

"Hiding from the bombers," she told us. As children, we weren't scared. We loved to watch the storm. And to count the seconds between the lightening and the thunder.

I also find in the transcript an incident that would certainly have been very frightening for a child.

"We were told that if we were out of the house at any time when the siren started, we should knock on anybody's front door and ask them to take us in. People had been told to give shelter in an air raid. And I often think now that you certainly wouldn't tell a child to knock on anyone's front door, but in those days of course it was very different. And we were on our way to school one day and the siren started, so my sister and I ran towards some shops, and only one was open. It was a hardware shop. We ran into the shop and there was a man in there, obviously the owner, and we said, can we stay until the raid is over, and he said certainly not, and pushed us out. So we had to go on walking with the raid blazing all around us and I don't know why we didn't try anybody else. I think we were too frightened.

When we told my father he was furious, and he immediately went to see this man. Later I heard him saying to my mother, 'well they couldn't have tried anybody worse because he was suffering from shell-shock from the last war'.

I didn't know what shell-shock was. I just knew it was something horrible. Fortunately we were never caught out in a raid again. But it's one of those things you remember. I remember the fear at being turned out into the raid, you know, thinking that we were going to be killed."

I once asked her why she and her sister had not been evacuated. She told me that at the time of the 'phoney war' her mother had taken Anna and Simone to the Scottish Highlands, leaving her husband to look after the house in Birmingham. They had stayed there for six months, only returning when the fear of invasion had receded. Anna told me that the separation had been so difficult that her parents had decided that they would stay in the city, whatever happened.

So these stories, and others too, have been part of our growing up. Part of what made Anna the person that she is.

And Dave?

There is another transcript. A transcript about Dave's war in the countryside. A war without sirens or cellars, and few bombs.

A very different war.

WAR IN THE COUNTRYSIDE

25th August 2018

. . . .

There's been no sign of Robbie for several days now. Dave is convinced that hunting cat is to blame, but tall son counsels patience. Perhaps Robbie has finished bringing up the young robins and retreated to the woods for a bit of a rest.

"He'll be back when the weather gets cooler don't worry."

"Them bloomin' cats. I've seen 'em in the garden. I know what they're up to. Robbie's too friendly for 'is own good."

In the kitchen Anna is writing the address on a birthday card for her friend Sheila. The envelope looks odd. I sneak a look when she goes to make a cup of coffee. It's covered with five pence stamps. At least ten of them.

"Anna do you need some more stamps for Sheila's card?" I ask.

"No deary, there's plenty of stamps on there."

I think a first-class stamp is sixty-seven pence, so we are seventeen pence short.

"Um, you may need a few more..."

Tall son and Dave come in from the garden.

"What's up woman?" says Dave.

"Nothing deary, just sorting out stamps on a birthday card."

Dave picks up the envelope, "What's up with the stamps then? Plenty 'ere."

Tall son does a quick calculation. "Seventeen pence short I think. If you want first-class."

"What!" blasts Dave, "What's a bloody stamp cost then?"

I google it. "Sixty-seven first class,"

Anna and Dave look at me in surprise.

"It'll get there on that," says Dave, "don't worry about that." He puts the envelope on the mantelpiece above the Aga.

"I dunno what's going on," he says, pulling off his Australian boots with much tugging, "I remember when stamps was tuppence."

"When you were young," says tall son, looking impatient, "but people aren't sending so many letters now, so it's got more expensive."

"Why aren't people writin' letters then?"

Dave looks baffled, but really it's a rhetorical question.

The truth is that things have changed. As they always do.

I've been reading the transcription of my conversation with Dave from thirty years ago.

It is wartime in the countryside.

'We 'ad plenty of food I tell you. Ducks and chickens and all sorts. Rabbits all over the place. Salmon and trout out the river. My grandfather taught me all the gun lore when I was very young; he taught me all the safety; pretty strict on me you know.

But then I started to go out on my own, and you know, when yer hungry you shoot pretty straight, especially when you ain't got the money for cartridges.

We 'ad a kitchen range where we used to do the cooking; sort of old kitchen range with coal, and we used to 'ave our young chicks under there in a box to keep 'em warm. I used to 'ave to go down to market regular you see and get young chicks. We used to get about twenty for about three and sixpence. That was our next year's chicken. Every year we'd kill 'em off and sell 'em and make a few bob, and we used to 'ave chicken once a year. Christmas. Never 'ad chicken like you do now. Chicken was a luxury then. We used to let 'em go off in the fields gleaning. When we cut the corn the chickens used to go off in the fields all day. It was double summertime then. Used to be daylight until about eleven o'clock.

And we used to 'ave this cock bird; 'e was the worst one out. You let him out in the morning, you 'ad to run for it. He'd pick on yer back and peck you, and 'e used to come out and drop his wing, then he'd go round the pen attacking everything in sight. Some nights we couldn't get him in, and if you went down the toilet - toilet was the bottom of the garden in a tin shed; a bucket we used to have and Dad used to dig the hole every week and rotate the crops. You wouldn't believe it would you! Well this cockerel 'e used to wait for you in the morning and if he 'ad a mind of his own, he wouldn't go to bed some nights you see, so he'd stay in the cabbages the bugger would. The first one down the privy in the rush, that bird'd come out and peck the backs of yer legs. And I mean peck. You 'ad bruises all up yer legs. I've seen him many a time runnin' around dragging the broom behind him, and I've seen our mum hit the cock bird with, like a hockey stick and knock him up in the air, and he'd still come back at 'er again; 'e was a sod 'e was; we had to give him away in the end.'

I remember Dave's mum Gloria. She was a strong plain-talking woman even in her eighties. She had brought up five children in wartime, pushing a pram three or four miles to the nearest town for shopping. It would have been a hard war for her, even in the relative safety of the countryside.

I'm late getting back from work tonight. I've washed up the supper dishes and just settled on the sofa to watch the ten o'clock news. A text from Shropshire brother.

'Sitting in the dark on war memorial steps. The peace is soothing.'

I text back, 'Where? Why?'

'Anna's driving me mad with her endless questions. And what do I share with Dave's friend Gordon? Yes. I'm always wrong. And can you tell Anna it's a warm evening. Been offered a hot water bottle at least three times today.'

Poor chap. It's not easy being with the old people. And it's true, the weather has got slightly cooler at last.

Anna probably thinks it's the start of winter in the countryside.

LASAGNE

1st September 2018

. . . .

Bedlinen is a problem. Anna and Dave are happy with their duvet covers; red check brushed cotton for Dave, and grey and pink flowers for Anna. But the difficulty comes when they need washing. How do you remove a duvet cover when you are frail and old and your knees have stiffened; your eyes are not as good as they used to be; your arms just don't have the strength. How do you put on a clean duvet cover for that matter. Even stuffing a pillow into a pillowcase can be a problem.

So this is my job on a Saturday. Once washed I carry them down to the line under the tulip tree. If there's a breeze Anna will worry all day that the washing might be carried away to the neighbours' gardens. If there's a breeze Anna will worry that it might be a forerunner of rain. And there's always the worry that I might tire myself out hanging them on the line.

But the weather is quiet today. A pale sun. A light breeze. Still no sign of Robbie, but Dave has a new friend. A striking green parakeet with a long tail and red beak.

"Where has it come from Dave?"

He doesn't know. But Alan first spotted the bird at his cottage across the field and told Dave that there are many of them in the wild now.

Supposedly the original parakeets escaped from the film set of 'The African Queen' in the nineteen-fifties.

Dave's new bird makes himself or herself at home on the bank, feeding on the nuts and fat balls and scattered corn from the corn bin. Dave's regular birds take no notice. Mr Pheasant paces up and down in the field behind the bank waiting for his wives. The sparrows peck at the corn Dave has thrown them. The rooks squabble in the field and perch on the fence posts.

At four o'clock I fill the Aga with lasagne, sweet potato, parsnips and apple crumble for our supper. Tall son is joining us. Dave has a problem with the electrical socket behind the sofa. The table lamp won't work any more. Tall son and Dave go off to investigate. Anna wants to help with the supper, but her hands are just not strong enough to peel and chop the potatoes and parsnips. I find it difficult to let her do the washing up as she doesn't actually use water any more. Just a quick wipe over with a dishcloth that has seen better days. It is true to say that Anna never did bother much with housework. Neither did my grandmother. Anna would polish the copper and brass until it shone, and arrange flowers in vases around the house. Everything looked in order and there was no clutter. But behind every object the dust and dirt gathered.

One day Dave took up the hoovering. His mother was aghast. But it seemed a practical job that Dave enjoyed. And then Shropshire brother found Sharon to do the cleaning in the cottage once a week.

I ask Anna to lay the table and she potters about with cutlery and slightly grubby table mats. And an array of sauces for Dave. And the salt, and grey pepper that always sends Dave into a frenzy of sneezing.

The lasagne is not browning. Nor the parsnips. Nor the apple crumble.

"Dave can we turn up the Aga just a little?"

Dave stomps out to the dining room, muttering about young people and their lack of knowledge of Agas. How the Aga has never browned anything he has ever eaten. How you have to be patient with an Aga. Don't hurry it.

But it's nearly six o'clock! And Anna is peeling satsumas. She is hungry.

We wait another half an hour. I check again. No difference.

Tall son lifts mini oven out of the long cupboard and onto the round table. We transfer the dishes from the Aga. That's better. Now we can see the lasagne beginning to brown. Dave and tall son return to the misbehaving table lamp. I warn tall son to keep an eye on the supper and I go down the garden to the washing line. Faded peg bag in one hand; laundry bin in the other. Anna finds her stick from the box by the front door and wanders out to the garden to watch. Across the lane the neighbour's dog hears me and starts to bark. Several cyclists pass by at speed towards the main road through the village.

"I think it's ready!" shouts tall son from the front door.

The top of the lasagne is starting to burn. The parsnips are starting to curl up. The sweet potatoes look dry. Why does mini oven do this? As soon as our backs are turned.

Anna and Dave enjoy supper though. Tall son has seconds of lasagne even though the top is burnt and the sheets of lasagne are slightly undercooked, giving it a rubbery texture. The apple crumble is dry, but Anna has plenty of ice cream with it. Dave opts for clotted cream. And plenty of red wine.

I've barely finished my pudding when Dave hurries off to his armchair to watch the television. Anna slowly follows with her glass of wine. Can they catch the end of the Channel 4 news?

Tall son and I are left at the round table. Empty plates and bowls and glasses. We wash up and put everything away. Outside the darkness is beginning to fall. Anna is slowly drawing the curtains. Hovering by the front door. She wants to lock up and settle down on the sofa.

"I think it's better to do lunch for them these days," says tall son as we walk down to our cars. "It gets too late for them."

I agree with him. Shropshire brother has said much the same. I drive home through the darkening lanes, the empty lasagne dish and crumble dish rattling together in the boot. Just lunches now then. They get too tired for late suppers. They want to eat early and then relax. It's a different pace now. The evening is for television and dozing by the fire.

In the lane that runs into the next village the bats dart and loop around the oak trees, their high-pitched sounds beyond our hearing. Somewhere in the woods behind the lanes a hedgehog shuffles, owls hoot and deer lift their heads to listen.

The night is young.

LEGO

2nd September 2018

My grandmother's house was tiny. One bedroom really. She had a bed in the dining room, and often slept on that. The galley kitchen was rather an add-on, like the conservatory that led into the courtyard garden. If something was unusual, my grandmother loved it. So the courtyard was decorated with artistic pots and curious wall decorations which made me think of an art gallery. We loved visiting. She had an old suitcase full of Lego which we would tip onto the navy blue carpet in the dining room and sit for hours, while she and Anna talked about friends, books, music and art. And drank tea.

And that's how it was on the day that Anna put down her cup and saucer, and said that she wanted to tell us something. I did listen, but I didn't want to stop looking for some Lego roof tiles for my Lego house. It was actually my grandmother who broke the news.

"You are going to have a little brother or sister," she said smiling.

My brothers looked puzzled. I was shocked. I knew Anna and John were divorced. And Anna lived with Dave. But didn't you have to be married to have babies? Had she married Dave and not told us?

"The baby will be born in the summer," said Anna, although no-one had asked the question.

So she wasn't coming back to John. To our house. Why would she want more children? Why didn't she just look after us?

I didn't ask any of these questions. I discovered the Lego pieces I was looking for, and then my grandmother found us some lemon bonbons.

Some years later my grandmother talked to me about Sigmund Freud. She was very interested in his theories, but seemed to believe that what happens to us early in our lives is forgotten. Completely forgotten. As if it had never happened.

Anna and my grandmother were extraordinarily close. They never lived more than a few miles apart. I cannot imagine that my grandmother ever said no to Anna. And so I can imagine Anna's internal rage these days when so many things are denied her. The ability to walk for miles. The ability to drive her car. The ability to go shopping for lovely clothes.

And now Anna has decided that she wants to take her tablets again. Dave is enraged.

"What do you want to take them bloody tablets for now you're alright?" he bellows.

Anna is calm but icy. "I haven't been sleeping too well."

I don't want Dave to get too upset.

"Anna you are so much better, so much more alert now. We can go out for coffee and lunch. It would be a pity to go back to how it was before."

"No, you don't know what you are talking about deary," says Anna, dismissing me. "The doctor gave them to me, so I should be taking them."

Anna has a point.

"I think the doctor was probably expecting you to check back with her from time to time though. To make sure that you still needed to take all of them. I'm sure the doctor wouldn't have wanted you to be so drowsy for so much of the day."

Anna rolls her eyes, "Make me some tea Dave please..."

"You really are so much better now," I say, "and several people have said so."

"No that's not true," she insists, looking at me as if I am quite mad.

Time to give up I think. There's a knock at the door, and I open it to a man holding a string of onions.

"Come on in Bob," shouts Dave, struggling to his feet.

The man looks at me curiously. "I'm Bob," he says putting the onions on the round table and holding out his hand.

It turns out he is a friend of Shropshire brother. He never realised Shropshire brother had a sister, he tells me. No, I say, I stayed here at weekends but never really lived here.

He sits down and Dave brings him a cup of tea.

"Anna you are looking so much better!" Bob calls across the room. Anna looks at him with suspicion in her eyes. I can't help myself smiling. What perfect timing! But I keep my eyes on the calendar I am making. This seems an odd thing to be doing, but the calendar I bought them last year was a mid year one, and they cannot understand what has happened to the remaining months of this year.

Bob and Dave are discussing onions. Bob lets the French onion seller store them in his garage. These are pink and mild, Dave says. Just how he likes them.

Perfect eaten raw with crusty bread and cheese. He breaks three or four off the string and pushes them across the table to me.

"You'll enjoy these," he says.

I sense that Bob likes to dominate the conversation, and that he would like me to stop my calendar design and give him my full attention. So I smile politely but carry on with my work. Anna listens, but says nothing.

"I've got to get down the sheds and get them logs split," says Dave eventually. We say goodbye to Bob and I heat up some soup for Anna's lunch. Dave disappears upstairs and then reappears in a pair of baggy pink trousers and his old white vest. It's a strange look.

"Summer trousers," he tells us, "got 'em at the discount store."

Anna and I drink soup and talk about family and friends. She manages two small cheese sandwiches as well. And some honey yogurt. The cottage is quiet. The fields outside the window are quiet. No cows.

Then the peace is broken as Dave reappears. Looking pale and sweaty.

"I've overdone it," he tells us. He sits by the open window and I make him tea.

"Come over all giddy." Anna gets up from her armchair and slowly crosses the room to give him a hug and stroke his arm.

"I've left all them logs on the ground. Got to go and get them stacked."

"I'll do it," I tell him, "just sit quietly until you feel better."

The logs aren't too heavy now that Dave has split them. I stack them on the bank. Not very neatly, but good enough.

After a while Dave joins me. He tells me that he and Anna had had a big argument about her tablets that morning. We talk about Dave taking Anna to her GP to talk about her medication.

The sun is warm again. I can see Anna sitting in the porch reading one of her catalogues.

"I'll tell you what," says Dave, as he locks up the woodshed, "I want to thank you for all that central heating work. In a couple of years I won't be able to do what I'm doin' now with them logs. I'm glad we've got proper heating now."

He limps up the garden in his strange pink trousers and baggy vest. Anna smiles to see him.

I'm glad about the central heating too. Dave told me he felt giddy when he was having a bonfire recently. I have a feeling the log splitting days may be coming to an end.

THE PURSE

8th September 2018

....

Dave is watering his plants when I arrive at the cottage. The pansies are fading, but the verbena is blooming and its little seedlings are pushing their way up between the paving stones outside the front door. The string of onions that Bob brought is hanging in the porch. Dave looks pleased to see me, but he doesn't look happy. He carries on watering the pots.

"We've had a bloody great row again."

"What about?"

"That bank card of hers. That one she keeps losing. She wants to keep it in 'er purse, but she'll just lose it again. Like before."

Earlier in the year Anna lost her purse in the supermarket. It was never found. Then she left her bank card at the hairdressers, and Dave had to drive her back to retrieve it.

"So I've put it on the table, and she's got to look after it today."

In the cottage Anna is looking worried.

"I want to take you out for a bit of lunch today, so I need my bank card, and he says I can't have it."

"It's on the table apparently."

We both look. There's nothing on the round table.

Dave stomps in from the garden.

"She'll just lose it again I'm telling you,"

"Where is it?" I ask.

"Where have you put it?" says Dave. His voice is angry.

"You haven't given it to me, have you!" says Anna defiantly.

"Of course I bloody have! I left it on the table."

"Ok it must be in the kitchen or something," I say. We all head out to the kitchen. "Perhaps you put it in your purse Anna?"

Dave reaches for her purse on one of the kitchen shelves. He unfolds it on the worktop. Library card. Supermarket loyalty card. Picture of Sydney brother as a toddler. No bank card. I sense Dave is about to explode.

"Let's have a cup of coffee and think about this," I say, trying to be diplomatic. "It's bound to be somewhere."

Anna walks slowly through to the dining room to put the kettle on the Aga. The atmosphere in the cottage is very strained.

"The birds haven't been down for your bread Dave," says Anna.

"Has your parakeet been back lately?" I ask.

"Nope," says Dave, "well just once, but I reckon there's other places in the village 'e likes to visit."

When Dave is sitting down with his floral mug of coffee, and Anna is settled with her red paisley mug in the armchair I try again.

"Well the card isn't in your purse Anna, or in the kitchen, so perhaps you took it upstairs with you when you went to the bathroom."

Anna has her purse on her lap and is turning it over and over, anxiously.

"I haven't seen the card deary, and that's the problem. He didn't give it to me when he said he would."

"Of course I did!" yells Dave, banging his mug down on the table.

"Stop!" I say loudly. "The card must be in the house somewhere. Let's not get over-worried. We'll have our coffee, and then I'll have a good look for it."

"If this doesn't stop I'm goin' a go screaming across them fields out there," says Dave, wiping his forehead with his cotton handkerchief. "She's gone mad!"

"No, it's alright. Anna has put it somewhere, and just forgotten. We can find it, I'm sure."

"Well I'm goin' down the boatyard now. Can't stay 'ere."

Dave get to his feet, reaches for his old cap and car keys and shuts the front door behind him.

"Let's go out for lunch," I say, sensing Anna's distress, "and don't worry about the card. We'll look for it when we get back. I'll buy lunch."

Anna brightens and smiles, "Oh no deary, no need. I've got some cash in my purse."

She indicates the purse on the little milking stool that sits by her armchair. Then she makes her way upstairs to find her outdoor shoes and handbag. I go outside to look at the front of the cottage that needs repainting. I've asked tall son to come and help with this. Anna appears at the doorway. "Are we ready deary?" She is holding her handbag and stick and has put on her black jacket.

"I'll lock the front door," I say, "have you put your purse in your handbag?"

Anna fumbles with the dark blue bag. Her thin arms get tangled in the straps. I lift the bag off her shoulder. I think I must try and buy her an across-the-body bag.

"No purse deary," she says, looking up at me.

"You had it on your lap, and then it was on the milking stool,"

"No deary, I haven't seen my purse today. And I've lost something else too, but I can't remember what it is."

I check the armchair and the milking stool, and upstairs I check the bathroom and Anna's bedroom. No purse. Anna looks so confused that I suggest we go out for some lunch and then sort out the lost items later. She holds onto my arm as we walk to my car.

"Am I weighing you down deary?" she says anxiously.

"No Anna," I say, "you are not weighing me down."

Anna is as light as a feather.

BOOTS

15th September 2018

. . . .

We enjoy lunch at the garden centre. Anna has a tuna and cheddar toastie, but cannot manage all of it. The staff are used to seeing me at the counter with half a sandwich or toastie, and kindly wrap the remainder in foil for Anna to eat later. Lunch is followed by a visit to the nursery's aquatic centre where Anna can observe the fish - bubble eye goldfish, glowlight tetras, black moor goldfish, and neon tetras. We stand by their tank and watch them drifting and darting, and Anna finds them calming to watch.

As we drive back to the cottage Anna worries about Dave.

"Things are not going very well deary," she tells me sadly. "We never argued like this until recently. We were always so happy together."

I try to remind her that Dave is her carer and that he wants to look after her. But that means he has to look after the finances. Including her bank card. And I tell her that she can trust him. And it's best not to argue about money. And most importantly… try not to be sarcastic. Dave hates sarcasm.

"But I'm not being serious deary," she says, "the sarcasm isn't serious. It's just to lighten the atmosphere."

I would like to say that the combination of her sarcasm and Dave's temper is a domestic powder keg.

But instead I just repeat that sarcasm doesn't work well with Dave. Better to let Dave look after the finances. And the bank card. Anna looks doubtful.

Back at the cottage she sits by the window in the pale afternoon sun and carefully examines the calendar, turning the pages backwards and forwards. Several times she asks me the day, the date, if I can remember who so-and-so is, if I've seen so-and-so lately. Often she asks me about people we haven't seen for many years. Or family members who are long dead. I search for the missing purse and the missing bank card, but to no avail.

Dave arrives back from the boatyard. He tells us he has had a good lunch with Gordon and now he's off to read the paper in the sitting room.

"Before you go Dave, I'm afraid Anna's lost her purse. I think we were hurrying off to lunch and she's just put it down somewhere."

I decided earlier that it was best if I tell Dave about the purse to avoid further arguments. He rolls his eyes when I tell him.

"She's gone mad."

"No, just forgetful," I remind him.

Dave goes through the drawers in the kitchen. Opens the kitchen bin. Looks behind the cereal packets in the cupboard, and under the cushion of Anna's armchair.

"What's all this then?" His hands are full of catalogues.

"I'm keeping them safe," Anna says. "Christmas is coming soon."

Anna was always well ahead with Christmas planning.

Dave sorts through the envelopes and opened letters and cards on the mantelpiece above the Aga.

"And this?" he says, holding up half a biscuit.

No-one answers, so he pops it into his mouth, picks up his newspaper and lumbers off to the sitting room.

"I give up. I just don't know any more," he mutters to himself.

As evening draws in I drive back to the city. It has been a bad day. I know that I will wake in the night thinking about them. Dave has promised to cancel Anna's bank card. We've talked about him just giving her a limited amount of cash each week. Perhaps if she insists on having a purse with cash in it we could put a tracker device on it.

So many things to think about.

The next day there are two messages on my landline when I return from the supermarket.

"Hello deary," says the first one, "I haven't seen you for a long time so I'm just ringing to see how you are? I've lost my bank card and my purse, and I'm just looking for them now. I'll ring you if I find them."

"Hello deary," says the second one, "I haven't found my bank card. Dave is going to cancel it for me with the bank. But I have found my purse. It was upstairs in my bedroom in one of my boots that I keep in the bottom of my wardrobe. I must have put it in there and forgotten about it."

I delete the messages. How curious. Anna put her purse in her boots. She makes it sound in the message as if it is quite natural to put your purse in your boots.

And perhaps for Anna it is.

WOOLLY BEARS

22nd September 2018

. . . .

Tall son is looking tired. Anna and Dave think this may be due to late nights, but he tells us that he was called to work very early this morning. I was hoping he might help me search the lanes for conkers but he is half asleep on the velvety sofa in the sitting room.

"What do you want conkers for deary?" asks Anna

"To keep the moths away," I tell her.

I think we may have had this conversation before.

"I 'ad that problem with the carpet up in the little room," Dave tells us, "bloody moths eaten all round the edge of that carpet. You can get a spray for 'em."

"I'd rather use conkers," I say, "and I think lavender works well too."

"Well I went round the edge of that carpet with diesel oil, and it worked bloody well," says Dave, "soon stopped eating that carpet they did."

Tall son opens his eyes, "Diesel oil! What was eating it Dave?"

"Woolly bears," says Dave. He is opening envelopes with a knife from the cutlery drawer.

"What's in the envelope Dave?" says Anna.

"Spanish lottery stuff. El Gordo."

Dave has been doing the Spanish lottery for several years. He has never won anything.

"Woolly bears?" says tall son looking puzzled, "did he says woolly bears?"

"Thought it was the driving licence," says Dave, "waitin' for the renewal. If I get stopped driving I shall die."

"That will make for an interesting post mortem," says tall son quietly.

There's a knock at the door.

"Come on in!" booms Dave.

It's Gordon, arriving for a spot of lunch with Dave at the pub in the next village. Gordon has walked up the lane, as he left his car down by Dave's sheds. He is very out of breath, and sits for a while before he is able to speak. He doesn't look very well. Dave makes him a strong coffee. They are not going to the boatyard today because of,

The traffic along the main road.

A regatta at the boatyard.

"All them people at the regatta, the roads are awful," grumbles Dave.

Gordon agrees. "This happens every year."

"There's something in the bag for you deary," says Anna, pointing to a bag on the leather trunk by the small window. "It's spotty."

Over the years Anna has often given me clothes that she doesn't wear any more, so I am not surprised by this. I have never had to buy a cashmere jumper or wool coat or elegant dressing gown. Nowadays her clothes are too small for anyone but Anna however.

"Yes, I can't remember what it is deary but it's spotty. You might like it."

I open the plastic bag and pull out a large cotton garment. What on earth is it?

Oh. Then I recognise the shape. Or lack of shape really.

"Anna it's a hospital gown!" I quickly stuff it back into the plastic bag.

"Why have you got a hospital gown?" asks tall son.

Anna looks vague. She is trying to fasten her watch. She always wears it over the cuff of her jumpers.

"That's from when she were last in the hospital," says Dave.

That was over a year ago.

"Well I should take it back with you when Anna has her appointment next week," I suggest.

"Silly rat, your daughter don't want that thing," says Dave affectionately.

"Well someone might want it," says Anna, who doesn't like to be proved wrong.

Gordon looks bewildered. Dave bangs down his coffee cup on the side table.

"Let's get going then mate," he says to Gordon.

"Are we going for a cream tea?" says tall son to his grandmother.

"Ooh yes," says Anna, "I'll get my outdoor shoes on. Take a key with you Dave won't you, in case you're back from the pub before us."

"Make sure you got that purse of yours in your bag," he says as he and Gordon head off to the pub, "or you won't be able to buy that cream tea!"

I think after creme caramel and chocolate cake, a cream tea is certainly one of Anna's favourites.

She takes tall son's arm and walks slowly to my car, with her stick in the other hand.

I lock the front door and put the key in my handbag. Safer that way. I don't want anything else to go missing.

Outside the weather is still mild for mid September. A group of sparrows hop about on the bank amongst the bird seed that Dave threw them earlier. The neighbours from the thatched cottage are walking their over-excited dog along the lane.

And there is the curious call of a strange bird coming from the tulip tree. A touch of the exotic in this very English village.

THE BANK

28th September 2018

. . . .

We are taking a trip to the bank. Anna's bank. We are hoping to open a savings account for her and to move money from her current account, so that if she loses her bank card again it won't be such a worry for everyone. It has taken me some time to persuade Anna to do this. She is reluctant to make many changes these days.

Dave has brought his disabled parking permit so that we can park in the centre of their local town.

"Park there," he orders, pointing at the pavement outside the bank.

"That's not a parking space," I say in alarm.

"Don't matter. I park there anyway," he says.

"Park there," indicating the town hall.

"But I'd be blocking the road! There's a mini roundabout here," I protest.

But Dave is getting exasperated.

"It's Saturday and it's getting busy. I've got a permit so we can just park so she don't have to walk far."

It's a small town. Saturdays are obviously busy, but hardly anything to worry about.

"Dave keep calm!" says Anna. She is worried about the bank trip and is clinging on to her seatbelt.

Hurrah. There's a space outside the estate agents. Not far to walk to the bank. It's not easy to get either of them out of my car. Dave's knees are stiff and painful. Anna is frightened of falling. I have suggested a wheelchair in the past, but Anna looked at me as if I had suggested a trip to Mars.

In the bank a notice informs us that there are no customer advisers in today. A shortage of staff.

"What's going on with banks these days?" demands Dave. He is trying to put Anna's walking stick out of the way before she trips someone up.

He and Anna sit by a low round table while I queue to talk to someone.

"Not enough bloody people working in this bank," says Dave loudly. A few people in the queue turn to look at him. He gets up from his chair and limps over to join me.

"I'm very sorry but there are not enough staff here today to open an account for your mother," says the young bank teller apologetically.

Dave's deafness means that, fortunately, he hasn't heard this.

"But we've come here specially. It's difficult for my mother to get out and about these days, and I am working during the week."

"You can make an appointment if you like," says the teller.

I don't want to hold up the long queue. "We'll have to come back another day," I say.

"But we just want to move some of 'er money to a new account," says Dave looking cross, "shouldn't take no time."

"Well you could certainly do this online," says the teller, "... if you do online banking?"

"Do what?" shouts Dave.

I steer him back towards Anna.

"What's that online banking?" says Dave.

"It's cold sitting by this open door," says Anna, folding her arms tightly.

I help her up and we walk slowly towards the stone steps down to the pavement. Anna has given up changing into going-out trousers, and her long velvet skirt brushes the ground. I have to hold her arm tightly.

As we reach the bottom step there is a hand on my shoulder. It is the teller again.

"If you would like to bring your mum back inside, I think we could get all the forms ready for her new account?" she says, smiling, "and then my colleagues would process the forms on Monday. It would save you coming back in again."

"Oh that would be helpful," says Anna.

Back inside, the teller takes us to a room off the main entrance. It's warmer there. She leaves us with three long forms to fill in and explains that she will need Anna to sign and date all the forms.

"Will you need to know how many husbands I've had?" says Anna looking up from her chair, "because I've had four."

"Oh God," says Dave quietly from the other side of the room.

The teller smiles. "No, just your signature and the date thank you."

Back at the cottage I explain that the bank will contact me with details of Anna's new account. She looks relieved and goes out to the kitchen, re-appearing with a big box of toffees that medical daughter had sent Dave for his birthday. We have just had lunch at the garden centre. Dave had a giant bacon bap and Anna had cheese on toast. She daintily ate the middle of the toast and left all the crusts.

"They're my birthday toffees woman!" shouts Dave.

"Not good for you," says Anna, helping herself to two pieces, "and don't shout Dave. We don't want a toffee war. Do you want some cake deary?"

I've noticed over the past year that Anna rarely finishes her main meal. And therefore allows herself pudding, followed by sweets and cakes. And perhaps that was always so. As a small child my memories of her cooking were not good. Chewy meat, overcooked vegetables, watery gravy. Lumpy nursery puddings. When she left us John struggled to cope with the cooking. We had boiled potatoes every evening, which I had peeled on my return from school. Certainly some meat. Then tinned fruit. At the weekend we went to the local butchers. John seemed to know all the staff there. And then the bakery where he bought jam doughnuts or fruit buns.

Things changed dramatically when John met the second Anna (the one who was also a model). Anna II had previously married an American and had lived in South America.

Her cooking was extraordinary.

FRANCE

6th October 2018

. . . .

I was in a bakery last week. The bread was wonderful. Doughy, wholemeal, filling, with a perfect crust. And cheese straws. And apple cake. And very good sandwiches. And I suddenly thought about Anna II, but I couldn't think why. I texted Shropshire brother. 'What sort of food did Anna II cook for us? I remember it was very different!'

After a while (he was probably at the races) I received a reply.

'Meatloaf. I loved the flavours, so unlike the bland meat or stew we had been served up to that point.'

And another text.

'Baked Alaska was another'.

Oh yes! Meatloaf and Baked Alaska. And I also remembered Chocolate Bavarian Pie. And Chicken Cacciatore, with tomatoes, rosemary and garlic. It was all delicious. I had never tasted such food before. But I pretended I didn't care about it. I didn't really like anyone in those days.

I have a picture of Anna II in my mind. She was very beautiful, with blonde hair, curious green eyes and flowing caftans.

242

She and her three children moved house three times in the years John was with her, and we always stayed with them. There was an expensive house outside the city with a long garden and a titled family next door. A rather cramped cottage in another city, where all five of us children shared a bedroom. And a large flat in a leafy suburb, beautifully decorated by Anna II, and very modern. The only thing that bothered me about that flat was the screeching owls that kept us awake at night.

I used to wonder how Sydney brother could have gone so far away from home, but his emails to me in recent years suggest he was looking for adventure, Pacific islands, sea fishing and surfing. And I think that growing up with Anna and Dave in the quiet village, living in the same house all your childhood, where there wasn't much money, well, it might make you thirst for adventure. Whereas all I wanted was a little more stability. To stay put in one house for just a short time. Because John liked to travel as well. And he liked to drive long distances. He drove Anna II to France on one occasion and when they returned he looked very sad. The next evening I was in bed. I couldn't sleep. And the au pairs were talking on the landing outside my room. Whispering really. But loud enough that I could hear. It was all over. Anna II had dumped John.

Last night I slept in the little room at the top of the cottage. Very much warmer than I remember, thanks to the new central heating system. I couldn't think where I was when I awoke, but then I heard the noisy rooks out in the fields, and the quietness of the lanes around the cottage.

Dave has gone to France with Gordon and two friends from the boatyard. They are stocking up with wine for Christmas. And olive oil of course. And it is a good opportunity for a big meal out. They took the overnight ferry and had booked cabins to sleep in.

Gordon was collecting Dave at quarter to nine. But Dave was still in his slippers, reading the newspaper when I arrived.

"Gordon will be here soon," I said, "have you packed your bag Dave?"

Dave looked surprised.

"I'll just lie down on the bunk," he replied.

"Toothbrush?" I said.

"Oh, I could do," he said, looking over the top of his newspaper.

But within a minute or two one of his boatyard friends was at the door and Dave was kissing Anna goodbye and putting on his old jacket and flat cap. No overnight bag then.

"Are you hungry?" I asked Anna, "I could make you some toast."

"That would be lovely deary," she said.

I found some wholemeal bread in the old wooden bin and put it into the wire Aga toaster. And while I waited for it to cook I suddenly remembered what else Anna II had cooked for us.

Waffles. Crisp on the outside. Soft and doughnutty on the inside. Sweeter than pancakes. Delicious with maple syrup. The five of us fought to eat as many as we could.

How could I have forgotten?

I found Anna sitting by the telephone. Shuffling through the pages of her little telephone book.

"I'm just looking for Sam's number dear."

"I guess he'll be having breakfast now," I said.

I found the number for her and she chatted to him for a while about the weather and the family. She was worried about Dave being away. I think it helps her to talk to family on these occasions. Several times she asked me,

"Is Dave coming back?"

"Tomorrow," I said, "don't worry, he'll be back tomorrow."

Then she rang eldest grandson. The phone was on loudspeaker and he sounded pleased, but surprised, to hear her voice.

And then she went up to bed. I carried her hot water bottles up the stairs because she has two. And very quickly her light went out and she was asleep.

FIREBRAND

14th October 2018

....

To celebrate Dave's successful visit to France, and as a late birthday present, we take him and Anna for Sunday lunch at a pub near tall son's flat. Roast chicken with Yorkshire pudding, roast potatoes, swede, red cabbage, kale and parsnips. Plenty of gravy. And a pint of Old Hoppy Hen. Dave is ecstatic.

"Best pub lunch I've 'ad in years," he tells anyone who will listen.

I ordered Anna a child's roast chicken lunch, but she barely managed to eat any of it, and piled her potatoes onto Dave's plate. Never mind.

We have pudding and coffee at tall son's flat. It's a passionfruit cheesecake and I cut a large slice for Anna. She eats all of it. They admire tall son's new bar stools in the kitchen, the secondhand sofa we found on Gumtree and the ottoman discovered in a furniture shop sale. Then we help Anna downstairs to the car while Dave goes to visit the bathroom. I wait in the car with Anna but I am surprised to see that there are tears in her eyes.

"Where's Dave? Has he gone?" Her voice is tiny.

"He's just coming," I tell her, "don't worry."

Her tears don't stop until she sees him limping towards us from the gate.

"Best pub lunch I've 'ad in years," he tells us again as he struggles into the car.

Anna reaches over to him from the back seat and leaves her hand on his shoulder all the way back to the cottage.

While they make tea I go out to the garden to bring in the washing. Unfortunately it doesn't look very clean. I suspect the washing machine needs descaling. Or perhaps they need to use a hotter cycle. It's all dry though because the weather is warm. There are bubbly white clouds over the fields and plenty of colour in the garden still. I notice that the mauve verbena has escaped into the fields. It surrounds the stile where James, the whipper-in from the kennels slept that New Year's Eve. All those years ago. Very drunk.

Back in the cottage Dave is entertaining tall son with stories of his wild youth. Anna is dozing in the armchair by the Aga after a busy day out.

"He were a firebrand that Mick. He were a lodger of ours. He got hold of that gang leader and his brother and he beat 'em up in the toilets and they left town. Never bothered us again. "

"Where was this?" I ask.

"Toilets at the milk bar," says Dave, "we used to go there after a night out for a Horlicks before bed."

Tall son snorts with laughter. The milk bar?

"And what's Horlicks?" says tall son.

But Dave is getting into the swing of this.

"George's caff was the worst. We used to go there in the Buick. The sailors they'd come up to the caff for a fight. One night we had to do a runner. Outnumbered. John, he'd hidden in a ditch.

Bob was in the back of the Buick and I drove off and John was yelling' 'Let me in! Let me in!' and he was holdin' onto the back door handle of the car and runnin' like mad to get away from them sailors."

He runs his hands through his white hair. "Anna! Got all them seeds in my hair again!"

"What seeds?" asks tall son.

"Dunno. I go down the sheds, and when I come back my hair's full of them brown seeds."

Anna is asleep now. Out on the bank I see a nuthatch on the bird feeder, and a new robin looking territorial.

"Well the worst night was at the dance out in the forest," Dave continues, "in the MGB. We got into a fight and me best jacket split down the back. Some bloke was punching these local troublemakers and draggin' 'em across the dance floor. One of 'em was just out of it. They tried to pick a fight with us but we got in the MGB and we just drove off fast. But I skidded and the darn car left the road and turned over three times. Hit an oak tree we did. There was a hissing noise and I said, 'get out quick' and we 'ad to go out the windscreen, cos that was broke anyway."

"Crikey, were you hurt?" I ask him.

"No we was alright. Then the farmer came along and 'e thought we was pinching implements. But 'e got the MGB back on the road for us. And we drove home."

I look at tall son in surprise.

"Another night outside the Byriver Hall I just woke up. Four in the mornin' it was. Frosty on that ground it was.

248

I'd 'ad a drink or two and got beaten up. Just dumped on the grass and it was four in the mornin'."

"It sounds to me like they were rough times," says tall son, who worked as a nightclub bouncer in his final uni year.

"Bit rough," says Dave stirring a sweetener into his tea, "but no-one got hurt. Not really hurt."

Really?

"Now you goin' to set that central heating clock for me?" says Dave to tall son, "then we can watch telly."

He gets to his feet and lumbers off with his mug of tea to the sitting room.

"There's nothin' good on the telly these days though," he says to tall son, "all quizzes and cooking shows and such nonsense. Nothin' exciting any more."

Anna has woken up and follows him, carrying her dainty mug of tea oh so carefully. One hand on the round table, then the wall by the front door and finally the mantelpiece in the sitting room. Then her seat on the sofa.

The television volume is too loud. But Dave can't hear it otherwise. Anna puts her blanket over her lap.

"Time to go," says tall son.

We leave them then. Dave is dozing. Anna looking at a fashion magazine. The garden is quiet and so are the fields. Still no cows.

But up on the bank I spy new robin watching us. Waiting for us to throw him some corn. Waiting for a sparrow or two to land on the bank above the cottage.

Spoiling for a fight.

METAPHOR

....

I did miss Anna II a bit. And all her family. Bernice and her younger brothers. Bernice and I could walk to school together, and share homework tasks. The best time was when her American father was visiting London, staying at a smart hotel, and Bernice and I met him there. He bought us Knickerbocker Glories for lunch, and gave Bernice a beautiful necklace, which I coveted. But what I missed about Anna II was that she could answer some of my questions. The most important one at that time being, why did someone leave the cake out in the rain in the MacArthur Park album by Richard Harris? Neither Anna nor John could answer that question for me. My grandmother, who read a great deal, had never heard the song.

But Anna II told me.

"It means something has been spoiled. It's a metaphor."

With that she swept out of the room, leaving me to ponder.

And today it's raining a little when I arrive at the cottage. But Dave's been busy. I can see that he has painted the back of the cottage and it's looking much better. We just need eldest grandson with a ladder to finish the job. The flowers in their various garden pots have perked up in the rain, and the lawn is clear of leaves from the tulip tree. All is quiet in the cottage.

Dave is reading the Saturday paper and Anna is looking at the calendar. It is Devon brother's birthday this month, and Anna senses that a birthday is coming, even if she cannot work out when.

There's a Christmas card on the mantelpiece.

"It's from a veterans association," says Dave when I ask.

"They're early," I say. It is only October after all.

Anna and Dave don't seem to agree. They look at me blankly.

The phone rings. Dave is talking (loudly) to Shropshire brother. The talk is of bloodhounds. Dave passes the phone to me and Shropshire brother explains that he is off to a bloodhound drag hunt.

"What is it?" I ask him.

Today apparently a pack of bloodhounds will follow the scent of three volunteers who will take it in turns to run through the countryside. Shropshire brother is writing a piece about it for a magazine.

Dave looks impressed, but he has never been enthusiastic about Shropshire brother's country pursuits, particularly horse-riding and hunting. Anna looks nonplussed. The cottage was always full of horse paraphernalia when Shropshire brother lived there, and the rest of us admired the beautiful horses he rode and raced, but couldn't match his passion.

"D'you remember when old Beauty was out in the field here?" says Dave. Anna remembers and smiles.

Beauty the horse belonged to the publican who lived down the lane at the pub which has been replaced by the new houses. Beauty's constant companion was Tom-Tom the noisy donkey.

"That donkey used to grab old Beauty's tail and run round the field with 'er," says Dave.

I think I remember staying at the cottage in the little room at the top. I woke up in the morning and looked out across the fields and Beauty was just lying there in the morning light.

"Old Windy Man buried 'er up the top of the field," says Dave.

"Why was he called that?" I say.

"That was 'is name," says Dave, putting down his coffee mug. "Now I'm goin' to get out my leaf blower and blow them leaves off that lawn of mine."

"Has the central heating been working ok?" I ask Anna.

"I think so deary," she says, "has it been working alright Dave?"

"What!" blasts Dave from the porch.

Anna repeats the question. I've noticed that with Dave's deafness he often doesn't hear a question the first time. So it has to be repeated.

"Don't know what's up with that heating," says Dave coming back into the dining room, "it comes on and then it goes off and then it comes on again. Can't keep up with it."

I explain about the thermostat which the engineers fitted at the foot of the staircase. How the thermostat communicates with the boiler to keep the cottage at twenty-one degrees, which is how tall son set it up.

Dave looks sceptical.

"Reckon that thermostat needs to be somewhere else. Reckon I need to move that thermostat."

Oh dear. Time to call out tall son.

The rain has stopped and the sun has come out. Dave whistles to himself as he finds the leaf blower in the back of the long cupboard. A couple of coat hangers fall off the rail as he backs out of the cupboard.

"Must get this bloody cupboard cleared out," he says to himself.

If Dave is getting the leaf blower out it means I need to shut the front door and close the windows. Anna and I have more coffee and eat small squares of ginger cake that I bought at the village shop that morning. The air is filled with the droning of the leaf blower. I wonder if I should move my car in case Dave decides it needs a wash and blow dry.

And then the cottage is getting warmer. Anna walks slowly to the box of sticks by the front door and takes out her walking stick.

"Do you want me to come with you?"

"No deary, I'm just going to sit in the porch."

She opens the front door. "I wish I could go for a walk on my own."

"I know."

This is all I can say.

Anna has been sitting outside occasionally ever since I told her about vitamin D. That was after she was taken ill in Australia and the doctor advised at least ten minutes of sunshine a day.

"Ridiculous!" Anna told us at the time, "Surely he realised I was from England!"

At the bottom of the garden Dave stands in a storm of fallen leaves. Above his head more leaves flutter onto the lawn. And Anna sits in the porch on the wooden seat and looks out across the fields.

Alone with her confused thoughts of walks in the past. Through the village. Up to Coffin Lane. Along the old tracks to the pub in the next town. Or even further afield with Dave.

I take her a cup of tea and the rest of the ginger cake and she opens her eyes and smiles. "Is my mother here yet?" She asks me.

"Not yet," I tell her, "I'll leave the door open in case you need me."

"Is it going to rain today deary?"

"No, not today Anna," I say, looking at the sky, "it won't rain today."

LEGS

27th October 2018

. . . .

Two days with the elderly parents this weekend. Saturday as usual. Then Sunday lunch in tall son's city.

Saturday morning and Dave is not going to the boatyard, or to the local pub with Gordon because Gordon has a job to do. He is cutting the grass.

"Been saying' e's goin' to do this all summer, and e' never gets round to it," Dave tells us.

"Is it a big garden?" I ask Dave.

"No course not," says Dave, "it's one of them modern houses."

I've made cheese on toast for Anna with gouda cheese. That was all I could find in the fridge. Dave is having fruit cake for lunch. The cake has a burnt look about it.

"Aga burnt it!" says Dave. He is surprised, but also a little pleased. It might stop the family being so critical. So the Aga has been taking lessons from mini oven. Dave scrapes off the burnt top and sides and seems to enjoy the taste.

"Look at them bloody rooks," he says, waving towards the field.

Out in the field the rooks are strutting around, and occasionally rootling in the cowpats.

255

"They're after leatherjackets," Dave tells us, "if my leg wasn't stiff this morning I'd be out there. Wave my arms and they'd be gone."

"Is your leg painful Dave?" asks Anna.

"Not like it was in that hospital," Dave says. He is talking about the knee operation he had the previous year. "I woke up in the night after that operation and there was blood everywhere. I bled a good pint or two I can tell you. Bed was covered in blood. Nurses came rushin' out with bandages. I felt terrible. Sickly. Next mornin' they wheeled me out and I just vomited everywhere. Floor, wheelchair, everywhere."

My cheese on toast has lost its appeal. And I've heard this account several times.

"I needed to build me blood up again. Not as bad as Les the leg though."

"Les the leg?"

"Yeah. A bloke I knew. Spent eight an' a half thousand quid on that operation, and then got one of them bugs that can kill you. E' was in that hospital a whole year. Come out in the end of course. But that's a lot of money."

He shakes his head.

"Nice hospital I was in though. It was a private one, but they did me on the NHS. Nice elderly volunteers and one lady she called me Young Dave. She said I was cheerful. There's a lady down the boatyard and she always says I'm cheerful. She's a very nice woman."

Across the room Anna scowls at him from her armchair.

"So you're going off with her are you?" she says coldly.

Time to go.

The next day we meet Anna and Dave at the pub at lunchtime. We are early, but they are even earlier. Dave is buying a pint and a tonic water with lemon, and Anna is struggling to sit at the big wooden table by the window. They are pleased to see tall son who has been on a short business trip to Canada and shows them photos of seaplanes and skyscrapers and mountains. There is also news that youngest grandson is back in England.

I order roast lunches. They can do a quarter-size child's meal for Anna.

"You'll never eat all them vegetables," says Dave when the meals arrive.

"May I just say what lovely eyebrows you have," says Anna to the young woman who serves us.

Tall son laughs. But she does have lovely eyebrows.

Anna passes her roast potatoes and Yorkshire pudding across the table to Dave, and then nibbles delicately at slices of roast chicken. Dave is immersed in a large plate of roast pork.

"Bloody good cracklin'" he shouts, holding up his fork to show us.

But Anna is not eating her vegetables. The tension is growing.

"Don't worry Dave," I say, as I see his face clouding.

Tall son tries to relieve the tension by talking about puddings.

"Yes, I'll have a pudding," says Anna.

The young woman with nice eyebrows clears our plates. Anna has hardly touched hers, but she is very interested in the dark chocolate pudding.

"And I'll have apple crumble," announces Dave.

Anna takes two spoonfuls of chocolate pudding and then slowly slides the pot across the table to me.

"Don't you like it?"

"You have some deary. It's very nice."

"No you eat it Anna," I say.

She slides it towards tall son, but he pushes it back.

"Here you are Dave," she says. He takes the chocolate pot and adds it to his apple crumble and custard.

"Custard's a bit watery," he says by way of explanation.

I give tall son a look that says, this is why Dave has an ever-expanding waistline.

I feel a ridiculous irritation with Anna. All my life she has been in a love-hate relationship with food. Fascinated by food. Frightened of food. But she has dementia, I tell myself. Of course things are going to be difficult.

Tall son has found a little terrier by the bar to talk to. Dave announces very loudly that terriers are a good breed. Unlike those silly dogs by the door there. The chihuahua by the door looks at him contemptuously.

Tall son helps Anna to her feet and finds her stick. By the pub door Dave lets out an enormous belch and I jump. Customers in the adjoining bar look startled.

We cross the road and I take a photo of Anna and tall son. Her stick in one hand, her other hand on tall son's arm. Unsteady on her legs. He is holding her handbag. Unselfconsciously.

Dave has headed off to the bushes at the back of the car park so we wait by his old red car, and tall son shows me how the boot no longer closes. Dave has another car of course, equally old, but probably more comfortable for Anna.

We help her in and exchange goodbyes. Dave starts the engine and tall son points out the one-way arrows in the busy car park.

"It's one-way Dave," I repeat.

"Yes I know that," he shouts.

We watch them drive away. The wrong way.

Tall son and I walk back through the park. It's warm and sunny and the river is sparkling.

The park is full of children, running, shouting, and climbing on the play equipment. Tall son strides ahead of me. I'm half walking and half running. He is talking about buying a dog. He wants a dachshund. How will a dachshund with those little dachshund legs keep up with tall son?

I am aware that we are walking so fast just because we can. Because being with Anna and Dave is so very slow that when they are back in their car, or back on their sofa, settled in their armchairs, we feel a sense of relief. A sense of energy.

I run to catch up with tall son and we leave the park and head back to the city centre.

CANADA

3rd November 2018

It's Devon brother's birthday. Anna has had a phone call to say that he and Alis and youngest grandson will be visiting the cottage. But she isn't sure when. I think I have time before they arrive to take my duvet to the launderette for a wash and tumble dry.

It's chilly but bright, and my car is in the sunshine, so I sit there waiting for the wash cycle to finish. It's a busy morning in the little row of shops. The hardware shop is one of those that stocks everything you could possibly need in the hardware line. From plant pots to matches. Drain cleaner to dustpan and brushes. The man who runs it is a distant relative of John's through his rather scary mother. I discovered this when I did a family tree on one particular family line and discovered they were horticulturists and nurserymen and had lived in the area for centuries.

I am deep in thought about distant relatives when my car door is opened abruptly and Dave climbs into the front seat. With difficulty, as his knee is obviously bad this morning. The car sinks with his weight.

"Thought I'd bring me duvet down and it could go in the wash with yours", he says cheerfully.

Oh dear.

"Well the wash has started Dave," I tell him, "and anyway my duvet filled the machine, so there wouldn't have been room for yours."

He gives me a puzzled look.

"Duvet's not that big surely?"

"Well, pretty big."

"When I got my duvet at that Dunelm shop it packed up pretty small," he insists.

I have to think for a minute.

"Er.. well that was a duvet cover Dave."

"Yes that's what I'm talkin' about," he says, "but if you've started the wash, I'm goin' to get me paper."

He opens the car door.

"See you up the house soon then. They're comin' up from Devon today."

At the cottage I carry the still damp duvet into the dining room to find the clothes horse. It should be in the long cupboard. Dave looks surprised.

"Bloody big duvet you've got there. Don't reckon mine would have fitted in the machine as well."

Just as well.

Devon brother is showing Anna and Dave photos of youngest grandson fire-fighting in Canada. Climbing into helicopters. Dangling from ropes over a forest canopy. Team photos. Fires at night. And very tall trees. On the round table is a half-eaten lunch of long sticks of French bread, and cheeses and pickles.

Youngest grandson is looking well. And his eyes seem to be much bluer than I remember. Alis agrees with me.

"They were green when I last saw him," she tells me.

"Will you go back to Canada?" I ask youngest grandson.

"Oh yes, I've got many friends there now," he tells me.

"Happy birthday," I say, giving Devon brother a hug.

"Oh I don't do birthdays," he says grinning.

Devon brother is a whirligig of energy and always has been. He finds the cottage oppressive. The quietness. The slowness. The sameness. He wants to take one of the dogs for a walk. Alis will take the other dog to visit her parents who live nearby. The only way I will get him to sit down and drink his coffee is to talk about politics, and the world, and the state of the British countryside. Dave is still marvelling over the photos. Anna is listening from her armchair. She looks a little worried.

"Have you brought the screens?" I ask Devon brother eventually.

"Yep I'll get them from the car," he says.

He's brought two screens to fit around the front and side of the new oil tank. Anna doesn't like to see the oil tank from the garden because, she says, it looks ugly. Dave wants a screen at the front of the oil tank to hide it from the road. He regularly tells us that his neighbour once had the oil drained from his tank by thieves.

Tall son has arrived from the city with his flatmate. He helps Devon brother to put up the screens on the bank while Dave goes off to find the leaf blower. The lawn is covered with leaves again. I hear shouts and laughter from the garden as the younger men steal the leaf blower from Dave and discover the fun of blowing the fallen leaves into piles and then dumping the piles in the field.

262

"Deary?" I feel a hand on my arm as I watch the leaf blowing through the window. Anna still looks concerned.

"What is it?" I ask her.

"Should I cook everyone something to eat now?" she says, looking up at me.

Poor Anna. It has been a long time since she cooked us all a meal. In fact when we were younger she told us that she would no longer cook for us when we reached eighteen. I wasn't sure what to make of that at the time. Her cooking wasn't very good, but it was still the sort of thing you look forward to when you go home to your parents. She was as good as her word though, and when we had family get-togethers we usually brought plenty of food with us.

"Don't worry," I tell her, "I think everyone has to go very soon. Before it gets dark," I add.

Devon brother appears with tall son. The two dogs are following them. Devon brother has his coat in his hand.

"Time to go," he says.

I wave goodbye from the garden. Devon brother is acting the fool. It looks as if he is dancing down the lane.

Back in the cottage Dave is watching television and Anna has put on the electric fire and draped her thin blue blanket over her lap. I will go home soon. Sydney brother and tall son are fond of saying that everything stops at the cottage at half past three. And that does seem to be the time that Dave settles down in his armchair to watch television. And Anna joins him.

"Not that there's anything worth watching," says Dave.

As if I had forgotten.

And yes, the light is fading a little. The fields are growing quieter. The day is coming to an end.

INVITATION

11th November 2018

· ·

It's time for a change. I have a busy weekend so perhaps Anna and Dave would like to come to my house for lunch on Sunday. Now that Anna is more mobile and alert I am sure it would be possible. Dave agrees. In fact he sounds pleased. I think they get a little bored together in the same house day after day, and so going out is a treat. And Sunday is a good day because the roads will be quiet.

I'm making fish pie, roasted sweet potatoes and red cabbage, followed by blackberry and apple crumble with cream. I've bought Anna a pot of profiteroles with chocolate and caramel sauce, which I think she will prefer to the crumble. It is a dry sunny day and quite mild. Some kind friends have brought me an elegant pot of bamboo for my courtyard garden, and we sit chatting while lunch cooks. Half past eleven, I told Dave. Fine, he said.

But it's twelve noon! I open the back gate so that I can see if they drive in. My friends sense my anxiety and say their goodbyes. Twelve fifteen. I can see the road from the front of my house. It's very busy. In fact it is ridiculously busy for a Sunday. The traffic is crawling past the house. Perhaps that's why they are so late. I ring the cottage. No answer. I ring Dave's mobile. No answer. I text Shropshire brother, 'Can I check Dave's mobile with you. They haven't turned up for lunch.' He sends me the number. No answer.

At twelve-thirty I hear the back gate rattling. I can see Anna's long red skirt as she tries to open the gate. I hurry out and help her into the house. Someone is banging on the front door, very loudly.

"Hold on, just coming!" I shout, as I help Anna to the sofa.

I open the front door to Dave. He is holding two carrier bags. Why on earth are they at different doors?

Anna is crying a little. "It's so nice to see you deary."

"Are you both alright?" I ask.

"it's just nice to see you deary," says Anna again.

No explanation as to why they are an hour late.

"Bloody busy in this city," says Dave, rootling in the carrier bags. He produces a huge bag of crisps, a box of chocolates and a Mary Berry bread and butter pudding.

"Forgot the bloody wine," he says to Anna.

"I would rather have coffee," says Anna.

"I need the bathroom," says Dave, putting down the carrier bags.

I make coffee and put the red cabbage in the microwave. It's a new favourite for Anna, after we had lunch at the pub with tall son recently.

Dave has settled down in the armchair with the Sunday papers. He hands Anna the colour supplement. I notice that he's left the light on in the downstairs loo. As I switch it off I also notice that I will have to wash the rug. What a dismal thought. I suppose men can lose their sense of direction in later life.

"Did you go to the boatyard yesterday Dave," I ask while we eat. Anna has a small plate of food on a green and orange patterned plate.

I've heard that a coloured plate encourages the appetite, rather than one that is plain white.

"Nope," says Dave, "Gordon's got something wrong with 'is back."

"Too much chocolate," says Anna helpfully.

Dave decides on bread and butter pudding to follow. Never mind, I can freeze the apple crumble for another day.

"I 'ad some lovely apple trees in my first cottage," Dave tells us, "not that my wife noticed mind you."

"Was that Fay?" asks Anna.

"Yep. She was too busy chasing blokes, she was. Made me mad."

"I'm not surprised Dave," I say.

He wipes his dinner plate with a piece of sourdough bread. "Mind you, I wish I 'hadn't hit her lover. 'E was bigger than me. Got out his car and I thought 'e was goin' to hit me, so I hit 'im first."

Crikey.

"What happened then?" I ask.

"'E was shocked, so I just drove off and left 'im. She tried to end it then."

"End the relationship?" I ask. I am slightly confused.

Anna is listening carefully, although she must have heard all this before.

"So 'e stole 'er car and drove round the town in it. She left 'er keys in it, stupid woman."

"What did you do?"

"I went to the police. Told 'em what 'e did. They didn't do nothing about it. Then she went off with 'im. So that was that. I just said, they can just get on with it."

He finishes his glass of wine. "Nice fish pie that was," he adds.

Anna seems to enjoy her profiteroles.

We settle down again with the Sunday papers, but after a few minutes Anna wants to use the bathroom. I wait in the kitchen.

"You don't need to lock the door," I say helpfully.

Anna locks the door.

I hear water running in the basin, and then a scrabbling at the door handle.

"Are you alright?"

"I can't get out deary, I think the lock has broken,"

I try the handle. The door is definitely locked.

"Hold on Anna," I say as I run upstairs to the main bathroom. It has the same lock; a thumb turn lock. Easy to turn. But maybe more difficult for someone as frail as Anna.

I call through the door, "Anna, turn the lock to the left. Use both hands if you have to."

There is a fumbling at the lock.

"It's broken deary," she says in a small voice, "I can't get out."

"What!" yells Dave, "What's up!"

"Um, I think you had better come and have a look Dave," I say.

Dave is a practical man. Short on patience. But practical nonetheless.

"Why did you lock the bloody door you daft..."

"Dave!" I interrupt, "don't upset her. Let's just work it out quietly."

My mind starts to race. Who shall we call? Tall son is in Ireland this week. Oldest grandson might be in the city. Or he could be anywhere. Do we call the fire brigade? The police? A locksmith?

"Dave, let me show you the lock upstairs."

Dave struggles with the stairs. His knees are stiff. With a lot of effort he pulls himself to the top, then inspects the bathroom lock with me.

It takes just as long to get back downstairs, but Dave has a plan. He pulls a selection of coins from his trouser pocket.

"One of these'll turn the lock from the other side," he says. Yes, the lock has a ridge on the outside. We might be able to turn it with the right coin. Ah yes, a ten pence coin. Dave fiddles with the lock , trying to get the ten pence coin into the ridge to force the lock open. Then he opens the door triumphantly and we see Anna's worried face.

"Don't lock the bloody door again you rat," says Dave fondly. He is quite pleased with his success. Anna needs to sit down with a cup of tea. And perhaps one of the mint chocolates that they brought with them. Her look confirms that she will continue to lock the bloody door if she wants to.

When peace has returned I suggest they head back before it gets dark. I help Anna out to the car while Dave inspects the plants in the courtyard.

When they've gone I read the newspaper that Dave left behind, occasionally looking out at the evening sky. My new pot of bamboo shivers slightly in the breeze as it tries to adjust to its new setting.

"Everything will be alright," I say encouragingly.

And I swear it gives me a look of sympathy.

GENERATIONS

17th November 2018

. . . .

John had a brother who lives in another city with his wife of many years. Their house has seen little change from the day they first moved in. Probably fifty years ago or more. In fact the family talks of the wallpaper that is decorated with birds.

"Have they still got the pheasant wallpaper?" is a regular question for anyone who has visited the house over the years.

I haven't seen them for several months. Anna and Dave, and my job have kept me too busy. But today tall son and I decide to call in on our way back from Ikea. The house, in a quiet suburb of the city, looks exactly as it always does. As if it is still in the 1960s.

To my surprise my cousin opens the door. He is a very tall man with long white wavy hair. Nowadays he spends most of his time in Denmark.

"Come in," he says, standing back from the door. Musical aunt is coming into the hallway and peers up at us. She is wearing one of her lovely knitted cardigans.

"Oh it's you dear," she says smiling at me, and taking my arm, "come and sit down by the fire."

It's not cold, but the gas fire is warming the sitting room.

The room is very tidy, which is strange because my uncle likes to have all his books and mathematical papers out on the table and the sideboard. But my uncle isn't in the house.

"I'll get you some tea, and then explain," says Danish cousin.

Tea arrives. Lapsang souchong, which John once described as 'like drinking a bonfire'.

Danish cousin explains that my uncle is in hospital, having fallen while running for a bus. Running? I do a quick calculation. Uncle is eighty-seven.

We decide that I will drive everyone to the hospital to see him. Musical aunt says that he will be pleased to see us. Tall son and Danish cousin stride through the hospital car park and all the long corridors. I follow behind with musical aunt.

We find mathematical uncle in a small ward. He is also wearing a hand knitted jumper. He is so thin and frail that I almost want to gasp. He takes my hand and tries to speak, but after a few words he stops. The ward buzzes with activity and noise and it distracts him. We all sit around the bed. Danish cousin tells us about hospitals in Denmark.

Tall son and I don't stay long, as my uncle looks tired. "Give your mother my love," says musical aunt, "we were great friends once." We hug. Danish cousin walks back through the corridors with us, and tells us that he will stay as long as he can. But he doesn't know how long that will be.

There is a message on my phone when I get home.

'Hello deary. Dave is having a fight with the Aga today. I hope you are having a good day. If you've won a lot of money, do give me a ring won't you.'

Anna sounds quite bright. And she is making jokes, as she used to do when she was younger. But I don't ring back. When I last saw my uncle he looked tall and fit and well. How can so much change in a few months?

After a few days I ring Danish cousin. He tells me that his father is home and has a bed in the sitting room and a nurse in attendance four times a day.

"I've been out once in three weeks," he tells me, "and that was round the corner to the local supermarket. I just can't leave them."

"Because they are too frail?"

"They both have dementia," he tells me, "both of them. My mother just asks the same questions over and over again. They've had a psychiatric assessment."

I am surprised and sad to hear this.

He tells me that he has spent a long time cleaning and sorting out the house. Getting the boiler serviced. Discovering a gas leak. Things have obviously become difficult. We talk about carers and sitters and nursing homes and costs. And the sort of help that is available to him and his brothers.

Tall son isn't surprised when I tell him. He knew something was seriously wrong with mathematical uncle.

And musical aunt reminded him of Anna.

"It was just like being with her," he tells me.

I agree. Musical aunt had a way of looking at us; a way of walking and talking; an absence. Just like Anna.

Poor Danish cousin. Both parents. A double dementia. I realise how lucky Anna is to have Dave. And how lucky we are too.

AU PAIRS

24th November 2018

. . . .

I haven't been to the cottage for two weeks. Anna and Dave were busy last weekend so I took the opportunity to see another branch of the family. It is hard to imagine Anna and Dave being busy, but in fact they had a party to attend. I had visited the week before, and the invitation was on the mantelpiece above the Aga, propped up amongst the old photos and the early Christmas cards. One of Anna's oldest friends was eighty. It was an all-day event and you were invited to pop in when you wanted, for a drink and nibbles.

There was a certain nervousness in the cottage however.

"I don't think I want to go," said Anna in a quiet voice.

"What am I going to bloody talk about," said Dave, scratching his arms. I think he has eczema, and stress makes it worse.

"Just go for a couple of hours," I suggested. I felt like a parent trying to get my shy child to go on a play date.

"Who's going then?" demanded Dave.

"I don't know do I," said Anna.

"Just have a drink and something to eat. You can plead tiredness after an hour or two."

274

All my life it has been like this. Anna not wanting to go to various social events. Is she shy? No I don't think so. Antisocial? Not at all. In fact once Anna is at an event she is friendly, helpful, welcoming. She seems happy to be there. And as for Dave, well, he likes to go out. He enjoys chatting to people. But he follows Anna's example. The "I don't want to go" example.

If I think of major events in my life, such as my graduation, or my wedding, I think of the stress of keeping Anna happy. Do I have to go? Will there be many people there? Will I know them? What will I say?

John was the opposite. He seemed to love parties, events, people calling at the house. He was a very sociable person. So when the au pairs brought family, friends and boyfriends to the house John seemed delighted. And the more people in the house, the more I learned about life. An au pair's relative who worked on the European Space programme. An au pair's boyfriend who talked to me about music. An au pair's boyfriend who took us all for days out.

Then one day I heard crying coming from the au pair bedroom. I stood outside the door, not sure what to do.

So I knocked very quietly. The tall au pair opened the door. The American au pair was sitting on her bed with her hands over her eyes. I didn't know what to say. I sat on the bed.

"It's alright. She's just a bit upset. She's worried about not being married. About getting too old, you know."

That was curious. The au pairs were twenty-six years old. It didn't seem that old.

American au pair wiped her eyes and blew her nose and put her arm round my shoulders.

"I'm being silly. Don't worry."

But I did think about it. A lot. Perhaps you should be married by the time you reached twenty-six? Would it make you very upset if you weren't?

And then one warm day in the school holidays John came home at lunchtime. Fetch your swimming things, he told us. We rushed upstairs and then down again. Swimming costumes rolled in our towels. My horrible clammy swimming cap which the swimming pool staff said we should wear. There was a young woman in the car, in the front passenger seat, and she came swimming with us.

Not long after that tall au pair told me that they would soon be leaving. I remember I was sitting on her bed when she told me, and I tried to pull the eiderdown over my face so that she wouldn't see how upset I was. Why were they leaving?

"Your father's getting married again," she said.

I remember the au pairs packing their suitcases and leaving. We never saw them again. Not that there was any ill-feeling. Not at all. It was just that nobody thought we might like to see them again. It just wasn't anything that anyone thought about.

Today when I ring the cottage Dave answers the phone.

"Did you enjoy the party?" I ask him.

"Didn't hardly know anyone," he says.

"And Anna?"

"She got a bit tired so we didn't stay long. Stayed a couple of hours and then we came on back and lit the fire. You going to be over later then?"

I assure him that I will be there. Dave is meeting Gordon at one of their favourite pubs. "You can get a bloody good lunch there for six quid," he tells me.

"See you later then. We've missed you," he says.

I laugh. It's only been a fortnight since I saw them. But I'm also pleased. Dave says what he means. He doesn't speak in riddles.

If life has its mysterious and elusive people, then Dave is not one of them.

GRANDMOTHERS

1st December 2018

During the preparations for the wedding John decided that I needed a wedding outfit. I was thirteen and lived in skirts and jumpers. Sensible clothes. I also had a few outfits, cast-offs, that Anna II's mother had brought me from a rich family she worked for. They were tweedy outfits with velvety collars, and I must have looked overdressed in our small town.

John took me to the city to meet rather scary grandmother. She worked part-time in a ladies clothes shop, so she knew what was fashionable. I left the shop with a black and white dress shirt-dress with black patent leather shoes. The wedding photos show a rather self-conscious young teenager, uncomfortable in her smart clothes.

I hardly remember the wedding day except that Shropshire brother and I were fascinated by the lunch menu which included tongue. Tongue of what, we wondered? Needless to say, we didn't eat it.

Today at the cottage, all is well. Dave is meeting Gordon for lunch, and Anna wants me to take her to the garden centre cafe. It's a damp cool day and I touch the radiators in the dining room to make sure the boiler is on.

"It gets so bloody hot I 'ave to watch the telly in a vest sometimes," says Dave.

"And that's not particularly attractive," says Anna.

I just smile. When I was staying with them I offered to get Dave some T-shirts or short-sleeved shirts from the charity shop. But Dave wasn't interested. He likes his vests. If the weather is warm he wears just a vest. Today he is wearing his brushed cotton check shirt. Very smart. And he has a burgundy neckerchief, held in place with a scarf ring.

"Carved it meself I did," he tells me. I look closer. "It's from a deer antler," he says, "Can't wear them polo necks. Not with a short stunted neck like mine." We laugh.

I have brought them a photograph of tall son's graduation, but it's difficult to find a place for it on the mantelpiece above the Aga because of all the other photographs and letters and cards. Anna moves things around to make room.

"Look at our dog Riff," she says, showing me a photograph of two teenage girls on a wide sandy beach. Riff is sitting between Anna and her sister. Everyone is smiling.

"And my mother," says Anna. She takes another photograph from the mantelpiece. A tall slim woman with wavy hair in a linen suit and nice earrings. Anna kisses the photograph. A child-like kiss.

"I miss her," says Anna, to no-one in particular.

The grandmother who lived in the tiny house by the church green, took the bus to the cottage two or three times a week to help Anna with cooking and looking after my younger brothers. She was as much a part of the cottage as the horse brasses and the rattling door latches and the birds on the bank outside. She always wore trousers, flat shoes and long tunics, and her hair was held in place with silvery-white or tortoiseshell combs. And she loved books.

About art and poetry and philosophy in particular. I still have several of them.

Bookish grandmother always had time for us. She taught us to read, to sew, to draw, to enjoy walks in the countryside, and to question what we read, and saw and heard. She looked forward to what exciting things might happen in the future. Things like space travel and cures for illnesses and new technology. She rarely mentioned the past, and if she did, it was usually to tell us something that would make us laugh.

Dave adored her. They talked about gardening, doing-up old houses, opera and country matters.

Anna adored her. Apart from holidays, I think they were rarely apart for more than a few days, and bookish grandmother never lived more than three or four miles away. She was always at the cottage on a Tuesday or a Thursday, or one of our visiting Saturdays. Always cooking or sewing or playing games with us. She was the most steadfast person in our lives. Her presence allowed Anna to look graceful, elegant and unruffled while the four of us children played and fought and made the sort of mess that children make. Sometimes I wished that I could have Anna to myself. And I am sure that my brothers did too. But Anna and my grandmother were as close as any two people could be.

We have a photograph of bookish grandmother sitting in the porch outside the cottage. She is holding onto one of the porch pillars. Not because of her frailty (and she was quite frail at this stage of her life) but because she was laughing. And when bookish grandmother laughed she often fell down and couldn't get up without help. She didn't break anything, and she put that down to her daily spoonful of cod liver oil.

She died over thirty years ago, but I think we all feel that somehow she is still advising Dave on garden plants, or sitting in one of the wheelback chairs in the dining room. Or out in the kitchen making someone a meal. Or playing Snakes and Ladders with Sydney brother in the sitting room.

Or just sitting in the porch looking out over the bank to the fields and the clouds beyond.

DIETS

8th December 2018

· ·

Dave is grumpy today. It's raining. A steady rain that won't let up. The bushes and hedges are heavy and damp in the garden. The lanes are muddy. Dave and Anna are sitting by the Aga with their coffee and the remainder of the Christmas stollen that I had brought on my last visit. Anna wants a glass of wine with hers, but Dave is reluctant.

"Got to save some for Christmas, "he tells her, "and you'll be sippin' wine all day long you will."

Anna gives him a cold look from her armchair.

Is it the rain that's making Dave glum?

In fact there is a list of things.

1. Dave has had no breakfast because he is on a diet.

2. Some people in France have protested about a campaign to get rid of rats in Paris.

3. Dave has read that Jersey Royals are being grown with artificial fertilisers in place of traditional seaweed. And Dave loves potatoes with every meal.

4. Members of Parliament are quitting over Teresa May's Brexit.

5. The neighbour across the fields wants to build a house in his garden. This will spoil Dave's view.

6. Anna has lost thirty pounds from her purse (again).

7. The hair thickener that he bought last week is not showing any signs of thickening his hair.

8. A ticket to a Harold Pinter play in London will cost Shropshire brother ninety pounds. The seat in question is behind a pillar.

9. Dave's car insurance has become more expensive. (So why have two cars?)

10. Anna wants a glass of wine. NOW.

"Dave don't you think it might be better to have a good breakfast, but eat less in the evening," I say.

"Dunno about that."

"Could I have a glass of wine now please Dave?"

"You'll get like my mother, you will," warns Dave, "she couldn't sleep without drinking brandy at bedtime. My sister had to stop Mum off in the end."

"Stop Mum off?"

"Hide the brandy," shouts Dave, banging down his coffee mug.

"And where's my grandson today?" he adds, "we 'aven't seen that boy for weeks!"

"He's got a new girlfriend," I say, "she's from Berkshire."

"Berkshire eh," says Dave, "I took 'er there to Greenham Common once. To the air show. She hid in the bloody car when the planes went over."

Hardly surprising really. Given Anna's childhood experiences.

Dave has finished the stollen. Anna eats slowly, cutting the piece into tiny portions.

"I'm off to see my horrible friends at twelve-thirty," Dave says.

"At the boatyard?"

"Nope. We're meeting at the pub this lunch. All you can eat for six pounds. Bloody good it is. Like a Christmas lunch."

"Do the wives go too?" asks Anna.

"Yep. Most of the wives," says Dave, "Just a few of us bachelors on our own."

Oh dear.

I think I will fetch the soup I've brought from my car.

"You are NOT a bachelor," I hear Anna say. There is frost in her voice.

"Well I won't 'ave no supper tonight then," says Dave, changing the subject. "Cos of the diet."

Outside the rain continues. It doesn't deter the sparrows on the bank however. Or the families out walking their dogs. Water runs down the lane towards the new houses that were once the pub. It's the heavy clay soil in the village that allows that, Dave says.

I think about Dave's diet. Probably too much bread and potatoes and crumpets at the end of the day. He'd better lose that excess weight.

It will be Christmas very soon.

LETTERS

15th December 2018

. . . .

"Someone slept in your bed last night!"

"What?" roars Dave.

"In your bed! There was someone sleeping in it last night!"

Anna looks genuinely concerned.

"What the..." Dave looks baffled.

For a moment or two he is lost for words. Then,

"IT WAS ME!" he roars again, "What the heck's the matter with you today?"

Anna puts on her detached look. "Cup of tea deary?" she says to me.

"Lovely," I say. Glad to change the subject.

"Dave, is that Robbie out on the bank?"

In the flurry of sparrows, pigeons, and Mrs Pheasant I catch a flash of red.

"Yep, he's back," says Dave, "down the sheds, then up here in the bushes. And he remembers me he does. Tame as you like. Eatin' out my hand. And that's Hoppy up 'ere too."

285

I see the rook's profile. He's on the old post. Just watching the other birds.

"Why is he called Hoppy, Dave?"

"Damaged 'is leg 'e did. Lifts it up when 'e perches on the post. I'm not feedin' old Hoppy as well. 'E can get lost."

""But I thought you fed all the birds," I say.

"Oh I feed 'em," says Dave, "but old Hoppy 'e can get worms out the field and look after 'imself. They're witchy, them birds."

Witchy.

I'm cleaning the windows so that Anna can see out across the fields from her armchair by the Aga. Then we will look for the Christmas decorations that I'm sure we stored under her bed last year. Out in the porch there is a driftwood mobile, made by Devon brother and decorated with tiny baubles. And a string of onions. And that's the Christmas decorations so far.

The phone rings and I hand it to Anna. "Yes, hello?... Hello?... Hello? There's no-one there," she says, holding the phone out to me.

"Give it to me," says Dave.

"WHAT!"

He shouts so loudly that Anna and I jump.

"WHAT DO YOU WANT?"

"No-one there…B******S!"

Crikey. That's telling them.

He slams the phone back on the base and stomps off to the kitchen.

"Gettin' all these calls from some company selling something. But I hope it's not one of my old ladies," he shouts.

"Who's that Dave?"

"Two old ladies in the next village that I look after. One of 'em fell over 'er rug yesterday. I 'ad to leave tea and drive down and pick 'er up when the emergency people called me. She's got rugs all over the place. Bloody daft. I told 'er, get rid of them rugs and you'll be alright."

"Was she hurt?"

"Nah. But she could do 'erself a mischief if she keeps them rugs there. I put 'er on the sofa and made 'er a cup of tea though. I'll take 'er some chocolates over. She's eighty-eight. Other one's ninety-two."

Anna sighs.

"You ordered the turkey then?" Dave asks me as he fills his coffee cup from the Aga kettle. "I hope it's free-range."

"Yes it's free range. Should be enough for all of us, with some left over for sandwiches."

"You'd better get two of 'em then," says Dave, heading to the front door to pick up the post.

Two turkeys?

"I don't think my oven's big enough Dave," I tell him.

"Hmmmmmm," says Dave.

Several Christmas cards. At least three of them are pictures of robins.

"I like them," says Anna, running her finger over the pictures.

"What's these letters here then," says Dave. There is a small pile of handwritten letters on the round table.

"I think they came yesterday," says Anna, "but I haven't read them yet."

She sits down and unfolds one of them.

"I am so sorry for your loss. I am thinking of you." She reads slowly, peering at the letter, turning it over and over. "Who is this from? What are they talking about?"

"We were very fond of her, it says. Who?" She hands me the letter. "The name looks like Kathy. In Birmingham. Do you remember her deary?"

"Kathy? No," I say, "I didn't live in Birmingham."

"Well, you said it's nearly Christmas. So why has she sent me such a sad letter."

I look at the date. It's nineteen eighty-six. Thirty two years ago. Thirty two years old.

"Anna," I say, "it's a very old letter. From Birmingham. Nineteen eighty six."

"Oh," says Anna. I can see from her face that she remembers the year that my grandmother died.

"Silly me," she says to herself, "they were under my bed."

"Well let's go and look for the Christmas decorations," I say. "I'll just finish the windows, while you drink your coffee."

Dave has been using the leaf blower and the windows are mud-splattered. It's cold outside. But at least the sun is shining and the air is still. Dave is crumbling bread crusts for his birds.

I can see Anna through the window. She is sitting in her armchair with the pile of letters in her lap. She reads them very slowly. Then she stops and stares for a long time at nothing in particular. I tap on the window and wave, and she waves back.

"I dunno what's she's thinkin' about," says Dave behind me. "If she's thinkin' about anything at all. Sometimes I wonder."

I soon find the Christmas decorations in two carrier bags under Anna's bed. The bags look like the mice have been nibbling them. There's a long string of plastic ivy, various red and green and gold baubles, golden fir cones, and a small wooden Christmas tree. Anna is delighted with the colours. I wind the ivy around the jars and bottles on the mantelpiece above the wood-burner in the sitting room. Anna dots the baubles and fir cones amongst the ivy. The little Christmas tree with the gold decorations sits next to the television.

Anna and Dave have not had a full size Christmas tree for many years. When we were children John would buy a real tree and my grandmother helped us to decorate it with home-made paper lanterns, and dots of cotton wool, to look like snow. In the last ten years or so Anna has preferred to just decorate the fireplace in the sitting room with the ivy and the baubles.

"That's better deary," says Anna, when we have finished. "Very nice. Shall we have a glass of wine then?"

The letters with their sad messages are forgotten for now. It's time to enjoy the days before Christmas.

MEN IN JUMPERS

16th December 2018

. . . .

Mathematical uncle is sitting in a wooden armchair, with what looks like an old Army blanket over his lap. I ask him how he is feeling. Am I interrupting his television programme? He takes my hand and holds tightly. Anxiously.

"No, I'm not..." he manages to say. But then falls quiet. Musical aunt and Danish cousin join us with a tray of coffee. The room is very warm. Mathematical uncle is wearing a thick wool jumper that my aunt must have knitted.

"We keep the fire on all the time," says Danish cousin. He and his mother sit on the old sofa facing us. "Dad sleeps down here now." He points to a single bed under the window on the other side of the room. A pressure relief mattress in a plastic wrapper is propped against the wall.

"They've just brought it," says Danish cousin.

"Who are all these people coming and going?" says musical aunt, "I don't need all these people in my house."

Danish cousin pours the coffee. It is very strong. I admire the little Christmas tree by the television.

"We've had the tree lights for so many years," says musical aunt. You can tell from looking at them because they are strangely pure and clear, unlike modern LEDs.

Danish cousin is telling me about a dentist in Hanoi who explained that the roots of my cousin's teeth revealed his Viking ancestry. I tell him that medical daughter was given an Ancestry kit which revealed some Scandinavian heritage.

Musical aunt is listening, but I think without understanding. Mathematical uncle is falling asleep. His hand lets go of mine, and his eyes close.

"My parents are going to my brother in Bristol for Christmas," says Danish cousin. He speaks very slowly and thoughtfully. But that's good. It will be a nice break.

Musical aunt looks pleased. "It's lovely there," she says.

"And then we must think about carers," says Danish cousin.

Musical aunt gives him a look that reminds me of Anna.

Medical daughter arrives the next day and we drive out to the cottage. It has been raining for several days now. Dave has forgotten that we are coming and left his old car on the drive. So I will have to park in the mud down by the sheds.

"I'm not eating. Not hungry," says Dave when I ask. Presumably still on the diet.

Anna wants something light. Mushrooms on toast?

"Lovely deary."

Medical daughter brings piles of fashion catalogues from the sitting room and sits beside her grandmother as they look through them.

"Have you tried them shit ache mushrooms?" says Dave.

"Those what dear?" says Anna, peering at him.

"Shiitake Dave," says medical daughter.

"Yeah whatever," says Dave who is looking for the frying pan. "I fancy a fried egg sandwich now."

That's good for the diet.

The dining room is soon filled with the haze of fried eggs. Anna and medical daughter are laughing at something. I'm trying to get the Aga door open to reach the macaroni cheese. It's barely cooked of course, but I really don't want to struggle through the long cupboard in search of mini oven.

"Are you coming here for Christmas?" says Anna anxiously, "I haven't got anything ready at all."

I reassure her that Shropshire brother is bringing them both to my house for Christmas lunch. Anna smiles with relief.

"It's amazing to think that Anna still makes jokes," says medical daughter on the way home, "and so clever."

"What did she say?"

"We were looking through her favourite catalogue. You know, the one with the long skirts and coats. And then we got to the end and it was all the men's clothes. So I said to her, we don't want to look at all the men's stuff do we? Although I do like looking at men in jumpers. And do you know what she said?"

What?"

"She said, yes, men in jumpers is better than meningitis! And she laughed!"

And we laugh now. Pleased that Anna is better in mind and body than last year. That she recognised medical daughter and enjoyed her company. That she is aware of Christmas coming.

We drive on through the darkness. A light rain on the windscreen. Clouds illuminated by the moon. My coat too heavy for the mild weather.

Christmas weather.

QUIET DAYS

26th December 2018

· ·

These are the quiet days between Christmas and the New Year. Mild, damp, muddy. Just like last year.

Christmas spread itself over several days as visitors came and went. On Christmas morning I hurried about the house getting everything ready for Anna and Dave's arrival. Should I tape over the bathroom door lock? I must remember to remove the rug from the bathroom floor. Have I got enough roast potatoes and sprouts to keep Dave happy? Anna won't eat Christmas pudding, so whereabouts in the freezer did I put the creme brûlée?

They arrive with Shropshire brother who has brought red wine and chocolate truffles. Anna and Dave sit quietly on the sofa while Shropshire brother and tall son open the wine. Red wine for us and Prosecco for Anna. Dave is strangely quiet.

"What's up Dave?" says tall son.

"Bunged up," says Dave miserably. He is definitely rather pale. "Can't eat much, so don't give me much."

"He had a massive bowl of porridge this morning though," says Shropshire brother.

Oh dear.

"We've got several vegetables with the turkey," I say, "and that might help. Are you drinking plenty of water?"

"Nope," says Dave.

"What about exercise?" says tall son, "walking would help."

"Nope," says Dave.

"Well we're off for a quick walk," says Shropshire brother looking at tall son. They hurry to the front door before I can object. This is not unusual. I put on the television for Anna and Dave while I tend to the vegetables. Carols from Kings College, Cambridge. I refill their wine glasses but notice that Anna is quietly crying. It's the carols.

"I'm sorry," she says sadly.

I change channels and Anna and Dave are soon engrossed in a wildlife programme.

The men return as I am cooking the gravy. They look sheepish.

"You've been to the pub I think."

"Just a quick one."

Dave eats well despite his internal difficulties. Anna toys with the turkey and vegetables. She wants to know where the rest of the family are.

Medical daughter is having Christmas with her boyfriend and his family. Eldest and middle grandsons are in Devon. Youngest grandson is in Australia with Sydney brother and his family. Apparently it is very hot there. Devon brother and Alis are driving up for Boxing Day with their dogs. Anna is happy. And she eats all the creme brûlée. Much to tall son's disappointment.

Boxing Day sees me loading the car with more food for a family lunch. We drive over to the cottage and Dave is in the garden looking like a different man.

"Found some medication in an old box. Took that. Hey presto!"

Anna is pleased to see us, but seems to have forgotten our Christmas meal yesterday. I unhook the cast iron frying pan for the bubble and squeak and put chipolatas and sticky toffee pudding in the Aga.

"Yep. It worked a treat," says Dave with his hands full of firewood, "it were explosive. Had to leap out of bed with alacrity."

"And who is alacrity?" says Anna haughtily. She really does have the hearing of a bat. But Dave is preparing the fire in the wood-burning stove.

"Are these yours deary?" says Anna holding up a very large pair of faded, holey Y-fronts. Tall son looks slightly shocked. "They're nearly dry deary."

She drapes them back over the Aga kettle.

"Time to eat," I say, trying to get the chipolatas out of the Aga. Something else is on this oven shelf as well. I wish I could remember to bring some oven gloves with me. Anna and Dave just use an old tea towel.

"Whatever's this?" I say as I pull out an old metal plate holding a pile of charcoal.

"What's that deary?" says Anna.

"It's your bloody fishcake!" explodes Dave behind me.

"Crumbs, how long has it been in the Aga?" says tall son.

"Since two bloody days ago," yells Dave, "I said fifteen minutes. Why don't you look at the bloody clock and take it out the oven?"

"Dave that's ridiculous," I say, "you need to be in charge of the timing. Or get an oven timer. You can't expect Anna to time the cooking can you?"

Anna is about to argue back. Dave gets grumpy in the winter. Stuck in the cottage too long. He likes to be out in the garden. And he doesn't like having to take charge of the meals. The atmosphere is darkening a little. Tall son looks at his mobile phone. I don't like getting cross with Dave. But sometimes he just doesn't think.

And then there's a shout and a scrabbling at the front door. Two Lakeland terriers rush in. Closely followed by Devon brother with wild hair, and Alis.

"There you are!" says Anna happily. Dave smiles. Burnt fishcake forgotten for now.

Time to celebrate the family.

NEW YEAR

5th January 2019

. . . .

There seems to be an argument going on in the garden today. Dave is busy filling the corn bin, but Anna is in the porch looking worried.

"Dave you have to take me to my doctor's appointment today!"

"It's not today!" shouts Dave, "Today's Saturday."

"Are you OK Anna?" She greets me with a kiss. "Yes deary, I can't drive any more because I haven't got my licence, so Dave has to take me to the doctor."

"But I took 'er sample down to the doctor yesterday," says Dave. He walks towards us and kicks the garden hose reel out of his way. "Doctor said we can ring in a couple of days. So I've told 'er to wait for that."

We go inside. Anna's coffee is getting cold on the round table, so I top it up with some hot water from the Aga kettle.

"Are you feeling OK," I ask her again.

"Yes deary, you know, the doctor is just doing her checks I think."

"Waterworks," says Dave helpfully.

"I thought you were seeing the consultant at the hospital in January though."

"Well I haven't heard from him."

Dave limps over to the mantelpiece where he keeps a stack of letters in their envelopes. He opens the top one slowly. "Here it is. Says they'll be sending an appointment in the New Year."

"So you need to wait a bit Anna and then you'll get an appointment in the New Year," I say.

"Well she kept on wanting to see the doc so I 'ad to take 'er down didn't I," says Dave.

"And what did the doctor say Dave?"

Dave looks blank, "Dunno."

"Oh so you didn't go in with her then?"

Anna looks disgusted. "Of course not!"

"So you don't feel ill or in pain Anna?"

I am struggling to work this out.

"No deary."

"But you didn't want to wait until you heard from the consultant?"

"Well he hasn't sent me an appointment has he."

I can see that this conversation is running out of steam. Anna is expecting an appointment with a hospital consultant, but she hasn't received one yet. That is because it is still December and not the New Year. So she has insisted that Dave takes her to see her GP. And that is because neither Anna or Dave really understands the difference between seeing a GP and seeing a hospital consultant.

"Would you like me to ring his secretary and see when you are likely to get an appointment?" I ask.

"No deary, I'll ring my doctor on Monday and make an appointment," says Anna, "she's a very nice lady."

Ah. So we are not waiting for the hospital appointment then.

"I'm off to see Gordon then," says Dave, "where's my keys?"

"Don't you want a coat Dave?" says Anna.

"When it's winter I'll 'ave one," says Dave on his way out.

Winter? It's January now.

Anna wants to have lunch at the garden centre, but when we arrive the doors are closed. A sign tells us it will open again in the New Year.

"We'll try the other garden centre," I say.

But everyone has had the same idea. The cafe tables are full. And there's a queue. I tell Anna that I will buy some soup and sourdough bread at the little supermarket on the estate. Anna seems quite happy with this. More interested in the crowds of people at the garden centre, and the car park full of cars.

"Isn't everywhere busy deary."

Dave isn't back until nearly four o'clock and I have looked at all the new catalogues and made Anna at least three cups of tea. The sky is begin to darken and from the sitting room window I watch the gathering of rooks on the telegraph poles across the fields. What was it Dave said last year? That they were meeting for a chat?

Then I see Dave limping past the sitting room window.

"I'm back," he yells as he opens the front door.

"Cup of tea Dave?" says Anna.

While he drinks his tea (strong and with a sweetener) Dave tells us about his day.

"I've bin to see old Charlie," he tells us.

"I thought you were having lunch with Gordon at the pub?" says Anna.

"Yep I did that. And then I went to see old Charlie cos 'e's not got long."

"What's the matter with him Dave?"

"His heart," says Dave, "and they can't do no more. So e's not got long. That's why I went to see Charlie."

"That's sad Dave," I say.

"Yep," says Dave, "all my friends are going." He struggles to his feet, heading off to the sitting room. "Let's see what's on the telly then."

"What's happenin' with that stick thing I'm waitin' for?" he shouts from the sitting room.

I tell him that tall son has got the Fire Stick and will be over to show Dave how to use it. Then Dave can watch Netflix to his heart's content.

Dave looks pleased.

"I'm a lucky man to 'ave such a great family," I hear him say as I find my coat in the long cupboard and head out to my car in the fading light.

THE VILLAGE

12th January 2019

. . . .

In the village people greet you, whether they know you or not.

At the shop tucked behind the village hall, where you can enjoy a coffee at one of the cafe tables with a piece of Maggie's lemon drizzle cake or a chocolate brownie. Or in summer outside the shop, looking over the recreation ground and the children's play area. People greet you as you walk up the lane to the telephone box library. Or on the walk we call 'round the church' pausing at the pond to watch the ducks and moorhens. Or further afield. Around the manor. Passing the old farmsteads that have been here for centuries. The old workers' cottages. And then the mixture of modern housing that has grown up since the end of the war. Or walking up Coffin Lane to catch the views from the top. And to watch the clouds.

Village life. The main road through the village simply leads on to other villages. It's rarely busy. You could drive through and see maybe two or three people walking to the allotments, exercising their dogs or riding ponies. And no-one else.

I read the monthly 'Village News' while staying at the cottage. Chris, Ian, Val, Judy and others run the village association.

The Chairman writes about the close-knit community, the Beer Festival, the Flower Show and the School Fair. The Editor calls for villagers' comments for a new letters page.

There's a churchyard upset, when the grave digger accidentally tipped rubble over an area of grass seed. A black and white photograph of elderly residents on a trip to the coast. Floral skirts, sunhats and walking sticks. News from cross-cultural friendships in Tanzania. Advertisements for pet portraits, get-togethers for village grandparents, the social club, the chimney sweep, seasoned hardwood logs and pilates classes.

Anna chooses not to join in with the village community. Perhaps she walked my younger brothers to school and back. Although I seem to remember them climbing over the stile and running across the fields with their school bags. She certainly visited the village shops on a daily basis. And at one time there were three such shops. She enjoyed taking us to the annual village fair. And she befriended some of the residents in the lane. But mainly Anna walked through the village. Her exercise. Sometimes twice a day with the dog. And greeted the other villagers on her walks, as they greeted her.

Dave, having grown up in the area, knows everyone. Their names, their nicknames, their parents' names. What they did in their youth, and what they didn't do. Dave would fix things for local people. Cars, engines, lawnmowers. And look after their gardens while they were on holiday. And feed their pets. Dave and his family have been in the area for so long that they can remember the thatched cottage across the lane selling for eighty-nine pounds. That was after the roof had collapsed. Dave can remember the lanes in the village being just gravel tracks.

"I remember the gravel tracks cos' I used to ride round on the milk van.

I'd jump off the back and take the milk bottles to the front doors. I did that every afternoon after school to make a bob or two," he tells me.

I don't believe Dave would have been happy living anywhere else. Perhaps by the sea? Who knows. He has always done the lottery to see if he can win a fortune.

"I'd 'ave an Aston Martin, a fleet of classic cars and a powerboat," he tells me.

And that's after he has given us all enough money to buy something nice.

"Get you that cottage in the country," he tells me.

Would I want to live in the country again?

Where nothing much happens. Where you need a car to get to work. Or the supermarket. Or the high street shops. Or a nice restaurant. Where you're stranded if it snows. Where everyone knows who you are. Where you can walk for miles and see nobody. Where you are always aware of the weather. The trees. The wildlife. The changes of the seasons.

The thing is, I suspect it may be different places for different ages.

SLEEP

19th January 2019

· ·

Shropshire brother rings me on his way home.

"I've been at the cottage. Just stayed the night after a race meeting. Anna seems very tired and not herself, and I think even Dave's worried."

I ring them. Anna answers.

"Just not quite right deary. Just tired I think."

"She's been sleeping on the sofa," says Dave in the background, "and getting up in the middle of the bloody night."

I tell them I will be there in the morning. I tell them if Dave is worried he must ring me at any time.

The weather is frostily cold. Hunting cat treads delicately through the grass by the allotments. At the cottage I hurry inside, but glimpse Robbie perched on cherub's head on the bank. Anna bought the little stone statue at the garden centre and it has sat on the bank for many years.

Dave is in the sitting room sorting out the Saturday newspapers. Anna is in her armchair by the Aga.

"Hi Dave!" I call, and give Anna a quick hug. She is shaking a little.

"Are you alright Anna?"

"No deary," she says, her voice breaking, "I've had a bad experience."

"What happened?"

"Dave was out... and I looked out of my bedroom window, and you know the stone seat..." Her voice falters.

"Yes, under the tulip tree..."

"There was a man... a man sitting there. Smartly dressed, and... well, I thought it must be important, so I came downstairs..."

"And what happened?"

"I went outside, and I went down the garden and... and I asked him if I could help and..."

I wait. The grandfather clock ticks. And the wall clock ticks. And Mr Pheasant calls from the bank outside.

"He... he turned his head away."

"He said nothing?"

She looks down and wipes her eyes with a tissue, "Nothing."

Dave comes out of the sitting room. He winks at me and shakes his head. His expression says, 'That was a hallucination'.

"Are my birds looking for their breakfast?" says Dave, looking out of the dining room window.

" I think I heard Mr Pheasant just now," I say, "but I haven't seen any of the females."

"They get up late," says Dave, "and that's why they miss breakfast. Sleeping too late they are."

Outside Robbie hops from the fence to the pots on the bank and on to the ground.

"I heard your pheasant calling, Dave," says Anna. Perhaps two minutes have passed since she told me about the man on the stone seat, but already the memory has gone. The fear has gone from her face. Now she is thinking about pheasants.

"Let's give them some corn," I say to Dave.

When we are outside I ask him about Anna.

"She didn't see no man," says Dave impatiently. "I found 'er outside in the porch when I got back from the shop. She's just lost the plot. Doctor's given 'er some tablets, but she won't take 'em."

Back in the dining room I ask Anna about the tablets. She looks confused so Dave fetches a small blister pack from the kitchen. Trimethoprim. A urine infection? The pack is unopened and five days old.

"These are antibiotics," I say, "so I think the doctor wants you to take them Anna."

"Ok," says Anna, "I need a glass of water though."

So no problem then. I'm not sure why Dave couldn't have done this.

Anna doesn't want to go out for lunch today so I make cheese on toast with chicken soup, and after we've eaten I bring her the colour supplement to look at while I check my emails.

But now she is full of questions.

"Do you see anything of your friend... um... I can't remember her name."

"Are you still in the Brownies deary?"

"Do you miss school these days?"

And a whole list of people whose names I don't recognise. I think they are friends and neighbours from Birmingham, which would be from the time when Anna was at primary school. I try to answer her questions.

"Um.. the friend I used to work with. Yes, we meet up and have a coffee sometimes."

"Not in the Brownies now… no…"

"No, don't miss school. I've been working for quite a while now."

But it gets tiring.

Neither the radio, nor the television, nor any of the catalogues distracts Anna from her questions. Often the same question, over and over.

"Do you want a hot water bottle deary?"

Then she falls asleep by the fire. I haven't seen her as sleepy and confused as this for several months. It's puzzling. Dave says he is not giving her sleeping tablets or anti-depressants. So it must be the infection. I must remind Dave to give her the antibiotics.

Or perhaps this is just how things are now.

She wakes when I lift the latch of the sitting room door.

"I need to visit the bathroom deary."

She puts aside her thin blue blanket (where did the green fluffy blanket go?) and gets slowly to her feet. One shoe is sliding sideways from her foot. Why does she insist on fairy shoes?

She climbs slowly up the stairs, holding on to both handrails.

"As Anna was walking up the stair..."

Anna turns and smiles.

She remembers the next line.

SNOWDROPS

24th January 2019

. . . .

A few days ago it was my birthday. Unfortunately I was working. I came downstairs to make some coffee and of course it was too early for the post, but there was an envelope pushed through the door. Hand delivered. I took it into the kitchen, put on the kettle and opened it. An invitation. For drinks and nibbles. At the brand new care home across the road.

Ah.

Well that certainly makes me feel my age.

And today. Well I have the day off as my car needs an MOT and I'm taking it to the garage near the cottage. Dave knows the owner and always takes his cars there. I rang Dave yesterday and asked him if he'd meet me there this morning.

"Course I will." The delight in his voice was palpable. I realised Dave stills needs to be needed. As far as engines, fishing, cars, shooting, tractors and chopping logs goes.

Dave is waiting on the forecourt when I arrive. He points to the ramps in the workshop, indicating I should drive in, but Harry comes out and points to a parking space instead.

"Leave the keys in the car," says Dave as I wind down the window, "You can go and 'ave a chat with Anna if you like."

310

"Where is she?"

"In the car," says Dave, "she made a fuss when I went to leave." He turns to talk to Harry about engines.

It's so cold today. I'm wearing two layers under my padded coat, with a woolly hat and fur boots. And also gloves. Anna is in the passenger seat of the old VW Polo. The inside of the car looks like a deserted building site. Anna is wearing a cotton polo-neck jumper and waistcoat and one of her long skirts.

I open the car door door. "Anna, let's get you inside out of the cold."

"All right deary," she says, reaching for my arm.

We walk slowly from the forecourt to the waiting room.

"Where's your coat?" I ask, as gently as I can.

"Er... I put a warm jumper on instead. Although it's not my jumper. I don't know whose it is."

The receptionist brings us a coffee. We watch the progress of my car on a monitor above our heads.

"Is that your car deary?"

Anna asks me this several times. Dave paces between the workshop and the waiting room. No doubt calling out instructions to Harry. Who appears not to be listening. The receptionist brings Dave a coffee and invites him to sit down.

Once the certificate is ready, Dave wants to buy me lunch. I haven't mentioned my birthday, and neither have they, but I think Dave had decided on lunch beforehand, and can't quite remember why.

We can sit by the wood-burning stove at the garden centre. There is soup on the menu. Anna is happy. And Dave can have a full English breakfast. So he is happy too.

"I 'ad porridge this morning, but I like a proper breakfast when I come 'ere." he tells us.

"And it's easy to park," says Anna.

The smile disappears from Dave's face.

"Bloody parking in town yesterday. Can't bloody park anywhere. Dunno why they want to do up the market place. All closed off it is. Bloody nightmare."

Anna nods in agreement.

"And I got a bloody parking ticket yesterday. Just went in the shop for ten minutes and forgot to open the blasted Blue Badge. It was on the windscreen shelf though."

"Could the parking warden see the badge though?" I say.

"Course 'e could see it. It was on the shelf. I come out the shop and I could see the warden chattin' away to 'er."

Anna sips her parsnip soup and says nothing.

"Course off 'e goes before I can get there. She didn't open the bloody Blue Badge did she?"

"He was very nice though deary," says Anna calmly, "we had a very nice chat."

Dave looks thunderous.

"Would anyone like some chocolate brownie?" I say.

"Yes deary," says Anna.

When I return to the table by the wood-burner they are discussing wartime bomb craters, so things have obviously calmed down. And Anna and Dave love chocolate brownies with a flat white coffee.

I give Anna a lift back to the cottage while Dave takes his own car.

"I'm sorry you had to wait at the garage this morning Anna," I say, "it was a bit too cold wasn't it. Dave says you didn't want to stay at home on your own."

"Oh I'm alright deary, Dave was just fussing you know."

As ever, Anna prefers to dismiss any difficulties.

"It would probably have been better if you'd had a sitter with you maybe. So you wouldn't have had to come out in the cold?"

Silence.

"Worth thinking about maybe? For next time?"

"Oh don't worry about me deary. You've got enough to think about. Dave doesn't mind driving me about you know. Look at all those birds up there!"

I look up to the telegraph wires that cross the main road from the pub to the field opposite. A dark line of rooks has gathered on them, huddled and a little chilled.

"They look cold don't they," says Anna.

And at the sides of the road, where hedge joins verge I see the little clumps of snowdrops.

Heads bowed, trembling slightly in the breeze.

But resolute.

HOLIDAYS

2nd February 2019

. . . .

Things are a little better. Danish cousin tells me that Christmas in Bristol with his brother was a success. Mathematical uncle is slowly getting back on his feet, and managing walks around the block. Apparently he's not talkative any more, and that seems strange. Mathematical uncle liked to talk. In the greatest of detail on most topics.

Danish cousin says that his parents now enjoy going out, and seem more alert, more aware when they are away from home. He thinks they are probably getting bored now. So he's hired a car. And all he needs is some destinations. We set a date when he will bring them to my house for lunch.

Anna too is a little better. More alert. Not sleeping so much during the day. Dave seems pleased to see me this morning.

"Don't reckon I want to go out for lunch."

"But isn't Gordon expecting you?"

"I was goin' to 'ave a nice chat with you," he says.

And chat he does. All about holidays he has had with Anna over the years. In Devon and Cornwall, Wales and Cheshire, the Lake District and Yorkshire. And in later years Croatia and Australia.

I realise that he hasn't been able to have a real conversation with Anna for a long time. He has all these words stored up, waiting for a visitor to the cottage.

"Can't believe 'ow many miles we used to walk. Walked for hours we did," he tells me.

"Couldn't live in Australia though," he says, "all them spiky trees. Couldn't put up with that."

"Couldn't live up north either. Too cold."

But the weather is very cold here today. Despite the central heating, Anna keeps elegant blue blanket on her lap and sits by the Aga. She heats a neck warmer in the bottom Aga oven and then drapes it over her fairy shoes. Dave and I offer to bring down her fur boots from her wardrobe, but she declines. When I look for them under her bed (just to make sure she hasn't thrown them out) I find she is keeping her alarm clock and watch in them. For some reason.

Mr Pheasant paces up and down the bank restlessly. I relent and throw him a handful of corn from the corn bin. Robbie joins him. And then a squirrel edges carefully along the bank. Watching and listening. Like a cartoon detective.

Dave has moved on to a new topic.

"I love waistcoats. Got three of 'em. Don't wear them so much now though 'cos we don't go out anywhere special. "

I remember they went out for a meal at least once a week. Usually to a pub where Anna could eat soup and a nice pudding, and Dave could have a hearty meal. And the beer was good. And the landlord friendly.

"Shirts of course. I love shirts."

Yes, that's true. Dave certainly has plenty of shirts. Sometimes ordered from the catalogues that lie around in the dining room and sitting room. Sometimes from the expensive shops in the nearby market town.

I listen to Dave talking about shirts. Anna sits quietly, watching Mr Pheasant on the bank, now joined by several females.

"Course when you lot were young I couldn't really afford that many nice shirts."

That's also true. I wasn't really aware of the lack of money at the cottage. I knew that often Dave worked very long hours, driving the diggers that constructed the A-roads and motorways and bridges. Sometimes a long way from home. If I look at photographs from the albums in the big kitchen drawers I can see that my younger brothers wore old clothes, probably from the charity shop where my grandmother volunteered. But at the time I was busy growing up and still puzzling about the strangeness of my childhood.

Because after the wedding, John's house was unusually quiet. The au pairs had gone, with their friends and families. Shropshire brother and I went to school, did our homework, saw our friends. He played football. I played hockey. We went to the cottage on Tuesdays, Thursdays, and alternate Saturdays. Then I went to a schoolfriend's birthday party and met my first boyfriend. He was from London and was boarding at a nearby school. Anna said he could come for tea at the cottage, and she drove me into town so that we could meet. Or to schoolfriend's parties.

But John was furious when he found out. I was never sure why.

So one afternoon I packed my belongings into two carrier bags, rang Anna, and went to the cottage. By now I was at sixth form college, and had to get a lift to the bus station in the local plumber's van each morning.

After a while I went to live with bookish grandmother in the local town. I could take the bus to college, and the train to London at the weekends to stay with my boyfriend's family.

Life at the cottage continued as it always had. But I had found somewhere new. A world away from everything I had known before.

UNDER THE WEATHER

9th February 2019

. . . .

I wasn't sure I could get to the cottage today. Snow fell heavily yesterday and the ground had frozen. It was difficult to get my car out on to the main road, but after a while I realised it was the same as last year. Being slightly further north I had experienced more snow than Anna and Dave. The journey was not as difficult as I had feared.

And now the village sparkles in bright sunshine. There is a dusting of snow across the recreation ground. People are out walking, enjoying the sun's warmth. Dave is up at the shop getting the newspaper and Anna answers the door looking worried.

We make some coffee and she tells me that she fell in the night.

"On the landing deary. I wasn't hurt, just shaken."

"Did Dave hear you? Did he help you up?"

Dave takes his hearing aids out at night, so hears almost nothing unless you shout at him. The occupational therapists tried to persuade him to have an alarm that vibrated to wake him, but he was having none of that.

"Oh yes dear, he helped me up."

The door opens and Dave comes in with a pile of newspapers and a carton of milk.

"Coffee deary?"

"Yep and one sweetener," says Dave. As if we didn't know by now.

Dave sits down heavily in the chair by the window.

"Don't feel right," he tells me. "Don't want to eat. Feel nauseous."

"Oh dear, and I hear Anna had a fall in the night."

Dave looks blank. "Nope. She's been down 'ere all night." He points to the armchair by the Aga. "Won't get to bed when I tell 'er. I come downstairs and she's sitting 'ere with cups of tea everywhere."

"Don't be ridiculous." says Anna.

"I'm not being bloody ridiculous. You're up half the night."

"Anna how about going to bed when Dave says it's the right time, and then staying in bed while it's dark outside."

"I do," she says coldly.

"No you bloody don't!" Dave is getting heated.

"Dave it's ok," I say, trying to calm the situation, "Anna, Dave is your carer and he's just trying to do his best for you. He's concerned that you might fall in the night. He'd sleep better if he knew you were in bed and not downstairs on your own."

Anna looks at me as if I am mad. "I AM in bed!" she says, her eyes narrowing.' "Just keep out of this!"

This is the Anna I remember from my teens. You didn't argue with her.

"I'm goin' to read the paper," says Dave getting to his feet and heading off to the sitting room.

We sit for a while in silence, thinking. The Aga kettle softly hisses and steams in the background. Out in the fields the snow lies in clumps. A blackbird hurries under the bushes on the bank. Then the telephone rings. It is Shropshire brother and after he's spoken to them the mood in the cottage lifts. Dave tells him with delight that eldest grandson has rung the cottage to check they are alright in the snowy weather. Youngest grandson is returning from a long visit to Australia. And Shropshire brother tells Dave he has had a recent trip to London to see middle grandson.

The sun is beginning to feel warm through the windows. I decide to make some egg sandwiches for lunch.

"Nice to hear from him wasn't it?" I say, as I take the phone from Anna.

"Yes deary," she says (argument forgotten), "did I tell you he's got a prolapse?"

I can't help laughing. No that is certainly not the case. But I don't tell her so.

"Egg sandwich Dave?"

"No can't eat nothing."

Dave is sitting on the sofa. In Anna's seat. Not in his armchair. That is odd.

"I'm goin' to chop some firewood. Need to light the fire."

I offer to get some wood from the sheds, but Dave says it needs chopping. He is not going to let me use the axe. When he returns from the sheds I put the firewood in the wood-burner, and light the newspaper. The fire bursts into life. But Dave is back on the sofa.

"Don't want any bread and cheese. Or any pickled onions. Don't even want a cup of tea."

I realise that Dave measures the gravity of illness, not by the symptoms he experiences, but by the foods that he doesn't want to eat.

I bring more logs in from the stack in the porch. It is icily cold and the air is still. I count seven female pheasants at the edge of the field, and throw them a handful of corn.

Then I bring Anna a plate of tiny egg sandwiches and a glass of red wine, and explain that I will have to drive home after lunch as I think there may be more snow coming. I don't tell her that I am worried about the road over the chalk ridge that can be difficult to get through in the snow.

I wash up and clean the teaspoons in the pot on the draining board. That never get cleaned otherwise. I wake Dave (still on the sofa) and tell him that I will ring them later in the evening, and that he must ring me if he feels any worse.

"Reckon' I just got some stomach bug," he tells me.

I leave them there, in the sitting room, by the fire. Dave is still in the old jacket he wore down to the sheds. Anna sits next to him, her glass of wine on the little oak stool. Pale-faced Monkey on the arm of the sofa. I don't think she realises that Dave doesn't feel well. That he probably isn't getting enough sleep with her wandering around in the night. That he is eighty-eight this autumn. That he isn't getting any younger.

But as I unlock my car I turn and take a final look through the sitting room window. The fire flickers and dances. Dave is asleep with his mouth slightly open. Snoring no doubt.

And Anna is holding his hand.

BLACKBIRD

16th February 2019

· ·

"Is that a blackbird Dave?"

The clear piercing song fills the garden this morning at the cottage.

"Early aren't they," says Dave, "but they like to sing after rain."

And we've had plenty of rain. The main roads were flooded in places, the grass verges dripped and the sky, although blue in patches, was grey and cloudy. I remember my late brother-in-law telling me that the reason he left England for Australia was our grey skies. They don't particularly bother me; I just appreciate the blue skies more when we get them. And I've already been walking. Through the village and past the turning to the pond and the old church; past the footpath that follows the Monarch's Way and the old chalkpit cottages on the very edge of the village. Then Coffin Lane, the narrow track with its high banks, the path worn down by centuries of horses and carts and walkers.

And up to the top where Shropshire brother recently took a rare photograph of us all. With the exception of Anna and Dave, whose walks up Coffin Lane are a distant memory.

When I get back Dave is talking to Anna about his forthcoming trip to France. But Anna is asleep in the armchair by the Aga.

"Dave, get some coffee going," says Anna sleepily as I shut the front door.

"You look very smart Dave," I tell him. He is wearing a striped shirt and navy waistcoat.

"Thought I'd make an effort for my little friends today," he says, "tho' we're only goin' up the usual pub. Don't reckon Chris'll be there though. E's got wife problems."

"What's that?" says Anna.

"She wants 'im doin' up that house they've bought, so she can 'ave a studio."

"A what?"

"A studio for 'er pots."

"She makes pots?" I ask.

"Yep. Costs 'im a bloody fortune. Always spending 'is money e' is."

He shakes his head, "No good marryin' a woman with artistic thoughts."

Hmmm.

"Came down last night. She 'ad all the damn lights on again," says Dave changing the subject.

"What time was this?"

"'Bout four in the mornin'"

"Well you've got LED's so don't worry too much." (Shropshire brother has told Dave this already. Many times.)

"Not natural though is it. Down 'ere in the night. Drinkin' all that tea. Eatin' toast. Cups and plates everywhere."

"Well Anna's got her emergency bracelet hasn't she. So she can press the button on that if she falls and you don't hear her. And you've got good neighbours. If Anna falls you can call them for help."

Dave ponders this for a moment or two. "Yep, better neighbours than we used to 'ave. That old roué. 'E was a one. Always fondlin' the lodger..."

What?

"They're nice enough now though. Them doctors over the road, they're alright. Very nice. Dog's got a flat nose though."

Right.

"Are you going to see some pretty ladies today Dave?" says Anna.

"What!" roars Dave, "I'm off. Don't need a coat. Mild enough out there."

"I think it's cold," says Anna.

Here in the countryside you are always aware of the weather. It looks in through the windows and the bullnose pane in the front door. It blows across the fields and ambushes you as you step outside the porch. The city has its distractions. Buildings, parks, cars and people. But here in the countryside it is uppermost in peoples' minds. What's the weather doing today?

"I saw that man again deary."

We are in the kitchen. I'm making cheese on toast, with tomatoes from the village shop, which Dave says are the best.

"The man in the garden Anna?"

"Yes." She shivers slightly and holds on the kitchen stool.

"Did you speak to him?"

"No, he was just sitting under the tulip tree."

"Can you remember what he looked like?"

She considers this for a moment. "He had red trousers."

"About how old?"

"About thirty. He's well-dressed. It must be important. Why he's sitting there. That's why I went down the garden again."

She takes off one of her earrings and rubs her earlobe. It's the pink and mauve flower ones I bought her last year. Anna prefers big earrings, and always clip-ons. That's why she often loses them. Under the sofa cushions, behind the jars in the kitchen, on the stairs and under the bed.

What is more upsetting for Anna now? For me to say, don't worry, this man isn't real. And therefore she is seeing things. Or to agree that sometimes a young man with red trousers sits in the garden under the tulip tree?

"I wonder... perhaps this man is just listening to the blackbirds singing," I say, "their song is beautiful."

(No bird sings like a blackbird, says Dave.)

"Mmmm." She thinks about this for a while. "Was that the blackbirds singing in the garden today?"

I nod.

"Yes... yes deary. That's probably it."

"Cheese on toast is ready," I tell her. "Brown sauce with yours?"

"Oh yes deary," she says smiling, "Cheese on toast is one of my favourites. We used to call it Welsh Rarebit I think. When my mother made it for us."

She settles herself in her armchair, and arranges the blue blanket carefully across her lap.

"And I think we should have a glass of wine with our lunch to celebrate."

What are we celebrating?

Who knows.

It doesn't really matter.

SMOKE

23rd February 2019

. . . .

I call in at the village shop on my way to the cottage. Maggie is doing her accounts at the big table.

"Just seen him," she says cheerfully, "he's just called in for the papers."

"I'm on my way there now," I say, "I just wanted some quiche if you have any..."

Maggie gestures towards the freezer at the back of the shop. "I love his stories don't you Freda?" Her assistant behind the counter nods in agreement. "He was telling us about his Dad having a horse and cart. He's got so many stories about the villages round here. And how's your Mum?"

I explain that Anna hasn't been feeling too good recently so we haven't been out to lunch for a few weeks.

"Yeah, she's hasn't been up here for a long time now," says Maggie.

My mobile rings. It's tall son. He's coming over to the cottage with Berkshire girlfriend and wants to take us out for lunch. I've just paid for the quiche and fruit cake. Never mind.

At the cottage Dave is talking about his youth.

"It was like a fog, you couldn't see yer hand in front of yer face," he explains to Anna, who listens attentively.

"I'm just tellin' 'er about the jazz club where we used to go. Yellow Dog it was. Cigarette smoke was so bad you just stumbled downstairs with yer pint in yer hand."

I do remember that everyone seemed to smoke when I was a child. And rather scary grandmother and other elderly relatives filled John's car with cigarette smoke, while Shropshire brother and I sat on the back seat rubbing our eyes.

"No wonder me sister's got emphysema," Dave adds, "all them pubs she used to run."

"Got in yer clothes. Got in yer hair..."

I remember that.

"Is it my hair appointment today Dave?"

"Bloody hell no, it's Saturday and I'm goin' to meet Gordon," says Dave getting to his feet.

Anna follows him to the front door. "Will I see you again?"

"Will you what?"

"Will I see you again?"

"Don't be daft," says Dave, giving her a loud kiss on her cheek.

And he's gone. Limping down the garden to his old car.

It is an established fact that Anna is always concerned about her hair. Is today her hair appointment? Will it rain on her hair? Will the wind blow her hair? Where is her headscarf?

My hair was a disappointment to my parents. As a child there was just too much of it.

328

"Why doesn't your hair look smooth and straight?" said John when I was a teenager. John's era was the 1960's when everyone's hair was floppy, shiny and long.

"Perhaps we could iron it," suggested Anna. I knelt down obediently at the ironing board while she ran the iron over my frizzy wavy hair. There was a smell of burning. It took a long time to grow out.

Shropshire brother had hair like mine, but boys in those days had their hair cut short and under control. Devon brother had hair like Anna, fair and straight, fading to blonde in the summer. Sydney brother had dark curls like Dave. He grew his hair long.

Tall son knocks at the door.

"Car's in the road… hurry up."

Anna leans on my arm and we slowly make our way to the lane. Anna is introduced to Berkshire girlfriend. And then we head to the local pub. It's full of customers. A busy lunchtime. The young people have steak and ale pie. And Anna sits quietly with a bowl of chocolate profiteroles, listening to them talking about work and holidays and apartments they've seen on RightMove.

Back at the cottage Dave has returned from his lunch with Gordon and is reading the Saturday paper in his armchair. More introductions. And then everyone sits down with cups of tea while tall son explains to Dave about Netflix.

"I like war films," says Dave. As if we didn't know.

Anna strokes tall son's arm, and then reaches across him to touch Berkshire girlfriend's beautiful blonde hair with its loose curls.

"Dave," says Anna, "Dave look at this girl's beautiful hair..." Her thin fingers gently stroke the blonde curls.

"Dave do you want to stroke this lovely hair?"

Berkshire girlfriend giggles. Tall son hides his face in his hands.

When my late father-in-law was diagnosed with Alzheimers, I remember a lunch at our house. I'd cooked roast beef. And he dropped his glasses onto his plate, and no-one had noticed. And he moved his glasses around the meat and the vegetables and the gravy with his fork. Until someone quietly picked them up and wiped them on their napkin.

And I've seen couples in the supermarket. A man holding his wife's hand and leading her up and down the aisles. And you can just tell that she has dementia. That she is relying on him to look after her. To be understanding. To be discreet.

This is not the case with Dave.

"What!" he roars, "would I like to do what!!!"

The good news is that Berkshire girlfriend is friendly and confident. This doesn't phase her.

"It's lovely hair isn't it," I say, "now who would like some more tea?"

"Yep I will," says Dave, holding out his Spitfire mug.

Subject changed I think.

The next day tall son calls me from his car on the way back from his girlfriend's parents' house.

"I met her grandmother today," he tells me, "and her great aunt. They came down from Manchester for a visit."

"How did it go?" I ask.

"Well," he says, after a moment of thought. "All I can say is that it was a lot easier for me to meet her elderly relatives than it was for her to meet mine."

COUSINS

24th February 2019

. . . .

I am busy making a cottage pie. The sun is warm on the kitchen window, and it's only February. I wonder if Danish cousin will be late for lunch. At medical daughter's twenty-first birthday party he arrived just as we were tidying up. He rang me yesterday and said that he has to fly back to Denmark later today to collect his young daughter and bring her to England for a visit. He didn't say why. So we agree on an early lunch.

Mash the potato. Grate the carrots. Soften the butter for the crumble mix. Radio 4 on a Sunday is all about Brexit. And more Brexit. And then the Archers. And then more Brexit.

The doorbell rings. Danish cousin with his parents. My uncle is walking now, a little shakily, but so much better than when I last saw him. Musical aunt is dressed in different shades of red and orange. They are smiling, but I can tell that they are a little confused as to where they are.

"I'll make some coffee," I say, helping mathematical uncle to the sofa by the french windows. The sun is so warm that I haven't needed the central heating today. I must remember that they like their coffee black, and very strong. Danish cousin follows me to the kitchen while I sort out the cups and spoons and a tray.

"Do you speak Danish now?" I ask him.

331

"Not really. So many people speak English." He tells me that his daughter slips between English and Danish without effort. But his English children find the language strange at times. For example, a "slut", he tells me, is a Danish word for a sale, as in a shop sale. A quick sale or final sale is therefore a "slutspurt".

The doorbell rings again. And on the doorstep is Bristol cousin, smiling. He greets his parents. Musical aunt is delighted. He greets his brother, and I wonder at how the men of the family are all so tall with such long legs. First Danish cousin nearly knocks over the coffee table, and then mathematical uncle does the same thing. I mop up the spilt coffee, and then the cottage pie is ready.

"If you get everyone to the table, I'll bring the dishes through," I tell Danish cousin.

The cottage pie is cooked to perfection. The carrots are steamed, the new potatoes boiled, and the sweet potato roasted.

"Did I tell you I'm vegetarian?" says Danish cousin.

Ah.

"Well… no… I don't think you did. I rang you to ask if there were any dietary requirements. I think you said your parents eat everything?"

"Yes, they do," says Danish cousin, "it's just me that's vegetarian."

"I can eat yours," says Bristol cousin helpfully.

"I'll just eat the vegetables, don't worry."

I sit next to mathematical uncle. He loves food, and looks pleased to see the cottage pie. I notice that he doesn't speak nowadays, which is curious as it used to be hard to get him to stop talking once upon a time. Sometimes it is as if he wants to speak, and his expression changes to one of anxiety. And then the words are lost, and he returns to his silence.

Musical aunt sits next to him, helping him unfold his napkin and find his wineglass. I mention that the radio is consumed with Brexit at the moment. This is probably not the best thing I could have done. A lengthy debate ensues between my cousins, narrowly skirting a real argument.

"Would you like some more cottage pie," I ask mathematical uncle.

He smiles and pats my hand in delight. How different this is from Anna. Dementia has not robbed mathematical uncle of his appetite. And musical aunt has eaten all her lunch as well. And they are just as enthusiastic about the apple crumble and ice cream.

Lunch over and Bristol cousin opens the french windows and the sun pours into the room. My uncle and aunt doze in its warmth. Danish cousin leaves for Gatwick via some friends in Brighton. Bristol cousin and I talk about the family and work. And it is all very civilised, and very different from my previous day at the cottage.

Anna wanted to go out for lunch. And then she didn't want to. And then she changed her mind again. But where was her purse? And where was her handbag? And in the meantime the fridge was in a mess. Something had leaked or melted or just disintegrated. What on earth was it? I was trying to lift out the glass shelves to wash them, but either Dave was standing in my way, or Anna was fiddling with the drawer containing her make-up and blocking my route to the sink. All the lipsticks without their lids. And the compact sponges mixed up with combs and hair lacquer. I thought if I made a coffee and sat in the dining room they might follow me there. And sure enough they did.

So I waited until they were chatting about friends and neighbours and sneaked off to the kitchen to continue cleaning the fridge. And within a minute or two they were back in the kitchen with me. Dave was sorting out the vegetables in the bottom drawer of the fridge.

Some were a long way past their sell-by date and looked very worn out.

"Don't matter. I'll put 'em in a casserole."

"We must get going," says Bristol cousin, getting to his feet. The sun is beginning to fade. My uncle and aunt follow his lead; my uncle shakily holding his wife's shoulder to steady himself. I take them out through the courtyard and they stop to admire the narcissi, and the handsome cordyline in the planter box that tall son made last year. Bristol cousin helps them into the car once we have said goodbye. But not before mathematical uncle takes my hand and holds it shakily but tightly. There is something he wants to say but cannot form the words. When I look at him I don't see John. There really is no family likeness, but at the same time there is something familiar. And then Bristol cousin helps him into the front seat.

And I wave as they drive away.

FALLING

11th March 2019

· ·

Dave FaceTimes me. It's Monday evening and I've just got home from work. He doesn't focus the camera on himself, so that for half the conversation I am looking at their ceiling.

"I've 'ad a rotten day. Bin at the hospital all day. I kept telling 'er to stay in for a night, but she won't listen to me."

What?

"Dave, what's happened? Why have you been at the hospital?"

"She fell over in the kitchen and banged 'er 'ead on the floor. Never seen so much blood. Blood everywhere there was. Took 'er to the hospital and they wanted to do scans."

"Why didn't you call an ambulance Dave!" (I can't believe he drove her to the hospital). "Did she lose consciousness?"

"I rang for an ambulance, but they said they didn't 'ave none available, so I 'ad to drive 'er in."

I find that hard to believe. I expect Dave was told there would be a delay. But Dave didn't want to wait.

"She's got a wound on the back of 'er 'ead but she didn't need stitches."

Then they said they'd scan 'er but she wanted to come home and she's won't listen to me. I tell 'er what's right but she won't listen."

"Shut up Dave. That's not true. You're making all this up!" Anna is indignant in the background.

"She's goin' off to bed now anyway," says Dave. The camera suddenly tilts back to his face. "I'll 'ave to take 'er to the doctor again in the morning."

I ring Shropshire brother. He is driving somewhere, as usual.

"I'll talk to Dave," he tells me.

He rings me back as I am washing the supper dishes. He sounds impatient. We are in agreement about the issues here. The cottage is no longer suitable for Anna and Dave. They should have moved ten years ago. Into town. Somewhere smaller. Easier to manage. All on one level. As we told them at the time. But they took no notice of us. Dave reasons that as he has fitted handrails throughout the cottage, that's all that needs to be done. My brothers tell me that Dave lives in the present. If I ask him what we will do when Anna can no longer manage the stairs, he tells me that they will deal with it when it happens.

There are things we can do now to help. But will they accept our suggestions?

Dave had come with us to the garden centre for lunch last Saturday. Gordon was working. Anna had looked tired when I arrived. Her eyes were smudged with make-up, including her trademark green eyeshadow.

"I can't find my make-up wipes," she had told me.

I found them on her dressing table. There were at least ten packets of them, most of them already opened, so I took one to her.

"That's better," said Dave smiling, as she wiped away the smudges, "now I can take you out for lunch."

Our short walk to the car, and then from the car to the cafe was slow and difficult. Anna's mobility has certainly deteriorated. Dave was impatient. "I'm having a full English breakfast," he announced.

I decided to bring up the subject of a wheelchair. I hesitated. Faltered. Tried to find the words. How do you tell someone who is so proud and elegant that they need to be pushed along in a chair by family and friends. And Dave was enjoying his breakfast, and Anna her beans on toast and flat white.

And then Dave wanted to look at crocuses.

"Them ruddy pheasants are eatin' the crocuses fast as they come up," he told us, "no sooner do I plant 'em but they eat 'em."

We walked slowly around the garden centre, gazing at the pansies and the hyacinths and stopping to admire the tall olive trees.

"What's this!!" roared Dave, "ten pounds fifty for fifty fat balls!"

"Dave!" I whispered loudly, "please!"

We were next to the cash desk. A fair-haired woman behind the desk looked at Dave curiously.

"How can they charge that for fat balls!! You wouldn't catch me paying that for fat balls!!"

Let's find the crocuses as quickly as we can.

Shropshire brother wants to bring in a sitter so that Dave can have more time to himself. A break from caring for Anna. He tells me that he will be driving down to the cottage this coming week and calling Social Services to try and set this up.

Dave will speak to them and explain the situation and Shropshire brother will distract Anna (probably with chocolate) so that she doesn't overhear the conversation.

He thinks that Wednesdays would be a good midweek break for Dave. And either he or I could try and be at the cottage when the sitter arrives so that we can make sure that Anna is happy with the new arrangement.

And that is the plan.

CERTAINTY

16th March 2019

. . . .

Dave seems happy with the idea of a sitter. I catch him in the kitchen while Anna is tidying her bedroom.

"Don't mind. Good idea," he says, "Yer brother's setting it up. And I could go and see my mates on a Wednesday and wouldn't 'ave to worry about 'er."

Good.

Anna says she is tidying her bedroom, but I think she is actually fussing about her hair. The bump on the back of her head means that she can't fix her hairpiece properly. So it hangs rather oddly to one side of her head. I suggested she might not wear it today, and let the wound heal. But I got a look that told me that was a stupid idea.

She comes slowly downstairs carrying her pyjamas and hangs them over the Aga rail.

"Would you like me to wash those Anna?"

"I have done, deary," she says firmly.

Ok.

Anna is cross with Dave for hiding the shrubs on the bank with a frost-proof covering. It flutters gently in the breeze like a tethered ghost.

"It looks so ugly," she says.

"It may be March but you can't tell in this country when there's goin' to be a late frost," he tells us. "The weather comes down across the fields and it'll kill my plants."

Anna scowls at him.

"And I've got plans for summer, so I want the garden looking good. I ain't got no boat now, so the garden's what I do 'ave." he adds.

"What plans?" I ask him.

"Sunflowers!" he says loudly, banging his coffee cup on the side table, "'Goin' to put them in round the front..."

He stops and stares at Anna.

"You've got my bloody socks on woman!" he roars.

I look at Anna's feet under her long velvet skirt. Yes they certainly look like Dave's socks.

"Were your feet cold Anna?" I ask, trying to diffuse the situation.

"Yes deary I expect so," she says, "but they're my socks, not his."

"They're MY socks," he shouts.

"Well there's a label on them," I say, "maybe that will help."

I sit on the little milk stool next to Anna's armchair. "Yes, it says... Nigel... Nigel Hartington."

Nigel Hartington? What is Anna doing with Nigel's socks?

"Your old boss?" says Dave in disbelief, "What you doin' with his socks,"

"Don't be ridiculous," says Anna, "they're my socks."

Dave shakes his head, baffled.

Nigel owned an interior design company and Anna worked part-time in the shop for a few years. It suited her well. Beautiful fabrics and fashionable objects for the home. In fact many of the pictures and vases in the cottage are from Anna's time at the shop.

"Perhaps he was throwing out some of his old clothes?" I suggest.

Why would Nigel have his name in his socks anyway?

But no-one is listening.

Dave is getting ready for his pub lunch with Gordon. Anna is waking from one of her sudden naps.

"Are you going to your own home tonight?" she says sleepily as Dave kisses her goodbye.

"Daft woman," he says, limping over to the front door.

"Robbie's out on the bank," I call to him.

"I'll give 'im some corn."

Robbie is sitting on cherub's head. I watch him fly to the cover of the bushes as Dave slams the front door. Then he hops nearer as he hears the lid of the corn bin opening. Dave is patient and gentle with Robbie, who lets him stand nearby as he pecks at the corn.

Anna is at the kitchen sink peering at the mirror and trying to re-pin her hairpiece.

"I've got an appointment with Mr McDonald soon. I can't remember when. He'll be able to do my hair."

"Well Anna, Mr McDonald is a hospital consultant."

"Yes deary," says Anna, "he does my hair very nicely though."

"I thought Janine was your hairdresser Anna," I say, expecting her to agree.

"No it's Mr McDonald deary, and he has a very nice assistant who lives at the top of the lane here with his mother. He gets on very well with Dave."

It's the certainty of all this that puzzles me sometimes. There is no hesitation or doubt in what Anna says.

"My memory…" she sometimes says wistfully. But that is rare. Most of the time Anna's reality is the only reality.

And now she brings me the RAF calendar from the kitchen. Looking for her next hair appointment. It's open in November.

We turn the pages to March and there's her appointment with Mr McDonald.

I wonder if he knows anything about hairdressing.

WINE

21st March 2019

. . . .

France called. And Dave answered. Another trip with Gordon to buy more wine and olive oil and French cheese. Before Brexit changes everything.

"Won't be worth going for just three bottles," Dave tells us.

I drive to the cottage after work and meet Dave walking down the lane.

"I'll be late back Saturday night I reckon."

"But you said two nights Dave?" I protest, "and I'm going out Saturday night."

"She'll be alright don't you worry," he says, thumping the roof of my car, "I'm goin' to the shed."

I watch him limping down the lane. He definitely said two nights, Thursday and Friday, and he'd be back in the early hours of Saturday morning. I am wondering if anyone else could sit with Anna on Saturday evening.

The kitchen is decorated with Anna's birthday cards, and she is pleased with the presents I have brought her. But confused.

"When was my birthday deary?"

"It was on Monday," I say, "but I was working."

"Look at them lovely flowers she's got," says Dave coming through the door.

"Oh yes they're from us," I say. Medical daughter had organised their delivery.

"Postman said they're from the grandsons," says Dave puzzled.

How would the postman know I wonder?

"No card with 'em," says Dave.

I go out to the dustbins. The brown bin holds the paper and cardboard. Sure enough there's the delivery box for the flowers. The paperwork still attached. I tear off the envelope and take it to Anna.

"Lovely deary," says Anna, admiring the picture of exotic birds on the card.

"So it's from you and the children," says Dave, "yep didn't think them boys'd send flowers.

"Men CAN send flowers," says Anna indignantly.

I open the bottle of Prosecco I have brought, and the box of triple chocolate cookies. Anna tips all twelve of them onto her plate. She unwraps the fluffy pillow cases, but looks puzzled by them.

There's a knock at the door and it's Dave's friends, Chris and Pete. Gordon will be arriving in ten minutes they tell us. When we see Gordon's car outside the cottage Dave puts on his best jacket and goes to kiss Anna goodbye, treading on her toes in the process.

He leaves without any overnight bag. No toothbrush, hairbrush or change of clothes. Just as before.

"That's a lovely stripey thing," says Anna, admiring the paper bag that held the Prosecco and biscuits. She says this several times over the evening, clearly more taken with the wrapping than its contents.

But she does go to bed when I suggest, and then I carry my bag up to the little room which was once my bedroom, and fall asleep quickly, despite the strange quietness of the cottage.

I am not sure where I am when I awake. It is so hot in the room. Then I realise that I have been sleeping next to the new radiator which is ridiculously big for the tiny bedroom. Just below the window I can hear Mr Pheasant calling, and when I look out of the window I see that everyone is on the bank waiting for breakfast. Robbie, Hoppy, two Mrs Pheasants, blackbird, several more rooks and a party of sparrows. Hurry up!

"What day is it deary?" says Anna several times. "Where's Dave?"

She has eaten half of the bowl of cereal I gave her and has now turned to the chocolate caramel squares and black grapes. Her jade green cashmere jumper is dotted with chocolate.

"Have you seen the mess next door deary?"

The mess is, in fact, the neighbours compost heap. They've cut back and tidied up the hedge, which now looks thin and bare. And it has revealed the bins and bags and garden tools that were previously hidden by the hedge.

"How could they let their garden get into such a state?" she says indignantly.

"I think it's their compost area Anna," I say, "the hedge will grow up again and hide it. And it's only really visible from the landing window isn't it."

Anna gives me a haughty look.

345

"It's different when you have to live with it deary."

The telephone rings. It's Dave. Having breakfast in Cherbourg.

"Can you put the brown bin out?" he shouts, "I forgot it. And get the newspapers from the shop. Forgot that too."

Before I can say yes, he has rung off. It's Friday. And he collects the newspapers on Saturday morning. Does he know it's Friday. Or does he think it's Saturday?

"What day is it deary?" says Anna.

"Isn't that a lovely present," indicating stripey bag on the blanket box.

"If I can find some washing powder we'll wash your bed linen," I say.

"Washing powder's in the coat cupboard I think deary."

The long cupboard, as always, is full of coats and jackets. I have to kneel down to see what's at the back of the cupboard on the floor. I'll just move the vacuum cleaner. I can't see any washing powder.

"What are all these boxes for," I call.

"Oh they're Dave's boxes I expect," says Anna.

There's at least six of them. Still kneeling amongst the coats, I pull open the top of one of the heavy boxes.

Oh.

It's wine.

It's full of wine bottles.

And so are all the other boxes.

WINE PART TWO

23rd March 2019

. . . .

I have no idea when Dave is returning. No point ringing his mobile as it will be switched off. That's if he even took it with him. But originally he said two nights, and that he would be back in the early hours of Saturday morning. So last night I slept on the sofa, thinking that if he did want a lie-in I wouldn't disturb him by walking through his bedroom from the little room.

But when I awake the cottage is quiet. I didn't sleep well. I could hear Anna walking about upstairs and my watch said two-thirty am. I had pushed Dave's armchair up against the sitting room door in case Anna tried to open it. On one occasion last year when I was sleeping on the sofa she had come in and touched my shoulder, and I had jumped and startled her. Several times last night I heard the rattle of the latch as she tried to open the door. So part of me was watchful, and that part of me is very tired this morning.

I can smell toast. Anna has made herself a cup of tea. She is dressed and sitting in her armchair by the Aga.

"Hello deary, where have you been? Do you know where Dave is?"

I tell her that he is in France, and he will be back today, although I am not sure when.

347

"And the sun is coming out Anna, so we will wash your bed linen today."

"Don't tire yourself out deary," she says. I think her own lack of energy and strength makes Anna think that everyone else must feel the same.

Her bed is a mess of blankets and throws. Pyjamas and dressing gowns. (Anna has several). And two hot water bottles. One on the floor and the other tangled in the duvet. The heavy dark curtains are still partly drawn. I cover her pillow with the new fluffy pillowcase and draw back the curtains to let in the sunshine.

Downstairs the postman is struggling with the letterbox but I can't find the key to open the door. A heavy parcel gradually emerges and falls onto the doormat. A catalogue no doubt. But no, it's a big jiffy bag and it has a label next to the address saying, "silk and cashmere".

"Have you ordered something Anna?"

"No deary. Do you want a cup of tea?"

I decline the offer. Anna seems to have forgotten how to make tea these days. She takes the teabag out so quickly that it barely has time to flavour the water.

Then I hear a key in the door and Dave is standing on the doormat.

"Six boxes of wine I've got in the wheelbarrow out there," he says with delight.

Wheelbarrow?

"And this is for you." He holds out a huge bottle of olive oil.

"We weren't sure if you would be back this morning," I tell him.

"Gordon and the lads wanted to go to Morrisons for breakfast on the way back, but I said I've got to get back to the missus." He gives Anna a hug. She is standing by the round table looking puzzled.

"Where have you been Dave?"

"What?" he shouts.

Shropshire brother and I think that Dave's hearing is getting worse. We can't have a telephone conversation with him now because he talks over the top of us, not realising when we are speaking. And even face-to-face I have to repeat everything twice. He tells me that he will make an appointment to see the audiologist. But when? And how does Anna manage?

"I'm just used to it I suppose," she says.

Dave tells me that his deafness is the result of working with heavy machinery on construction sites before the use of ear defenders. And then Frank's brother fired a 12-bore shotgun next to Dave's right ear.

"Never bin right since then," he says.

Dave wants to tell us about his trip. And particularly all the meals they enjoyed. The crepes, the tartes citron, the frites, the cassoulet, the soup a l'oignon and the red wine. But Anna has this morning's parcel to open. It's her birthday present from Dave. And it's a long navy skirt. But very crumpled. I get out the iron and the old ironing board that pinches your fingers if you're not careful. Anna is delighted when her skirt is ironed and smooth and goes upstairs to try it on.

"Are we going out for coffee Dave?"

"Looks alright that skirt," says Dave, "nice colour on you."

Anna looks pleased and turns slightly, so that we can get the full effect.

"Yes, and I'd like to go out for coffee now," says Anna, stroking his arm. "You can come with us deary," she says, turning to me.

"I'll stay and make some lunch," I tell her. I've bought some chicken and mushrooms to make a casserole.

"Bring yer stick," says Dave indicating the box by the front door, "don't want you staggerin' all over the place."

The cottage is quiet when they've gone. Just the ticking of the grandfather clock, and the slow hiss of the Aga kettle on the warming plate.

While the casserole cooks (very slowly) in the Aga I read the newspaper and drink my coffee. When I look at my watch it's nearly one o'clock. I go to the window, but there's no sign of anyone. Have they gone for coffee and decided to stay for lunch? Did they hear me saying I would be making a casserole? Perhaps Anna has spotted the chocolate brownies. Or Dave has ordered a full English breakfast.

I go outside to sit in the porch and admire the willow tree on the bank, its buds like dozens of bottle brushes. The sun is warm and Dave's pansies are happy in its warmth.

It's like being a parent of young teenagers again. Will they be home for lunch or won't they?

I decide to enjoy the solitude.

GUILT

5th April 2019

. . . .

Last weekend I helped Dave carry the old teak garden bench up from the sheds. It had been pushed into a corner at the end of last summer, and hidden by a huge stack of logs. We placed it against the outside wall under the sitting room window and brushed away the cobwebs. Dave stood and admired it for a few minutes. Then I called Anna to come and enjoy the sunshine, but she said it was too windy and cold. So Dave and I sat there and looked out across the fields.

And today I've been to the garden centre and bought a long cushion for the bench. It's cream, with a green floral pattern. I hope they like it. I park outside the sheds and walk up the lane with the cushion under my arm. Dave is just driving out and sees me and waves. But he doesn't stop. Anna is in the dining room making a cup of tea.

"He's gone up to the shop deary," she says, "we need more milk."

I try the bench cushion for size and it is perfect.

"It's comfortable to sit on now," I tell Anna. But she is not listening.

"I need to go to the doctor I'm afraid."

"Is it your head Anna?"

She puts her hand up to the back of her head.

"Yes, the bump is still there," she says. I can see the worry in her eyes.

"It will take a while to go down," I say, "it was obviously quite a bad fall."

"I'm worried," she says, "I think it may… it may cause damage to my brain."

"Well I think after your fall the doctors would have said something to you."

"Oh yes," she says. She takes a deep breath. "Yes they would have done."

I can hear whistling out in the lane, and then a shout.

"Well that's alright isn't it!"

Dave looks pleased. "Nice cushion out there. Did you bring it? Wasn't expecting you today."

He likes it. That's good.

I make them both some coffee and pull a chair up to the round table. Now I will have to tell them.

"Dave, Anna, I'm afraid I can't come over tomorrow, as usual. I'm going to visit a friend and I'll be away for the whole day. I'm really sorry but it's the only opportunity I have for the next couple of months."

"I'll get on with the garden then," says Dave, "got plenty to do out there. Don't want to leave 'er on 'er own."

"Have you seen my hot water bottle Dave?" says Anna changing the subject.

"Your what? Hot water bottle? Nope. Under yer bed I expect."

I volunteer to go and look for the bottle.

Underneath the bed there are several carrier bags, Christmas decorations, some pyjama trousers and two hot water bottles.

As I'm upstairs I will have a quick check from the landing window on the state of the neighbour's compost area.

"So I'm not goin' to lunch with Gordon tomorrow then," I hear Dave say. "Bin let down again. Stuck here again. I need a day off."

Oh heck.

I make more coffee.

"Dave, your neighbours next door... I know they would come round and have a cup of tea with Anna if you wanted to go and meet Gordon and the others. And what about the lady across the lane who recently retired. I can't remember her name. Didn't she offer to come and sit with Anna occasionally?"

Anna looks cross. "I don't need anyone to come and sit with me."

"She's stubborn, that's the problem," says Dave, brushing biscuit crumbs off his lap. "Bloody stubborn."

I have two thoughts at this point.

Why hasn't Shropshire brother followed up his initial phone call about getting a sitter, as he said he would?

Why doesn't Dave just tell Anna that he wants a break from caring, and so she needs to have someone with her. Friend, neighbour, sitter, whoever.

Once home I call Shropshire brother. He is driving somewhere.

"I've just been too busy," he tells me, "but I will send an email. Don't worry. If Dave has to miss a lunch one week that's just the way it is. Don't feel guilty."

But I do. And I don't know why.

I wonder if we look after our parents in their old age because we are grateful to them for looking after us when we were young. It is our turn to do the caring. Or does the child in us still see them as our caregivers and so must be protected? Perhaps we want to set an example to our own children of how we would like to be treated when we are old and frail.

It is hard to imagine the cottage without Anna. It seems that whenever I have visited she has always been there. Sometimes ironing. Sometimes polishing the silver and brasses. Sometimes cooking Dave's tea. But more often than not, just drinking coffee or reading one of her books. If I arrived on my own she would sit and chat. If I arrived with the children she would find them drinks and snacks and games to play.

But if Anna and Dave visited my house, or any other house she would be content for a few hours, and then become restless and anxious.

"We must get back Dave. We must light the fire. I must get your tea."

And Dave would get unsteadily to his feet. Not really wanting to leave so early. But ready to drive her home.

So am I grateful to Anna for looking after me when I was young? Or for helping when I became a mother and one of my children was ill? And I had to go to work. Or when I was ill? When their father worked away in London.

Probably not. Anna has never been that kind of mother.

That's doesn't stop me from texting tall son.

'I need to ask you a favour. Could you take Anna for lunch tomorrow so Dave can meet Gordon etc at the pub?'

Then I sit down to watch television and wait for his reply.

EARS

13th April 2019

. . . .

I'm sure Dave said he had an appointment with the audiologist today. I tried to ring him to check but he just couldn't hear me.

"My ears 'ave got worse I reckon," is all he could say.

I decide to go to the cottage anyway. I've repotted a bamboo plant in my courtyard and have the spare pot in the boot of my car for Dave. Hopefully he'll like it. Eldest grandson is at the cottage with two dogs that he is looking after for his aunt. A big dog and small dog. He and Dave are drilling something in the sheds. Anna greets me looking tearful.

"We've had a bit of a row," she says, "I've lost my purse."

Again? Or is this another purse?

"Perhaps it's upstairs in one of your boots," I suggest.

"No dear, I've looked there."

"Well I'll search for it, don't worry," I say.

She tells me that Sydney brother has phoned and is coming over to England soon.

"For a dance," she says.

"It's a long way to come for a dance."

356

"Yes deary, but it's somewhere he can meet girls I think."

She smiles to herself, "It's what you do when you're twenty-one isn't it."

I think Sydney brother might be fifty-one actually, but I don't say anything. Anna is often in the late nineteen-eighties these days.

Eldest grandson and two dogs appear in the porch. Dave is just behind them.

"Under 'er bed is a right mess," he shouts, "and she's lost 'er purse again."

"Yes, Anna's just told me," I say, "but what's under her bed?"

"Everything!" he shouts, "and the hot water bottles 'ave leaked all over the carpet."

"Well that's nothing to do with me!" says Anna coldly.

"I'll sort it out," I say, "would you like some coffee Dave?"

"We haven't finished down the shed yet," says eldest grandson.

"I'll 'ave a coffee first," says Dave.

The next hour or so is spent cleaning under Anna's bed. Everything is decorated with cobwebs. Anna tries to help but I am worried that she will trip over the vacuum cleaner or the many carrier bags that I have discovered. And we realise that Dave has yet another job ahead of him, and that is to fill Anna's two hot water bottles at night. She must have left the stoppers loose and they have spilled their contents over the bedroom carpet. No sign of her purse unfortunately.

And then while Dave goes to his appointment I make some lunch of home-made mushroom soup with bread, and some of the very smelly Camembert cheese that he brought back from France.

Anna asks many questions about friends and family from her childhood in Birmingham.

As I can't really answer them I find it easier to distract her with what's going on outside the window. The sunshine, the pheasant family looking for Dave, Robbie and Hoppy on the bank looking for corn, and the empty fields waiting for the cows.

Dave returns and sits on his chair by the window.

"Says I've got infection in both ears," he tells us.

"Who's that dear?" says Anna.

"The audiologist bloke!" says Dave loudly, "and I don't know how I've got an infection 'cos I clean 'em out mornin' and night."

"Every day? What with?" I ask him.

"My flannel."

Ah. I think the flannel may be the problem. When I was staying at the cottage last year I noticed that Dave's flannel often fell off its hook into the bath. Or Anna mistook it for her flannel. And nobody ever thought of putting it in the washing machine.

"I think it might be an idea to buy a new one Dave," I say, "and when you collect your antibiotics have a chat with the GP about washing your ears."

"Reckon we'll get that seat cushion out now, " says Dave changing the subject, "lovely day out there."

I find the seat cushion on the bed in the little room. I am not sure why it has travelled upstairs. Dave and I sit outside with our cups of tea and enjoy the warmth of the sun.

"Have you heard back from the sitting service Dave?" I say. I have to repeat the question loudly. Dave is more interested in telling me about the evening scent of the jasmine on the bank.

And the fact that Mr Pheasant can't have his way with his wives because it's not the right time for that sort of thing.

"The sitting service Dave?"

"Oh yes, they called me. I told 'em that we're doin' alright. We don't need their help. Though we might do at some point I said."

What! How can he say that? I cannot imagine what Shropshire brother will say when he hears what Dave has told them. So many phone calls and emails to try and set this up.

Anna appears in the porch with a plate of toast and blackcurrant jam.

"Would you like some toast and jam dearies?"

Toast and jam. Hmmm.

Shropshire brother is going to be very cross.

Very cross I think.

RATS

21st April 2019

. . . .

Shropshire brother gets my message and calls me. He is driving somewhere. He is cross. He reels off a list of race meetings. Hereford, Wincanton, Lingfield Park, Aintree. This means he is very busy and cannot really sort out Dave's misdeeds.

He follows our conversation with a long email to the family which explains how he has tried to set up a sitter for Anna, and how Dave has thwarted his plans. Sydney brother thinks that Dave might be worried that Anna will be taken into a care home, if he is seen to be not managing and needing help from social services.

I drive over on Easter Sunday. Yesterday I had family visiting and Anna's friend Sheila looked after her while Dave went for lunch with Gordon. The sun is bright, but the air is cold. Weather from the east, said the forecasters. But the blossom is out and the woods running alongside the main roads are streaked with bluebells. And that is sad, because one thing Anna loved was to come with us up to the bluebell woods at this time of year. We would make our way up to the Red House, hidden away off the footpath. Dave told us that a family had lived in this cottage when he was young. We always marvelled at the idea of living in a wood.

Dave is reading yesterday's newspaper and Anna greets me at the door. She is wearing odd earrings. One a bright silver rose pattern and the other a dull whorled pattern.

I have brought a new pair for her which I found in the market. They are cream with a diagonal gold line. She puts them on immediately. Dave hears the Aga kettle hissing and popping and puts down his paper and comes to the dining room for a coffee. He is soon busy reminiscing about the old days. A peculiar tale of one of his contemporaries who got three women pregnant.

"How did 'e get away with it?" marvels Dave, "and 'e was married too. You wouldn't catch me doin' that. And 'e was a lazy bloke too. Wouldn't get on the ice. Wouldn't skate. Not 'im. Just stood at the edge smoking a cigarette."

He follows this topic with a long discussion about mobile phones. Are hands-free mobiles safe to use while driving?

Anna dozes. She is not interested in these topics.

"How is Anna's walking at the moment Dave?" I ask.

"Shaky. She fell over between the sofa and the bookshelves the other night. Couldn't get 'er out. She was alright though cos the furniture's soft. It's a thick carpet too. Best place to fall. Couldn't get her out though."

Anna has a curious way of waking when she hears her name.

"What have I done?"

"Nothing you rat. I was just telling 'er about you fallin' and gettin' stuck in the lounge."

"How did you get Anna out in the end Dave?"

"Well..." He scratches his arm thoughtfully. "Just waited till the end of my programme and then I could concentrate on gettin' 'er up and back on the sofa."

Crikey. At least there doesn't seem to be any harm done.

"Did you get a rhododendron for the pot I brought Dave?"

"Yep. Come out and 'ave a look."

We go out into the sunshine. There are many blue pots filled with pansies of all colours. Dave is proud to show me his new plants. The rhododendron fills its new pot in a pink cloud of blooms.

"Robbie's looking for you Dave."

We go to the corn bin and Dave takes out a handful, and a piece of soft granary bread. He holds out the bread and calls to Robbie, who hops down from the bushes and pecks delicately at the bread.

"E's got a family down the sheds," Dave tells me.

But Robbie flies back up to the bushes and we watch him feeding another smaller robin.

"Well I never," says Dave, "young are up 'ere already."

It's too chilly to be outside for long so we go back to the warmth of the kitchen, and watch Robbie through the window.

"Problem I got 'ere with rats," Dave tells me. He points to the tangled branches and brambles where the garden meets the edge of the field. "That's where they got their nest."

"Could I have some more tea deary?" calls Anna from the dining room."

"I've got to get 'em in a pile," says Dave.

"How will you do that?"

"Sardines I reckon. Got lots of tins of sardines. She don't eat 'em any more."

"The rats will go for sardines?" I ask.

"Yep, I reckon," says Dave, "and then I've got 'em."

"Could I have a kiss please Dave?" Anna is at his elbow. He laughs happily, shrugs and kisses her. "Always wantin' kisses these days."

It's time to change Dave's bedclothes. Dave and Anna come to help, but stare in bewilderment at the process.

"Where's the clean cover then?" says Dave, as I shake up the duvet.

Dave you've just watched me put the clean duvet cover on the duvet!

With the bedclothes in the washing machine it's time to leave. Work tomorrow.

Once home I start a shopping list. My phone pings with a message.

It's another email. With another problem.

Sharon the cleaner at the cottage has a new job.

SPARROWHAWKS

27th April 2019

. . . .

Dave is discombobulated. He is talking to Gordon on the phone. "She's turning' the house upside-down. I'm gettin' out of 'ere. See you at the pub at twelve-thirty then?"

"Dave, why are your shirts here in the coat cupboard? And here's some of your trousers as well!"

I think I can see the problem. The long cupboard is full of clothes because Dave is using it like a downstairs wardrobe. It's probably getting difficult to carry the clean washing upstairs, whilst holding on to the banisters either side of the stairs. And if you add in all Anna's coats and jackets...

I must admit I'd had enough of hearing that the long cupboard was not the right location for a portable toilet.

"Why not?" I asked them.

"It's so full of coats deary," said Anna.

"There's nowhere else to put 'em," said Dave.

"Nowhere at all," agreed Anna.

I told them that in fifteen minutes or so I could create enough space in the long cupboard for the portable toilet that Dave feels they might need.

"What if she can't get up the stairs?"

"Exactly," I agreed," so I will clear these coats and jackets, and you will be surprised to see how much space there is."

While I clear the cupboard Dave finds the catalogue of useful things to show me. The best-seller loo is called, 'When You've Got to Go.'

"I reckon that's all she needs," he says.

I notice that he is quietly taking his shirts and trousers upstairs. To hang them in his wardrobe. Where they should be. But every jacket and coat that I show Anna she wants to keep.

"Yes deary, I want to keep that one too," she says.

"But this coat is so long. And so heavy," I say, holding up a check Jaeger coat that would easily sweep across the floor if I wore it.

"Yes but I'm bigger than you deary,"

Really?

"And what is your name deary? she calls from her armchair by the Aga.

I tell her my name. She looks puzzled. A flicker of memory in her eyes. "Was that always your name?"

I explain that she gave me a different name when I was born, and I changed it when I got married.

"A good job you did that deary," she says, "much nicer."

Right.

There's a carrier bag by the door ready for the charity shop, and a pile of 'coats to keep' on the chair. I take some of them upstairs. Anna has two wardrobes in her bedroom.

One of them is full of Dave's shirts for some reason. The double wardrobe is Anna's. There is space for at least six of her coats.

"Sharon gave us some lemon drizzle cake if you'd like to try some deary."

Anna is struggling to reach the stairs.

"Where's your walking frame fatty!" roars Dave.

"Look," I say proudly, "lots of space in the cupboard for the portable loo now."

"Yeah but where's the oven?" says Dave.

Oh. I've left mini oven glowering on the bench outside the front door. When I've put mini oven back in its place there is still room for a portable loo. I'll ask my brothers to get one sorted.

I cut some lemon drizzle cake and sit at the round table.

"So I've got some news for you both," I say. "with Sharon leaving next week you'll be without a cleaner. But I've spoken to your sister, Dave, and she's found a nice friendly cleaner called Lorraine who'll come on a Wednesday morning for two hours."

I sit back, smiling. Dave looks puzzled. Anna is drifting off to sleep.

"Yeah but Sharon comes on a Tuesday..."

"Yes, and..."

"Well we'd want this new one to come on a Tuesday."

"Why's that?"

"Dunno really. Just got used to it."

I can't help sighing. Loudly.

"I'm sure you'll get used to Lorraine coming on a Wednesday," I tell him. "Just give it a few weeks and you'll have forgotten all about Tuesdays."

"There's that sparrow hawk!" shouts Dave in alarm. We look from the window across the fields. "'She better not be after my birds!" He holds on to the side of the coffee table and pushes himself up from the chair. "I'm watchin.'"

We go outside and stare at the sky.

"She comes across them fields like a Spitfire," Dave says, "Gamekeepers used to kill 'em once. Can't do that now."

"They were nearly extinct weren't they Dave?"

Dave agrees. "Yep there's more of 'em now. But where are the yellowhammers and the goldfinches and the chaffinches? That's what I want to know. Never see 'em in the garden now. Used to see 'em all the time."

Anna's woken from her nap. "Can I have a cup of tea Dave please?"

We go inside. Leaving the sparrowhawk still flying low over the fields. Twisting and darting through the trees in the distance. Her tail long and slim.

Her yellow eye watching.

WHEELCHAIR

4th May 2019

From the bathroom window I can see that the willow tree on the bank is blooming. Furry catkins, tiny buds, and now the tree is in full leaf. In the field beyond the bank Mr Pheasant paces restlessly back and forth in the long grass. Downstairs Anna is making another cup of tea and Dave has just returned from the village shop with the Saturday newspapers. He has found the pikelets I brought with me. I thought they would remind Anna of Birmingham.

I go downstairs with a pile of washing.

"What's this then?" says Dave holding up the pikelets. "Co-op eh?"

"Yes I found them this morning," I say, "I popped in to get some milk."

"That's aner-thema to me," says Dave, and grins. "Do I mean that? Aner-thema?"

"The Co-op?"

"Yep, my mum wouldn't 'ave gone in there when she was shopping."

I've heard something similar from Anna in the past.

"Do you mean anathema Dave?"

"Yep that's it!"

I think that maybe Dave gets these words from Shropshire brother.

"Well I'm going to put these bath towels and flannels in the washing machine," I tell him.

He stands aside so I can pull the kitchen stool away from the washing machine door. The heavy walnut stool is always in the wrong place. Anna insists on keeping it, but I am not sure why. I have never seen anyone or anything sitting on it except for Anna's two hot water bottles, and a pile of tea towels that have seen better days.

"That washin' you put out last week blew away," Dave tells me, "so I've lost the pegs somewhere in the lane. 'Ad a look, but can't find 'em."

Oh dear. I tell him I'll have a search for them later.

"How are your ears now Dave?" I ask. I've noticed that his hearing seems better today.

He tells me that the antibiotics have cleared the infection and he's not washing out his ears with his old flannel any more.

"Now we've got the shower I can just hold the shower 'ead up and spray it in the old ears," he says, "it does the trick. It's one powerful shower." He holds the telephone up at right-angles to his ear to show me what he means.

Crikey.

The phone rings. It's Gordon, making sure Dave is joining him for lunch. And Brexit talks.

"Don't reckon he'll ever get a girlfriend now," muses Dave after the phone call. ""E did 'ave a girlfriend once but his mum put a stop to that."

"Why did she do that?" asks Anna.

"Dunno. Wanted 'im to stay at home and look after 'er, I reckon. So it's too late now. And 'e eats too much chocolate like I've said."

"Perhaps he'd do for you deary," says Anna looking at me.

Hmmm. Delivered so elegantly. The sort of comments that could easily start an argument. That probably did start an argument with her sister Simone.

It's just irony. That's what Anna would say, if challenged.

"And what's this rubbish about David Walliams' wife?" shouts Dave from behind his Saturday newspaper.

"Who's that?" says Anna.

"Second swipe at love! Whatever that means. I'll tell you what,"says Dave getting heated, "I wouldn't get mixed up with showbiz women."

I can believe that Dave.

"Wonder what 'appened to that boyfriend you 'ad before you got married," says Dave, changing the subject. "I liked 'im. "E was odd."

Oh.

I feel as if I'm sixteen again.

"Well I'm quite happy on my own, don't worry," I tell them.

Anna is creeping towards the kitchen. One hand on the Aga rail, and the other reaching out for Dave's arm.

'You could get married again though deary," says Anna. "After all I've had four husbands, and Dave's had three wives."

"She tells everyone that!" shouts Dave. The middle of the Saturday newspaper slides onto the floor under his chair. The colour supplement follows it.

"I've got hedges to cut!"

Dave bends down with difficulty to retrieve the papers. "Gotta get on with the garden I 'ave. After I've seen Gordon of course."

"Give me a kiss Dave," calls Anna, back in her armchair.

He plants a loud kiss on her cheek and then flings open the front door.

"'Ad an 'ell of a fight on the oil tank the other day..."

Huh?

I follow him out to the garden.

"Mr Pheasant 'e got taken on by a younger male. Fightin' for the females they were. Younger one won. Mr Pheasant was very cross."

"He looks a bit on edge today Dave," I say.

"Yep he's worried. Keeps lookin' over 'is shoulder."

I tell Dave I might walk up round the church when he gets back from lunch. There'll be lambs in the field at the top of the lane.

"Yep churchyard's lookin' nice with the bluebells out," says Dave, "wanted to bury my old man up there. Bloody vicar said no."

"Why Dave?"

"I dunno. The old man hadn't lived in the village for a long time. We moved down the town when I was a nipper. Down by the salmon leap. I loved it there. Catching minnows and all in the river."

"Your father was a local man though Dave."

"Yep, he built the chapel 'ere in the village. 'E was an engineer. Didn't earn much in those days though. Then the waterworks moved us up the next village and gave us the bungalow."

Oh yes. The bungalow in the fields. Where the drunken men fell over on their way back from the pub.

I don't know whether Dave talks so much about his early life because he enjoys doing so, or whether he wants me to know all the details in case they are forgotten when he is gone. Maybe a bit of both.

And talking about the past is probably a welcome relief from the present. The difficulties of looking after someone who rarely remembers anything for more than a couple of minutes.

Later in the week I ring the cottage to check how they are. Dave isn't happy. Anna has lost four things since the weekend.

Two watches that Dave bought her. Her panic alarm bracelet. And her top set of teeth.

But I have some good news for him. The Red Cross have a wheelchair they can borrow. For twelve weeks.

"Anna can try it out and see how she gets on," I explain. "It will make things a lot easier when you go shopping in town. Or out for coffee. And on Saturdays I can take her round the church, or even round the manor. And up to the village shop for coffee."

The only thing is.

As I will be at work, Dave must remember to collect the wheelchair between nine-thirty and eleven-thirty on Friday.

ROUND THE POND

11th May 2019

. . . .

Devon brother is under Anna's bed.

"Can't see anything," he calls.

"Neither can I."

I'm searching through the old wooden chest of drawers. One drawer is full of beautiful cashmere jumpers. Lovely colours. A tangle of pink and teal and blue.

We shake out the duvet and pillows, and the layers of blankets that Anna insists on sleeping under.

"Nothing," says Devon brother.

"No, nothing," I agree.

"It's so difficult," I tell him. "if I ask her when she last had them, of course she can't remember. And if I ask Dave he can't hear me properly. And then... well, he can't remember either."

Devon brother looks thoughtful, "we could look inside her shoes. Dave says the cleaner found them in her shoes last time."

Ten years ago I would never have imagined that I would have to make regular searches of Anna's bedroom for missing purses, debit cards, earrings.

And now her teeth.

Devon brother has made a surprise visit to the cottage. I found him sitting at the round table drinking coffee and chatting with Dave. Anna in her armchair by the Aga. Dave was clearly cross about the missing purse, the missing watches, and the missing teeth.

"It's lovely to have my grandchildren visiting," said Anna when I arrived. Devon brother laughed, but I suppose I am used to this.

Shropshire brother (driving somewhere) had rung me that morning.

"It's cold out today," he told me, "don't think you should take Anna out in the new wheelchair."

But Devon brother has wheeled the new chair around the kitchen and dining room and is keen to try it out in the lanes. With Anna of course.

"No point searching for teeth all day. They must have gone out with the rubbish. Let's go for a walk."

"Let's have some lunch first," I say.

Devon brother is not a patient man. He is a whirlwind of energy and political discussion. And strong opinions about the countryside. But for now he has brought French bread and a wonderful soft cheese, and I warm the mushroom quiche I've made in the Aga (while Devon brother marvels that it is still working, albeit temperamentally).

"Cleaned it all out the other day," Dave tells us as he heads off to meet Gordon for lunch.

While we eat, Devon brother tells us about youngest grandson, soon to start training as a paramedic in Scotland. And he has joined the Army reservists, much to Dave's delight.

Anna picks delicately at the quiche and bread, and out on the bank Mr Pheasant calls continuously for his many wives.

Time to try out the wheelchair. I find Anna's warmest coat and the green furry throw.

"You push," I tell Devon brother, "until Anna's used to it, and then I'll have a try."

"It's cold…" complains Anna in a tiny voice from under the furry throw.

"Keep in the sunshine if you can," I tell Devon brother.

Now there's a car coming.

"I'm just going to wait in that drive on the left," says Devon brother. But the wheelchair won't turn to the left. It refuses to budge from the centre of the road.

I start to giggle. Devon brother is getting mad with the wheelchair. The car slows and waits.

Finally the wheelchair turns. The car draws up next to us and a young couple look out at us and smile.

"Are you alright," says the male passenger laughing.

"Sorry, it's our first outing with the chair," I tell him.

"Are you enjoying it?" he asks Anna.

She looks at him from under her long fringe. "No."

I realise what a strange picture we must make. Two middle-aged people fighting with a wheelchair in a country lane. Giggling and laughing. Because when I am with my brothers we can slip back into childish behaviour. Old memories coming back. And I feel quite happy that we can take Anna out on a village walk again.

Today the sun is bright but the air is cold. Devon brother has borrowed Dave's old country jacket which is too wide for him.

We walk as quickly as we can, but stop to show Anna the bluebells and the village pond and the lambs in the field by the telephone box library. But I'm not sure she is really seeing them. Not in a meaningful way.

Back at the cottage I make cups of tea while Anna sits out in the sunshine with Devon brother. She thinks he is tall son, and constantly refers to him as such. He doesn't seem to mind. I wheel her into the dining room when she says she is cold and help her into her armchair for a nap.

Devon brother and I sit on the garden bench with its new cushion and drink our tea. Overhead the sparrowhawk patrols the fields. And fearless Robbie darts about between the bank and the willow tree.

We talk about the cottage. When it has to be sold. One day. Who would buy it? And all the sheds. And the walls that need painting. And the floors re-carpeting. And the damp patches. And the little room upstairs that you can barely stand up in. And the Aga. Would someone want to do up the cottage? To bring it into the twenty-first century?

"I must get going," says Devon brother, and he goes to say goodbye to Anna and to Dave, who has enjoyed a good lunch with Gordon.

"A very nice salad I 'ad," he tells us.

A salad?

"Call me if you need me," says Devon brother as he disappears out to the lane.

And I stay sitting on the garden bench looking out at the honeysuckle and the fields. Until Dave comes to join me.

To talk about his beloved garden.

FERRETS

18th May 2019

. . . .

Dave's not going out to lunch today.

"I'm goin' to stay here and have a chat with yer brother," he tells me.

"What about Gordon?" I ask him.

"Nah, he's got paperwork to do. Works all hours 'e does for that company. When I told 'im I 'ad family coming 'e said don't worry e' was going to get on with the paperwork today."

Shropshire brother arrives at lunchtime with a fold-up bed and some smart luggage. He is wearing a nice green cashmere jumper. We have beans on toast and mugs of coffee while he and Dave talk about digging through chalk hills to build roads. In his younger day Dave drove diggers and started work at seven in the morning.

"I 'ad chalk everywhere," he tells us, "in me eyes, in me ears. Everywhere. And the noise of the machines! I 'ad no ear defenders."

I bring Anna a creme caramel from the fridge. She looks pleased. As I pass the kitchen windows I see two turtle doves on the bank looking hesitant.

"Doctor says I'm to 'ave new hearing aids," says Dave, "reckons these don't work now."

I'm pleased to hear this.

"I see you have some doves here now Dave." (I have to say it twice).

"Yep. And a bachelor pigeon too," he tells us.

"It must be cold outside for them," says Anna from her armchair.

"Daft woman," says Dave smiling.

Shropshire brother has been in Ireland writing about horses. He tells us that he and his partner visited friends who have young children.

"The children were very well-behaved," he tells us, "but the whole sitting room was like a toy room. Toys everywhere."

"Do children really enjoy that?" I ask him. "I mean, isn't it too much for them?"

"In my day..." says Dave. Shropshire brother grins.

"We wouldn't 'ave got away with that," says Dave. "We 'ad to be tidy. Same as at school. Some master'd give you the cane if yer desk was untidy."

"I got the cane at school," says Shropshire brother, "only once though."

"What for?" Anna asks him.

"Some older boys heard that I'd got a betting scheme running in the school and they made me show them how it worked. But they got caught. And then they blamed me. I looked in the mirror after the caning and I had three stripes across my bum."

"Good heavens!" says Anna.

"Well I got the cane regular." says Dave. "It was because I were often late for school. One master 'e really 'ad it in for me 'cos of that."

"Why were you late Dave?" we ask.

"Cos me ferret got stuck down the rabbit hole. Wouldn't come out. 'Ad to wait for 'im to get bored and come out."

Huh?

Dave blows his nose loudly and goes back to scratching his arms. His eczema is bothering him.

"But why were you ferreting Dave?" asks Shropshire brother.

"For rabbits of course!" shouts Dave, "I could sell 'em for a bob to the teachers. And take 'em home too. Mum would be pleased with a rabbit or two."

"So you were catching rabbits before school," I say, "and then you went to school. But what did you do with the ferret then?"

"'Hung 'im on me peg in a sack," says Dave. Obvious really.

How school has changed in Dave's lifetime. I try to imagine the health and safety implications of hanging a ferret in a sack in the cloakroom today.

"My mate at school though, 'e put his ferret in his desk, bloody idiot. Made a right mess of the desk it did."

"So you'd get the cane if you and the ferret were late for school," I say.

"Yep. Mr Brand. That were the master's name. 'E went mad with the cane one day and just hit everyone in his path. Caught me across me face, right under the eye." He points to his face. "I got 'ome and Dad said, 'what's wrong with yer face?' and I told 'im. Next day Mr Brand come in to school with a black eye. 'E used to drink in the same pub as Dad, so you can guess what Dad did to 'im."

Crikey.

"You 'ad a ferret didn't you?" says Dave, turning to Shropshire brother. "Lovely one that was. Jake wasn't it?"

"Yes Jake, that's how I met my first girlfriend. I used to take Jake to the top of the field and let him run around and when he was tired he'd run back to the cottage. But one day he ran next door instead. So I went round there and called over the fence to the girl who was sunbathing in the garden. 'Could I come and get my ferret please?' Do you know what she did?"

"No..." we say.

"She went over to the flowerbed where Jake was playing and just picked him up and carried him over to me. And I thought gosh, wow!"

We laugh.

"And now," says Shropshire brother, "let's go out for tea. To the forest. We'll take your new chair Anna, so I can have a go at pushing it."

"She don't want to go in that," says Dave.

"Shhhhh Dave," says Shropshire brother. "We'll put it in my car. And we'll see."

I find Anna a jacket to wear. It's warm in the sun. She looks for her handbag, but Shropshire brother says that he's paying for tea. No need for her bag. Or purse. Not that we know where it is.

We help her out to the car. She walks very very slowly now. And painfully.

She will have to accept the wheelchair now.

Fingers crossed.

FOREST

18th May 2019

. . . .

The forest in May. The lanes we drive through in Shropshire brother's fast car are strewn with grandmother's lace. Late bluebells, nettles, dandelions and hawthorn. And something we called 'sweetheart' when we were children, but I don't know its real name.

And then the ancient oak and beech woods. Dave tries to tell Shropshire brother which roads go where, and which roads connect with other roads. But Shropshire brother knows all the forest ways and doesn't listen.

"Where are we going?" says Anna after a while.

"Nettle Hill Hotel," says Shropshire brother, "not far now."

He stops the car in an isolated car park amongst the trees. "We'll walk a little way."

"I'll need my stick," says Dave.

We help Anna out of the car and into her wheelchair, fastening the lap belt and folding out the foot rests.

"Dave!" calls Anna as Shropshire brother takes off at great speed along the forest road. But Dave is left behind, walking slowly and leaning on his stick. He didn't exercise his legs after his knee operations, and they have stiffened over the months and years.

I am running to catch up with Shropshire brother. This is very similar to the wheelchair outing with Devon brother. Too fast!

How will we get the wheelchair over the cattle grid? Is this the drive up to the Nettle Hill Hotel? Look at the beautiful copper beech trees at the top of the drive! It looks very quiet here. Aren't there any guests?

And then the hotel itself, an imposing old hunting lodge. The enormous gloomy bar is full of chunky old oak furniture, and antlers and stag's heads line the walls.

"There is no-one else here," I whisper to Shropshire brother, who is struggling to push Anna's wheelchair over the thick dusty carpets. Not even a landlord or bar person.

And then out of the darkness we see an old white-haired man with a tea towel and tray in his hands. Shropshire brother goes to the bar to order tea, and returns with a tray bearing an old metal teapot and some utilitarian crockery. The handle of the teapot is cobwebby. I do hope we are not going to eat here.

I pour the tea. "Where's the scones and jam then?" shouts Dave.

Shropshire brother changes the subject. We talk about his forthcoming visit to France.

"It made me think of Fawlty Towers," I tell him when we are back in the car. "The hotel that time forgot."

"Yep, that's why we didn't have anything to eat," he agrees, "and so now we are heading to Mario's."

"Good," says Dave.

Mario's is an unassuming bungalow in a quiet village.

The garden is full of customers sitting at picnic tables eating ice cream under an enormous electricity pylon. We leave Anna and Dave in the car and head to the counter.

"I'm buying," says Shropshire brother, "coconut or lemon meringue? I'll get the oldies lemon meringue I reckon."

He directs me to look at an old photograph on the wall behind us. Mario, newly arrived from Italy with his wife and several children, smiling at the camera. From their clothes, I'd say it's mid nineteen-forties.

Shropshire brother strides across the room.

"Dave tells me he went out with Mario's daughters when he was young."

"Which one?"

There are several pretty Italian girls in the photograph.

"All of them!" laughs Shropshire brother.

Of course.

We take the ice creams back to the car. Home-made lemon meringue with chocolate flakes and cigar-shaped biscuits. Anna and Dave are very happy.

Anna watches the children playing on the lawn next to the car park. And a toddler sitting on the grass with her ice-cream.

Shropshire brother looks at me in the driver's mirror. I know what he is thinking.

Anna is enjoying her ice-cream and the children playing playing in the sunshine. She knows Dave is with her. We are delighted that she co-operated with the wheelchair.

But she doesn't really know anything else. What day is is. What time it is. Where she is. Or that we are her children.

And that is just a little sad.

LOVE

1st June 2019

. . . .

"Your hair needs a flippin' wash!"

Dave's right. Anna hasn't been to the hairdresser for two weeks now. The wound on the back of her head, where she fell, is still healing. Dave takes her to the nurse at the surgery every few days to have it dressed. But Anna's hair is falling in her eyes in lank strands.

"It might be better to give it a gentle wash here Dave," I suggest, "over the sink."

Anna has always washed her hair in the sink so I am thinking that it would seem familiar to her. Even though there is a newly-fitted shower upstairs in the bathroom.

"I want to go to the hairdresser," says Anna frostily.

"Well when your wound's healed Dave will take you again. But just for now I'll fetch a chair and Dave can wash your hair for you over the sink."

Anna slowly gets to her feet, holding on to the Aga rail to steady herself. Good. I run upstairs to fetch shampoo, towels, comb. Quick, before she changes her mind.

Dave helps Anna to the chair. Then he fills the sink with water. It takes several minutes to get her comfortable and secure enough to lean back.

"Just call me Teasy Weasy," says Dave laughing and stroking her forehead.

"Teasy who deary?"

"She's supposed to be takin' antibiotics from the doctor to get this wound healed," says Dave.

"I AM taking them," says Anna crossly.

"I keep gettin' 'em mixed up with my tablets," says Dave, pointing to a pile of prescription medicines on the window sill.

We need to sort this out.

Dave is a surprisingly gentle hairdresser and Anna sits calmly for him.

But wait... what is he washing her hair with?

Surely not the pan scourer!

Unbelievable.

Dave has finished shampooing and is kissing her forehead.

"That's better isn't it little one," he says gently, popping the pan scourer back in its dish.

Anna smiles. So he kisses her some more.

For heavens sake oldies, can we get on with this! I've got lunch to make.

Then he takes her out to the garden, sits her on the bench and carefully combs her thin hair in the sunshine.

"Ow, ow, ow!" says Anna as the comb tugs on the tangles in her hair.

I'm trying to sort out the mess of tablets and lotions. Packets and tubes and tubs. And I've quietly taken the pan scourer to the dustbin.

"Dave are these skin lotions for Anna?" They don't seem to be labelled.

"Nope they're mine. Got 'em for something on me arm. Doctor said I 'ad to put the cream on it. It's all written down somewhere. Nice doctor she is. Checked me all over. I 'ad to take all me clothes off. And I've not done that for a woman for a long time I can tell you."

Right.

The sun is warm and Anna dozes. I make coffee and Dave and I sort through the medications. Then Dave goes outside to feed bachelor pigeon and a new robin.

"And I reckon I've seen a linnet on the bank 'ere too," he tells me.

And while he heads off to meet Gordon for lunch (a salad of course) I make Anna some egg sandwiches with tomatoes. And then suggest a walk around the church.

"I'm not sure I could manage that today deary."

In the long cupboard I find her new wheelchair resting against mini oven.

"I'll need my jacket," she tells me when I wheel it into the dining room.

Today we can go as slowly as we wish. We can stop in the lane and admire the purple azalea in the neighbour's garden. The honeysuckle climbing through the hedges. The village pond, still and very green.

Two drakes and five ducks circling the duck house in the centre of the pond. Lambs and their mothers at the gate to the big sloping field. Rooks everywhere, cawing and arguing.

And when we get back to the cottage I am tired. It is surprisingly hard work to push a wheelchair, even with a very frail person in it. But Anna is happy.

"That was a nice day out deary," she says smiling and closing her eyes against the bright sun in the garden. "We must do it again."

SPAIN

8th June 2019

. . . .

I haven't seen Anna and Dave for two weeks now. I was invited to Spain. A villa near Cadiz. And I thought, yes, that is a good idea. Tall son isn't far away and can check on Anna and Dave.

But he and Berkshire girlfriend were flying to Mexico.

Shropshire brother could stay at the cottage for a couple of days perhaps.

"We're off to France for my birthday," he told me. The signal was bad. He was driving somewhere.

Devon brother is always happy to help.

"Alis and I will be in Italy, I'm afraid."

Oh.

Medical daughter sounded impatient when I asked her.

"I'm busy on the geriatric wards!" she told me.

So eldest grandson is in charge.

And all is quiet. No messages.

Just the blue bubbling of the swimming pool. Tall stately palms above our heads, and the strange cries of birds I do not know.

But we sprinkled toast crumbs on the lawn this morning. And soon sparrows came down from the pine trees.

And later in the morning as the sun rose higher in the sky I saw a familiar figure.

A blackbird. Watching. Hopping.

In the morning heat.

LUMBAGO

15th June 2019

. . . .

Dave rings me during the week. He sounds very pleased. He asks whether I had a good holiday and then declares,

"I've found 'er teeth!"

"Where Dave!"

"Under the chest of drawers in 'er bedroom in one of those 'andbags. Bit of a secret compartment with a zip, it was."

That's odd. Devon brother and I searched the bedroom thoroughly. I can only imagine Anna must have moved the handbag after we'd gone home.

"That's great news," I tell him, and make a mental note to cancel her dental appointment at the hospital.

"Er 'ead's not good though. I took 'er down the doctor's on Saturday 'cos she 'ad an appointment, and I 'ad an appointment for me ears there, and the bloody place was closed!"

"But it was a Saturday Dave?"

"Well the appointment was up at the hospital, but we got muddled, so we went to the wrong place."

Oh dear. This is not uncommon. I have a conversation with medical daughter that evening about elderly people and their appointments. They forget them. They can't physically get to them. They go to the wrong place. They go on the wrong date. Or at the wrong time.

"Perhaps we need a system where the GP surgery rings them before the appointment to check they are coming," I suggest.

"Mmmmm." Medical daughter is probably thinking of the cost of such a system.

"We just get a text from our GP surgery," says my colleague at work.

Dave does have a mobile phone, but never switches it on.

"And now my back's bad. Pain goes all down me leg. Can't stand up proper," Dave tells me, "lumbago I reckon."

Lumbago. Probably sciatica if the pain is affecting his leg too.

But when I arrive on Saturday morning all is calm.

Except for the wind.

"Look at that wind!" exclaims Anna, again and again. "The poor trees… they're bent double."

Dave is limping, but not too badly.

"Them painkillers doctor gave me are alright I reckon. Take the edge off the pain they do."

"What about some stretching exercises Dave?"

"Stretchin' eh?" Dave thinks about this for a while, "what's that then?"

The new cleaner didn't turn up during the week so I need to vacuum upstairs and downstairs.

Then change the bedlinen, put on the washing, clean out the fridge and help Dave wash Anna's hair. Remember to throw out the pan scourer.

The wound on the back of her head is still sore and needing regular dressings. The morning passes quickly and then Dave is off to the boatyard to meet Gordon for lunch, and to visit Alan, the gamekeeper/builder who isn't well.

I heat up some carrot soup, while Anna sits in her armchair staring out across the fields which are full of pale grasses.

"No cows...," says Anna quietly.

"Plenty of birds out on the bank though," I tell her, "and I can see a squirrel on the nut feeder. Dave won't be pleased." I open the kitchen window and the squirrel darts away into the field.

"Yes, we were given some squirrels," says Anna absently.

And then there's a knock at the door and I open it to Joan, an old friend of Anna's, who hasn't visited for many months. She rang me recently and explained that she didn't know anything about dementia and felt worried about visiting on her own.

"I don't want to visit her unless you're there," she tells me.

And she has brought two bags of fruit scones. Anna looks pleased.

Joan tells us that as she is nearing eighty, she is selling her house and moving nearer the town. Her house is too big for her. Her garden is too big for her.

"Which town?" says Anna.

Joan names several, and tells us that she hasn't decided yet.

I leave them to catch up and go out the garden to check the washing. The garden is full of colour.

Purple aubretia spills over the stones supporting the bank. Yellow, purple and pink pansies fill the pots outside the front door. And the tulip tree is decorated with dozens of pale green and orange flowers. Joan comes out to join me.

"Anna's dozing now. I'll say goodbye."

She turns to go. "But I'll come back another Saturday. If you're here."

I put on the kettle, but the hissing and popping wakes Anna. It's half past four

She struggles to her feet.

"I'll just pop upstairs..."

When she returns she is carrying her green handbag. Then she goes to the long cupboard and looks through her jackets and coats. Finally selecting a jacket that matches her handbag. Then to the kitchen drawer to find her make-up. When I go out to the kitchen I find all the scones have been cut in half and arranged on plates.

"I'll just put on some make-up deary."

Where is she going?

"I'll have to phone my mother," she says.

I move to another chair so that she can find the red book with all their telephone numbers in. But Anna is distracted by a new brochure for garden plants that arrived that morning.

"Are we going soon?" she says eventually.

"Well, it's evening now," I say, "and Dave will be back soon to tell us about his day. He'll wonder where we are if we go out."

"Oh yes deary," she says, "but I'll just go upstairs and find my purse."

She walks slowly, carefully, purposefully to the stairs. She has to get ready. It's that time of day. The anxiety is growing. She needs to go home.

Sundowning.

SUMMER

22nd June 2019

. . . .

The last days of June. The early days of summer. Still no cows in the field. Dave reckons the farmers are leaving the long grass for hay. It means that Mr Pheasant disappears when he has finished his breakfast on the bank. Only the top of his dark green head can be seen. Hunting cat can steal through the long grasses. And the squirrels can avoid Dave's morning checks from his bedroom window.

"Stealin' all the nuts from the feeders, them bloody squirrels," he says irritably. And tells us that all the neighbours are saying the same thing.

No clouds. The sun is very warm. Anna can sit out on the garden bench and dry her hair. But I have to keep moving this bench in and out of the sun. And being wooden it's heavy. First she is too hot. Then too cold. And she seems puzzled by things she sees in the garden.

"What's that metal thing deary?"

"The rake Anna."

"What's that's up on the bank deary?" (pointing)

"The oil tank Anna."

"How did that chicken get up on the bank?"

"I think it's just enjoying the sunshine." (it's a ceramic chicken that Anna herself put there years ago).

I noticed on my arrival that Anna no longer wears her make-up; the familiar green eye-shadow and lipstick, or her clip-on earrings. Or asks if we can go out to lunch, or even coffee. It's some weeks since we went to the garden centre for lunch.

I am sweeping the patio, clearing away the patches of soil that Mr Pheasant dislodges in his dust baths on the bank. And the bits of dried leaves left over from the autumn. And I stop to gather my breath, and think that the cottage garden is at its nicest in June, like so many other gardens in England.

Shropshire brother rang me during the week on his way home from somewhere to do with horses. We talked about Anna of course, and how we wished that she could be somewhere more practical, where she could be more cared for. Spoilt even. Shropshire brother tells me about a ninety-three year old man he knows of, whose luxury nursing home fees are thirteen hundred pounds a week. The cost each year seems extraordinary. And Anna would need a specialist nursing home.

And at the same time we wondered whether Anna herself would want this. Certainly she always liked the finer things in life. But to be in an unfamiliar place. To be with many other elderly people with dementia. To be away from the cottage. To be parted from Dave?

And while I am thinking about this as I sweep, I hear Dave's old car driving into the carport. Bachelor pigeon hurriedly flies off across the field and Robbie perches on the old staddle stone, waiting for another bird to disturb the fat ball feeder and shower pieces down to him.

"Oh you're out in the sunshine fatty!" shouts Dave. Anna looks pleased to see him.

"Where have you been Dave?" He sits on the bench beside her.

"Just out for lunch with Gordon. 'Ad a very tasty prawn salad and half a pint of lovely cider. And Gordon, well 'e 'ad Yorkshire puddings of course."

Just Yorkshire puddings?

"Then 'e 'ad chocolate pudding. An I said, Gordon, all this is no good for you. Won't do you no good."

Anna listens attentively.

"'E don't listen to a word I say of course. I reckon it's 'is mum's fault. She wouldn't let Gordon go out with a girl 'e wanted to go out with. Reckon that's the problem."

Presumably that was some years ago. And how many times have I heard this story?

Sweeping finished, I go inside to make a pot of tea. Through the open window I see them still talking in the sunshine. Anna holding Dave's hand.

"I don't think either of them would be happy being apart," I say.

To no-one in particular.

SALAD

29th June 2019

．．

The hottest day of the year so far. Dave's plants are flagging. The nasturtiums have collapsed over the sides of their pot. The new begonia in the chimney pot has wilted. Anna tuts at the struggling pansies.

I wore my lightest clothes today. I'm thinking about the heat from the Aga. But at least the front door and all the windows are open. Anna, in a polo neck and long wool skirt, is making coffee. Dave is reading the Saturday papers. The first thing I notice is a new photograph on the mantelpiece. Black and white and creased on one corner.

Surely not?

"Is that your wedding photo with Cecil?" I ask Anna when Dave has gone to the sitting room.

"Um, yes deary."

It's clearly from the nineteen-fifties. Anna in a narrow-waisted full skirt with a short jacket, and decorated headband. Cecil in a smart wide-trousered suit smiling broadly. It's his wide smile that makes me think of John. So similar.

"Does Dave mind you having that photo on the mantelpiece?" I ask innocently.

"No deary,"

And that's it. No further explanation. Anna, who never goes into detail about anything.

"I've moved 'er 'ospital appointment," Dave tells me. "Washing machine won't work and the bloke's comin' Monday, so I couldn't get 'er there."

Oh.

This appointment is at the hospital where I work. Anna's GP is sending her there to get her head wound checked as it is not healing properly. I have arranged to take some time off work to meet them and go with them to the appointment. It's a hospital some distance from the cottage, in the next county, and unfamiliar to them. But now Dave has changed it. And the washing machine only works on one cycle anyway!

"And me leg's still bad."

He sits in the chair by the window. "Can't lift the bloody leg to do the exercises the physio gave me. They reckon if I do the exercises I won't need them painkillers."

"And Gordon says 'e can't meet me today 'cos of that motorway being closed. Reckon 'e worried about gettin' stuck in long queues."

"Never mind Dave," I say, "it's very hot out there and the roads are full of traffic diverted from the motorway. So Gordon's probably better staying at home."

But Dave's not listening. "What's all this stretchin' about anyway? Me leg's just not moving proper."

"I've brought a fish pie," I tell them, "what veg would you like with it?"

Dave's face brightens. "Fish pie! Reckon I'd like a nice salad. She won't though. Fatty never eats salad."

All I can find at the bottom of the fridge is lettuce, spring onions, tomatoes and red pepper. All past their best. But Dave looks astonished when I put the bowl on the round table.

"Well I never!" he exclaims, "I'd 'ave never thought of puttin' all them together."

This is strange. I thought Dave had a salad every Saturday at the pub with Gordon.

Anna picks at the fish pie, discarding the potatoes. But then has a large bowl of rhubarb and cream.

"Reckon I'll 'ave that again for supper," says Dave carrying the left-over fish pie and salad to the kitchen.

We sit out on the bench in the shade after lunch. On the bank the purple verbena and the hollyhocks are vying to be the tallest. Dave has to keep getting up to feed the birds on the bank and top up their water bowl. Every so often Anna offers to fetch me a blanket or a hot water bottle.

"Daft rat," shouts Dave.

"Don't call me a rat," says Anna coldly.

I distract them with photos of the family on my mobile phone.

"And me phone's not working either," Dave tells me, "I like to 'ave it with me. Just in case. Don't really use it though."

That's probably why it's not working now. I promise to call tall son about this.

"And I got this shampoo that you leave in for ten minutes and it's supposed to make yer 'air thicken up."

"Is it working deary?" asks Anna.

"Nope. Well it's makin' the sides thicker but not the top. It's the top where you want it thicker don't you."

He pulls at his white cottonseed hair.

"When you think I 'ad golden curls once. All the girls loved my 'air."

"Golden curls Dave? I thought you had very dark hair?"

"I'm talkin' about when I was a teenager. Had golden curls on me chest as well. And mainly dark curls too of course. The golden curls was streaky like."

Streaky like?

"What do you mean Dave?"

"Dunno. But I reckon I know what it was. I was washin' meself all over with Tide. And I reckon it was Tide that was bleaching me 'air."

Crikey.

"Would you like some tea deary?" says Anna.

I go into the kitchen to help her. "I'll get the milk."

What's this at the back of the fridge?

I take out the bottles of sauces and vinegars and dressings that Shropshire brother must have left here. He loves cooking. Oh dear. The back of the fridge is thick with ice. And deep within the ice is... what exactly? I scrape off some ice with my fingernail. A bottle of garlic sauce. Packets of pastry. Encased within a fridge igloo.

I think we may have a fridge problem.

To add to the list.

HOSPITAL

6th July 2019

. . . .

"Whose birthday is it then?"

The mantelpiece is filled with cards. One, a pencil drawing of a blackbird, is a card I recognise. Yes, I sent it to Anna for her birthday. But that was four months ago.

"Mine, I think deary,"

"Very nice Anna. Coffee?"

I marvel at her wool polo neck and long skirt, with Dave's blue stripey socks. Dave is busy flinging open the windows in the sitting room.

"Bloody hot today," he says to Robbie who has perched on cherub's head, waiting for breakfast.

"Er 'ospital appointment's on Tuesday then," he says, joining us in the dining room.

"Um Thursday I think Dave."

"What's that for Dave?" asks Anna.

"For them doctors to look at yer 'ead wound," says Dave.

"I'll meet you in the car park at eleven Dave. I can bring a wheelchair and get Anna to her appointment."

"On Wednesday is it?" says Dave.

"No Thursday," I say again.

"Or is it Tuesday your appointment?" he says, looking at Anna.

It's too hot to discuss this further. So I fetch the calendar and put it on Dave's lap.

"Says 'ere Thursday," he shouts, "so I reckon it must be Thursday."

"Is that my hair appointment?" says Anna.

Outside the window on the bird feeder the sparrows are happily pecking at the fat balls. But there's a sudden flurry of wings and two young starlings fighting to get at the bird feeder. The sparrows scatter to the bank.

"Got lots of them young starlings now," says Dave, "didn't 'ave them 'ere for a long time, and now they're all back again."

There's a knock at the door and Gordon comes in. Slowly. Out of breath. He must have walked up the lane.

"Hot isn't it," says Dave. "Cup of tea?"

I make Gordon some tea while Dave starts a discussion about Brexit. Gordon doesn't look as if he wants to discuss Brexit.

"We'd better get going Dave if we want some lunch," says Gordon, putting down his mug. "Can you be here at the end of August if Dave and I go over to France. Might be the last time before you know what."

I put the dates in my diary.

Anna and I are sitting in the garden when Dave returns from his lunch. It's too hot to go for a walk. Too hot to sit inside.

But I have managed to make a macaroni cheese for supper. One of Dave's favourite suppers.

"Am I going to the hairdressers's on Thursday Dave?"

"No. We're goin' to that hospital to get yer 'ead sorted out like I told you."

Silence. Just the sounds of horses' hooves in the lane.

Then I feel her hand on my arm. Very gently.

"I'm frightened deary." Tears in the corners of her eyes.

I hold her hand. "What are you frightened of Anna?"

"What's going to happen to me..."

"At the hospital?"

Silence.

"Well the doctor will just examine the wound on your head. Dave and I will be with you."

"No... not the hospital. I'm frightened of… the end… the end of me."

There's a roar of laughter from Dave. "Daft woman! You're not goin' to know nothing about it. Be like goin' to sleep. I'll hold yer hand. And if I go first you can hold my hand can't yer."

Anna doesn't look comforted by this. The talk of her hospital appointment has started this anxiety in her. As it has done before.

Usually she talks likes this when Dave is out. In the garden, or the shed, or at lunch with Gordon. If I ask her to explain her fear, or wait for her to tell me more, there's nothing.

"I'm still worried deary." Her grip on my hand becomes tighter.

"What you got this fear of death for?" shouts Dave. "Sometimes I think yer gone anyway. When I open yer bedroom door in the mornings."

I want to tell Dave to shut up. That's my first thought. And then I wonder whether it's his old country way to see death as a natural part of life. That's how he grew up. Your grandparents came to live in the family home when they got too old to cope alone. And that's where they died. Buried in the churchyard up past the pond.

And if it's a bird or an animal, suffering or in pain. You just get your gun from the cupboard.

Anna throws him a cold look and gets unsteadily to her feet. One fairy shoe sliding sideways as usual.

"I'm going to the bathroom," she tells us quietly.

"Let me kiss yer weathered hand then," says Dave grabbing her fingers and kissing them.

"I do everything don't I," he tells her. "I even take out yer teeth at night and scrub 'em, and 'ave 'em all ready for you in the mornin'. I'm 'ere to look after you. So stop worryin'."

He kisses her hand again and she holds on to him tightly.

"When she gets like this I sometimes play 'er some opera to calm 'er down," he tells me. "My Beloved Father. Do you know that?"

I have to confess I don't know much about opera.

"I didn't 'ave one of course. But she did."

He strokes Anna's hand.

"That's why she cries."

SLUGS

11th July 2019

. . . .

Thursday morning. I am standing in a disabled parking space at the hospital. Where's Dave? He said eleven o'clock sharp. It's so busy here that if I don't save this space they won't be able to park.

But then I see him, limping towards the hospital entrance, his white hair standing on end. He must have found somewhere else to park.

"Dave!" I shout. He can't hear me of course, so I run towards him.

"She's over by the entrance sittin' on a bench," he shouts. So I change direction and find Anna sitting with a young female nurse. Anna seems to be turning out her handbag onto the bench.

"I'll go inside and find a wheelchair," I tell her. But she seems more concerned at finding her lipstick.

"We'll get 'er inside and then find a chair," says Dave, joining us, "do 'er good to 'ave a little bit of a walk."

"If you give me the appointment letter I'll go on ahead and book you into the clinic Dave."

Dave fumbles in his old shirt pocket. "Too bloody hot this shirt is in this weather," he tells us.

I take the folded letter to the reception desk. And then I read it. And then I see that the appointment was five minutes ago.

And we are not even in the clinic. How can this be? Dave told me the appointment was today.

The receptionist looks sympathetically at Anna and Dave struggling to sit on the fold-out seats outside the Costa cafe. "I'll ring the clinic and explain," she says.

I feel the eyes of the waiting queue on my back. They can sense my agitation.

"Was the appointment definitely for today?" asks the receptionist.

I check the letter again. Oh no! It was last week!

I beckon to Dave and he lumbers to his feet.

"Oh I brought the wrong bloody appointment letter," he says, "must be the earlier one. I changed that one to today." He turns and walks back to join Anna.

"So sorry," I tell the receptionist. She sighs. "Never mind dear."

The queue behind me smiles.

I buy Anna and Dave a flat white and open some chocolate biscuits I bought earlier. This cheers Anna immensely. Then we walk very slowly to the clinic. I have found Anna a comfortable wheelchair. Dave holds her hand, so we have to stop and move to one side whenever a hospital bed or trolley approaches. The corridors are long and every obstacle we approach produces a small cry from Anna, "Oh dear!" "Look out!" "Oh no!" "Help Dave!"

"Look at all these pictures," I say, pointing to the hospital art group work on the corridor walls. Anna stares disinterestedly at the country scenes, the gardens and the painting of cats and dogs. She has always preferred abstract art. But Dave loves them.

"Wouldn't mind one of 'em on the kitchen wall," he tells us.

We are shown to a small examination room. There are two small chairs and a bed with a curtain.

"Hold my hand Dave," says Anna quietly. We are all a bit nervous.

"What's that slug doin' on the floor by yer foot?" says Dave.

Slug?

"Dave, that's the door stop," I tell him, "just relax."

(Dave always has an eye out for slugs. They ruin your plants. One evening he tells us he gathered up eighty of them from the garden).

The door opens and in comes a young Asian doctor. He shakes our hands.

"I'll just examine this head wound of yours," he tells Anna.

"Ow, ow, ow, ow, you're hurting me!"

The doctor pauses. "The wound isn't infected. There's nothing sinister here. I think you should leave the dressing off during the day. Which position do you sleep in?"

Anna looks at him blankly.

"On your side... on your back?"

She says nothing. Dave can't hear the conversation.

"I think Anna sleeps mainly on her side," I say.

"She has dementia," I add quietly.

There's a squeak from Anna. "Do I!"

"And that's a lovely skirt you're wearing today Anna."

I am changing the subject very quickly.

Anna smiles and strokes her skirt. The doctor looks amused.

"Where are all my wedding rings?" she says, looking at her empty hand on her lap.

Oh no. Please do not feel it necessary to tell the doctor that you have had four husbands. And Dave three wives.

But the doctor is putting a new dressing on Anna's head.

"Ow, ow, ow, ow, Dave, Dave." She reaches out her hand to him. And her other hand to me.

"You've got yer family here with you," says Dave, "it's all okay."

"Family is very important," agrees the doctor.

"We're 'ere to look after you," says Dave.

"Yes, we're looking after you," I agree.

"Shut. Up," says Anna giving me a cold look.

Right.

I wheel her out of the clinic, with Dave holding on to the wheelchair for support.

"Can I say how very pretty you look," she calls to a young female doctor in a red dress with a full skirt.

"And so do you," calls the doctor.

"Don't be ridiculous," says Anna, as we head back to the main entrance.

I help Anna into the car and see them out of the parking space, reminding Dave of the one-way system in the car park (probably to no avail). I am left with the empty wheelchair.

Time to get back to a very busy office.

Probably more restful.

LINGERIE

20th July 2019

· ·

Dave has been shopping for lingerie. But he doesn't pronounce this as you might expect.

"So we got 'er two bras, didn't we rat," he explains, "she can't do 'em up at the back now, so we got 'er ones that do up at the front."

Anna listens carefully, ready to silence Dave with a chilling look.

"Can't 'av 'em droopin' can we!" he laughs.

Dave will never learn that you might be able to make a passing mild criticism of Anna for her housekeeping, or her cooking or lack of general knowledge. But never her looks, her clothes or her make-up. But he seems oblivious to her withering stare.

"Plenty of your birds on the bank today," I say, changing the subject, "and what's that one on the feeder. It has a black bib and white cheeks?"

Dave stares hard out of the window. "It's a coaltit I reckon. Don't see many of 'em in the garden these days."

"Coffee anyone?"

The fridge needs sorting. Again. On the top shelf an opened packet of bacon lies atop the yogurts. A plate of defrosting raw fish nestles close to the open bowl of stewed rhubarb.

There is a decomposition of something in the salad drawer. Dave was interested to see me covering food with lids and silver foil when I stayed at the cottage last year. I thought he might try this himself, but it hasn't happened so far. Anna has never shown the slightest concern for food hygiene.

"Don't fuss deary," is all she would say. And my grandmother was the same. Their kitchens were tidy, but except for a daily wipe down with a cloth, they were never properly cleaned. The cloth would wipe the sink and worktops. And the floor if necessary.

Spitfire mug for Dave. Poppy mug for Anna. And mine is the one I carefully hide on the top shelf every week.

"Don't wear yourself out deary," calls Anna from her armchair. She says this whatever I'm doing. But never to Dave or my brothers. I think it might be a little passive aggression. If she cannot do things now, she is going to suggest that I will struggle to do them as well. So I usually change the subject.

"Biscuit anyone?"

"Trouble is, yer used to a lot of attention aren't yer,?" says Dave, "And yer miss it of course." Dave can be surprisingly perceptive.

"But I still love yer," he says, "whatever. An' now I'm off for a salad with 'orrible Gordon."

"Don't eat too much Dave," calls Anna as he stuffs his car keys into his pocket and kisses her goodbye.

"Got somethin' rattlin' in me boot I got to sort out," he tells us as he opens the front door.

"Anna, we'll go to the garden centre for lunch next time," I say, "now that your head is healing."

She touches the sore place on her head tentatively.

415

"When you can wear your hairpiece again you'll feel more like going out for lunch."

"Yes deary." She leans forward in her chair, "and what are you looking at? Yes, you out there." Who is she talking to?

I turn to look out of the window. It's ceramic chicken, surrounded by pink and red hollyhocks.

"We should take your birthday cards down soon Anna. It will be easier to dust the mantelpiece then." The photograph is still there from last week. Anna notices me staring at it.

"He's a handsome man isn't he?" she says.

"Cecil?"

"Yes, don't you think so..."

"I do. He reminds me of my father. Perhaps it's a Welsh face?"

"Well he's very helpful to Dave," she says.

"How so?"

"He comes over and helps him in the sheds deary. Several times a week I think."

"That's nice of him."

I realise I am waiting for her to smile. Just a slight smile. A smile to let me know that she is joking.

Anna always liked a prank. To fill the toes of Sydney brother's wellington boots with strawberry and orange cremes. The chocolates that everyone rejected from the box of Quality Street at Christmas. To sew up the arms of his shirts that she posted to Australia when he first left home. To decorate my car with 90th birthday balloons while I was at work.

But no. Anna may, for that brief moment, have been joking about Cecil. Or she may have been saying what she believed to be true. But in the next moment she'd forgotten what she'd said, and so I will never know.

She is staring out of the window again. This time she is watching Mr Pheasant walking away across the field. I go closer to the window. He has lost all his tail feathers and looks strangely despondent for such a proud bird. Is that moulting? Or fighting? I make a mental note to ask Dave.

"I think he wants some corn deary."

"Mr Pheasant?"

"No that chicken on the bank deary."

I take a few grains of corn from the bin outside and sprinkle them on the bank in front of ceramic chicken.

And through the wavy glass of the old dining room window I see Anna smiling.

Briefly.

MIDLANDS

27th July 2019

I've been visiting medical daughter and her fiancé in the Midlands, and meeting up with Birmingham cousins for supper. The weather was so hot. When I rang Dave to say I would be at the cottage on Saturday he sounded very pleased. And relieved that he could join Gordon for their salad lunch.

He reported that tall son had been to the cottage, setting up Dave's new mobile phone, fixing something to do with the television, and taking Dave and Anna for supper at a nearby pub. And eldest grandson had been doing the gardening, trimming some of the overgrown bushes. I breathed a sigh of relief.

And when I arrive at the cottage they are pleased to see me. Dave sitting with the Saturday newspaper and Anna in the kitchen putting on mascara. I fetch her a piece of kitchen towel because the mascara has dotted her nose and cheeks, and seems to have missed one eye completely. Dave comes out to the kitchen. I notice his limping is more obvious. And then I notice his new shoes. Light tan brogues. As stiff as a board. He notices my gaze.

"Yep new brogues. Got 'em in a catalogue. Reduced from a hundred and fifty to seventy-five. Bloody good eh?"

"Yes..." I agree, "they'll take some wearing in won't they?"

"I'll wear 'em out to lunch today," says Dave, "an' I'm cutting back on lunch, 'cos I'm cutting back on eatin'."

As he says this he takes the last of the mini chocolate brownies from the round table.

"An' we've washed 'er 'air this morning, so she looks nice. An' the back of 'er 'ead is nearly all healed isn't it rat."

"Reckon I'd make a good male nurse," he adds. "Can't imagine wantin' to be one though."

He heads off to his car after kissing Anna goodbye, and treading on her feet as usual.

"I don't know where my combs keep going," says Anna, "people just walk in and take them."

I search the kitchen drawers and find a round hairbrush. Anna holds it tentatively. Then carefully brushes her fringe.

I make mushroom soup and toast. Anna eats it all. Then strawberries and ice-cream. While I am sweeping the patio outside the front door Anna comes out to sit in the porch. In the shade. The new oil tank has been encased in a bamboo coat (for aesthetic reasons) and Dave's trailing plants are starting to disguise the newly-built wall beneath it.

"Our mother's were friends weren't they deary?" says Anna.

"Um yes Anna. Can you remember my mother's name?"

"Everyone called her Mick."

Ah. Anna is back in Birmingham.

"Have you seen Terence lately?"

"Uh... no..."

"We were all friends when we were young weren't we." She lowers her voice. "And Terence was rather spoilt, if you remember. But we were friends."

"And you're a faithful friend aren't you," says Anna, pointing at a spot on the patio with her walking stick.

I put down the broom. "Who is this?"

Anna traces the edges of the old paving stone. "Here's his nose, and his eyes. And here's his head and his body."

I look carefully. But all I can see is a rectangular paving stone with a broken edge.

She is smiling. I have no doubt that she believes I am a friend from Birmingham. But I am really not sure whether she is also playing games with me.

We hear Dave's car in the carport. He limps into the house and returns in his old sailing shoes.

"Don't reckon I'll drive with them brogues again."

I'm not really surprised.

I make tea in our favourite mugs and we sit on the bench next to the bank. Dave crumbles fat balls for Robbie's youngsters who dart from the bushes on the bank to the staddle stone outside the kitchen window, and then onto the top of the green boiler. The conversation includes youngsters and mobile phones, Brexit (of course) and the hollyhocks that have seeded themselves in a tub reserved for nasturtiums.

"Still not cuttin' that field," says Dave, "no cows either. Haven't seen them farmers for a while. Can't have a bonfire with the field that dry."

"And look at them daisies of yours!" shouts Dave, pointing at the tub of yellow gerbera under the window. The wooden tub has started to rot away, spilling soil around its base, but the flowers are bright and sunny. "What you lookin' at?"

Anna takes no notice. She doesn't hear him.

She is staring at the paving slab again.

Talking to her new friend.

GREEN WOODPECKER

3rd August 2019

. . . .

I hear the laugh of the green woodpecker as I take the washing out to the line hanging from the tulip tree. It makes you stop what you're doing and just listen. A strange sound in the English countryside, and apparently a warning of rain to come.

As I drove into the village today it was full of life. A bouncy castle and children's slide on the recreation ground, surrounded by excited young villagers. Residents on the allotment, or in their gardens. One man up a ladder clearing his gutters. A portly man in an orange teeshirt power-walking. Roses everywhere. And small red apples spilled onto the lane from the tree over the hedge.

Dave is washing Anna's hair in the sink when I arrive. Robbie and the young robins look hopefully towards the kitchen window.

"Fronds of 'air, like seaweed," Dave tells me in his curiously poetic way, as he pours water over her head from an enamel mug.

"Ow, ow, you're hurting me," says Anna.

I make them coffee and notice several sparkly Christmas bags around the kitchen and dining room. I sneak a look inside. Incontinence pads? I can only think that perhaps Anna likes to keep them in pretty packaging.

Dave wraps Anna's hair in a hand towel and helps her to her armchair. I notice again that she can only walk by holding onto one of us, or with her frame, or by holding onto chairs, tables and door handles.

"She don't get out the car now," Dave tells me, "I just leave 'er in it and do the shopping. She's got the radio."

"Don't talk about me behind my back," says Anna, "it's spiteful."

"You're sittin' right 'ere you rat," says Dave, "so nothin's being said behind yer back." He takes a noisy slurp of coffee, followed by a belch. "Spiteful as an adder, was what our Dad used to say."

"I've never heard that expression,"

"Old Brusher Mills in the forest. Used to collect adders. 'E 'ad a big top 'at an' a big beard, an' a sack on 'is back, full of adders.

"What for?" says Anna with half-closed eyes.

"Sold 'em to the hospitals 'e did. So they could get out the venom and make cures for snake bites and such."

"I don't think I've ever seen an adder in the wild," I say.

"They keep outta yer way if they can," says Dave, "unless you disturb 'em. Went fishin' in the forest one day, by one of the rivers and saw a nice patch of leaves by an old tree stump. Got settled there and got me fishin' rod out. Then I felt something movin' about under me bum. Leapt up, and there it was!"

"An adder!" I am horrified. "You were lucky not to be bitten."

"Yep," agrees Dave. "It would kill you if you was a weak constitution."

"So no real danger for you then Dave."

Dave grins, showing the gaps in his teeth.

"If you want to see 'em you can put out a metal sheet or a corrugated sheet and they'll go underneath it for warmth."

"I'd rather not," shivers Anna.

"Drop of rain comin' I reckon," says Dave, "you got that washing out?"

I head out to the garden with the wash bin I bought last year. Anna and Dave were delighted with it. Up to that point they had simply left the washing on the kitchen floor.

"My pansies'll be pleased," says Dave, behind me.

The washing is nearly dry. I stand for a few moments under the tulip tree, looking out across the fields beyond the hedge. And listening to Dave admiring his sunflowers.

TODAY

10th August 2019

. . . .

Dave is talking (loudly) about something he has read in the newspaper, and Anna and I are listening, and then she slowly tilts to the right, her arm falling over the edge of the sofa. My mind wanders. Perhaps it's the heat of the day.

I feel that Anna often seems more cheerful when she is talking about the things she sees that we don't. The tiny orchestra on the kitchen windowsill. "What are they playing?" I ask her. And she tells me that they haven't played a note yet. The little white dog jumping up and down on the table. And the walk through the village that she took before I arrived today. Our reality puzzles her. Frightens her even. People she doesn't recognise. News she doesn't understand. Conversations she can't follow. Only made better if she is holding Dave's hand.

And I realise that I could continue to tell you how Anna's illness progresses; how she deteriorates. Perhaps they have to accept sitters, or even carers. Perhaps Anna can't get upstairs any more. Perhaps she can't get downstairs. Perhaps she has to go into a nursing home.

Or I could go back in time and tell you how Anna disapproved of my first boyfriend and how we became quite distanced from each other.

How anxious and difficult she was about my wedding where she would have to meet John's family again. How John and his new wife had two children, and how he died far too young. How Devon brother and then Sydney brother went abroad and Sydney brother made a new life in Australia. How I never met Anna's sister or her adopted sister, and never found out why they were not close. And how Anna made some links with her cousins and then lost them.

Or I could just leave things as they are now. As they are every afternoon.

Dave in his armchair with his Saturday newspaper. Anna on the sofa turning the pages of one of her catalogues. The clocks ticking. The kettle on the Aga hissing. Mr Pheasant calling from the bank by the field. Hunting cat in the bushes along the lane.

Perhaps I should leave the last word with Dave.

One evening just before I left to move into my new house, we were watching television. Anna had gone to bed.

"I'm going to miss you," said Dave, leaning forward in his chair. "Our little talks. I enjoy telling you about the past, the RAF, my Mum and Dad and where we lived. Nights out with the lads. The war and the GI's."

"Me too," I agreed.

He looked into the fire and was quiet for a moment.

"One thing I just wish," he said.

"What's that Dave?"

"I just wish I'd written it all down."

Printed in Poland
by Amazon Fulfillment
Poland Sp. z o.o., Wrocław

54057899R00256